LESSONS FOR
EXTENDING
FRACTIONS

GRADE 5

THE TEACHING ARITHMETIC SERIES

Teaching
ARITHMETIC

LESSONS FOR
EXTENDING
FRACTIONS

▲▲▲▲▲

GRADE 5

MARILYN BURNS

MATH SOLUTIONS PUBLICATIONS
SAUSALITO, CA

Math Solutions Publications
A division of
Marilyn Burns Education Associates
150 Gate 5 Road, Suite 101
Sausalito, CA 94965
www.mathsolutions.com

Library of Congress Cataloging-in-Publication Data
Burns, Marilyn, 1941–
    Lessons for extending fractions : grade 5 / Marilyn Burns.
        p. cm.
Includes index.
    ISBN 0-941355-43-8 (alk. paper)
    1. Fractions—Study and teaching (Elementary) I. Title.
QA117.B86 2003
    372.7'2—dc21

                                                    2003013256

ISBN-10: 0-941355-43-8
ISBN-13: 978-0-941355-43-8

Editor: Toby Gordon
Production: Melissa L. Inglis
Cover & interior design: Leslie Bauman
Composition: TechBooks

Printed in the United States of America on acid-free paper
07 06 05   ML   2 3 4 5

A Message from Marilyn Burns

We at Math Solutions Professional Development believe that teaching math well calls for increasing our understanding of the math we teach, seeking deeper insights into how children learn mathematics, and refining our lessons to best promote students' learning.

Math Solutions Publications shares classroom-tested lessons and teaching expertise from our faculty of Math Solutions Inservice instructors as well as from other respected math educators. Our publications are part of the nationwide effort we've made since 1984 that now includes

- more than five hundred face-to-face inservice programs each year for teachers and administrators in districts across the country;
- annually publishing professional development books, now totaling more than fifty titles and spanning the teaching of all math topics in kindergarten through grade 8;
- four series of videotapes for teachers, plus a videotape for parents, that show math lessons taught in actual classrooms;
- on-site visits to schools to help refine teaching strategies and assess student learning; and
- free online support, including grade-level lessons, book reviews, inservice information, and district feedback, all in our quarterly Math Solutions Online Newsletter.

For information about all of the products and services we have available, please visit our Web site at *www.mathsolutions.com.* You can also contact us to discuss math professional development needs by calling (800) 868-9092 or by sending an e-mail to *info@mathsolutions.com.*

We're always eager for your feedback and interested in learning about your particular needs. We look forward to hearing from you.

A DIVISION OF MARILYN BURNS EDUCATION ASSOCIATES

CONTENTS

ASSESSMENTS

BLACKLINE MASTERS

INDEX

ACKNOWLEDGMENTS

A special thanks to Annie Gordon and her students at Marin Horizon School, Mill Valley, California, and to Danielle Ross and her students at Park Elementary School, Mill Valley, California, for allowing me to try out ideas in their classrooms.

Thanks to Maryann Wickett for reading the drafts of lessons and giving me clear, honest, and helpful feedback and support.

Thanks also to Enrique Ortiz, University of Central Florida, Orlando, Florida, for his article, "An Activity Involving Fraction Squares," from the December 2000 issue of *Teaching Children Mathematics,* which inspired the lesson in Chapter 11.

INTRODUCTION

The first Teaching Arithmetic book that I wrote about fractions, *Lessons for Introducing Fractions, Grades 4–5*, was published in 2001. I had concentrated my classroom teaching on teaching fractions to fourth and fifth graders for about six years before completing that book. I included in the book those lessons that I knew to be especially effective for helping students just beginning to study fractions build a foundation of understanding and skills. My goals included helping students learn to name, represent, compare, and order fractions and also helping them develop a firm understanding of equivalent fractions.

I was pleased with these introductory lessons and with the positive feedback I received from teachers who taught them. However, I knew that more was needed to further students' beginning learning. For example, while students were able to compare fractions with "friendly" denominators that were either the same or multiples of one another (for example, three-fourths and five-eighths), some students would falter when comparing other fractions (for example, two-thirds and five-eighths). Even students who were more facile with fractions still needed more experience and additional practice. Furthermore, the book gave very little attention to combining fractions, and I knew that the students needed to learn about all of the operations with fractions—addition, subtraction, multiplication, and division.

I kept three goals in mind when working on this second book, *Lessons for Extending Fractions, Grade 5*: to help students cement their understanding, to give them experiences applying their skills in new situations, and to teach them strategies for adding and subtracting fractions. For all the lessons that I taught, I kept a detailed record of what I did and how the students responded. I also saved all of the student work and pored over it to analyze what students learned and what they didn't yet understand. I realize that this sort of effort and documentation is unrealistic for full-time classroom teachers, so I'm pleased to offer here what I've learned from my experiences to help you build your students' understanding and skills about fractions.

I think it's also important to note that this book does not address multiplying and dividing fractions. This was not because I was avoiding these important skills, but rather because I felt they deserved more careful and detailed attention. Therefore, I have devoted an entire third Teaching Arithmetic book, *Lessons for Multiplying and Dividing Fractions, Grades 5–6*, to these two topics that have vexed teachers for years.

As always, I learned a great deal from the students I taught. In class one day, Sandro, sparked by the idea from a classmate, Alan, shared that he was thinking about counting in fractions. This was during a lesson on comparing and ordering fractions. (See Chapter 2, "In Size Order.") I was curious. I have found it helpful for students to count fractions with the same denominators; for example, they can count by eighths—one-eighth, two-eighths, three-eighths, four-eighths, and so on. But Sandro had a different idea. He shared the counting sequence that he had in mind— one-half, two-thirds, three-fourths, four-fifths, and so on. I recorded the sequence on the board:

$$\frac{1}{2}, \frac{2}{3}, \frac{3}{4}, \frac{4}{5}, \frac{5}{6}, \frac{6}{7}, \frac{7}{8}, \ldots$$

Sandro explained, "See, whenever you make both numbers one bigger, the fraction gets bigger." Sandro was referring to the numerator and denominator of each successive fraction.

The class became interested in Sandro's idea. At the moment, it was hard for me to be sure how to respond. I am always pleased when students suggest ideas, but I'm not always able to understand how they're thinking or to know how best to respond. I've learned in those situations to be honest with the students.

"I've never thought about this before," I said. "It's very interesting and seems to work. Let's talk about it some more at another time." Sandro looked pleased at having thought of something that was new for me. I knew that when we count, either by ones, twos, fives, or tens, for example, we count in even intervals, and I also knew that Sandro's sequence didn't follow this convention. However, I realized that his fractions were indeed increasing each time, a realization that came to me quickly because of all the time I'd been spending thinking about and teaching fractions. I returned to Sandro's idea at a later time, curious about whether the students could come to this conclusion.

"As Sandro is counting, do the fractions increase in size?" I asked.

Hope responded, "I think they're getting bigger. I know that seven-eighths is bigger than one-half, because four-eighths makes one-half. So I think they're getting bigger."

"Two-thirds is bigger than one-half, and it's what comes next," Jake added.

I knew that it was easy for the students to compare fractions when one of the fractions was one-half, but not to compare all fractions. "What about from five-sixths to seven-eighths?" I asked, pointing to two fractions in the sequence. "Is seven-eighths more than five-sixths? Talk with your neighbor about this." I chose seven-eighths and five-sixths rather than seven-eighths and six-sevenths because I knew that the students were not as comfortable thinking about sevenths as about sixths and eighths.

Conversation broke out. Some students reached for pencil and paper. I circulated and listened. Most students seemed convinced that seven-eighths was larger than five-sixths, but some weren't sure why. In a few moments, I called the class to attention and repeated my question, also writing it on the board:

Is $\frac{7}{8}$ more than $\frac{5}{6}$?

We had a lively discussion that gave me insights into students' understanding. Some students argued that you could tell from making a drawing of two circles or two squares, showing seven-eighths on one and five-sixths on the other. "You can see that seven-eighths takes up more space," Eva said.

"I don't think you can be sure of that," Sadie said. "A drawing isn't accurate." Sadie was repeating what I had often told the students.

"There are more pieces in seven-eighths," Philip said. "There are seven pieces, and there are only five pieces in five-sixths."

"But the sixths are bigger pieces than the eighths," I countered.

"Oh yeah," Philip conceded.

Bo was eager to share. "I know seven-eighths is bigger because if you have pizzas, with seven-eighths you have a littler piece of pizza left over, so it has to be more than five-sixths." Several others nodded.

"They would have to be the same size pizza," Sandro said. There were more nods.

Emmy added, thoughtfully, "I think Bo is right because they both need one more fraction to make it a whole, and one-sixth is bigger than one-eighth."

Conversation broke out again in the room. When I called them back to attention, I gave the students a writing assignment. I thought that having specific information about each student's understanding about how to compare seven-eighths and five-sixths would be valuable information. I said to the class, "I'm interested in Sandro's idea, and I'm also interested in what each of you thinks about seven-eighths and five-sixths. I'd like to have you do a quick writing assignment. And while you're working, I'll be thinking about Sandro's counting idea so that we can explore it more." I wrote on the board:

How would you convince someone that $\frac{7}{8}$ of something is more than $\frac{5}{6}$ of the same thing?

I read the students' papers that evening. Of the twenty-seven students, all thought that seven-eighths was larger. However, only twenty-one were able to give a clear argument. Elizabeth, for example, wrote: $\frac{3}{24} = \frac{1}{8}$. $\frac{1}{6} = \frac{4}{24}$. *So $\frac{1}{8}$ is smaller than $\frac{1}{6}$. So $1 - \frac{1}{8} >$ $1 - \frac{1}{6}$. $1 - \frac{1}{8} = \frac{7}{8}$. $1 - \frac{1}{6} = \frac{5}{6}$.* Daniel wrote: $\frac{7}{8}$ *is more, because $\frac{8}{8}$ is a whole and is like $\frac{6}{6}$. When you draw $\frac{7}{8}$, you're leaving out $\frac{1}{8}$ which is smaller than $\frac{1}{6}$. So $\frac{7}{8}$ is closer to a whole than $\frac{5}{6}$.* He included a drawing. (See Figure 1.)

Of the six students who didn't give a clear argument, Maddy's paper was typical. She drew two circles and wrote: *Now as you can see I have made some examples of*

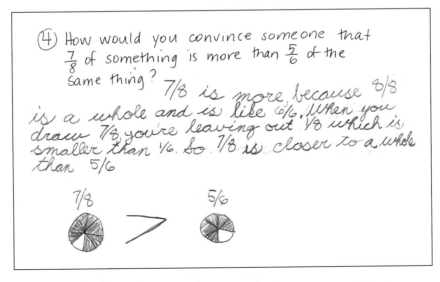

▲▲▲▲▲▲Figure 1   *Daniel's argument was clear and convincing.*

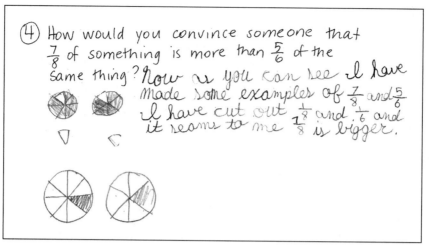

▲▲▲▲▲▲**Figure 2** *Maddy's paper showed her inability to explain why $\frac{7}{8}$ is more than $\frac{5}{6}$. Her explanation was typical of the students whose understanding was fragile.*

$\frac{7}{8}$ and $\frac{5}{6}$. *I have cut out $\frac{1}{8}$ and $\frac{1}{6}$ and it seams to me $\frac{7}{8}$ is bigger.* (See Figure 2.) Kyle also wrote an unconvincing argument. He wrote: $\frac{7}{8}$ *is bigger because $\frac{8}{8}$ has $\frac{4}{8}$ on each half, and $\frac{5}{6}$ is smaller because $\frac{6}{6}$ has $\frac{3}{6}$ on each half.* Figures 3 and 4 show two more students' thinking.

Getting students involved in thinking about fractions and the relationships among them is an important challenge for our instruction. Creating lessons to accomplish this is another challenge. And having the depth of understanding ourselves to be able to deal with all ideas that come up is still another challenge. I've written this book to help you meet all of these challenges. (See Chapter 7, "Fraction Sequences," for how I created a lesson around Alan's and Sandro's ideas that you can try with your students and for an explanation of the mathematics involved.)

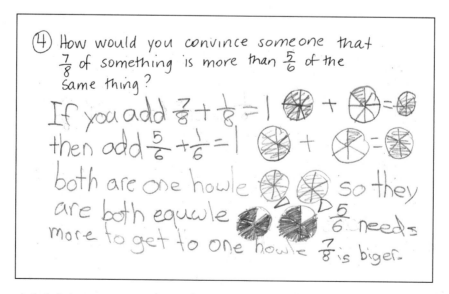

▲▲▲▲▲▲**Figure 3** *In his paper, George showed that his math understanding was better than his spelling.*

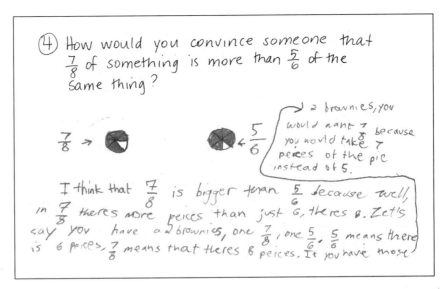

▲▲▲▲▲▲Figure 4 *Philip resorted to brownies and pies but didn't construct a convincing argument.*

If you are planning to use this book with students who have not had the experiences in my prior Teaching Arithmetic book, *Lessons for Introducing Fractions, Grades 4–5*, I strongly suggest that you teach at least the lessons from that book that engage students with fraction kits, Chapters 2 and 15. Fraction kits are referred to in a number of these lessons; they're an invaluable tool for building students' skills with naming and comparing fractions and for developing an understanding of equivalence that allows students to learn to add and subtract fractions with ease. If your students have not experienced fraction kits, I urge you to start there. If you do not have a copy of the prior book, we've put all the information you need about fraction kits in the booklet, *The Fraction Kit Guide*, accompanying this book.

Goals for Fractions Instruction

Our goal in teaching fractions is to give all students the chance to learn how to

▲ name fractional parts of wholes and sets;
▲ represent fractional parts using the standard notation, including proper fractions, improper fractions, and mixed numbers, and also with concrete and pictorial representations;
▲ recognize equivalent fractions and represent fractions and mixed numbers in equivalent forms;
▲ compare and order fractions;
▲ make reasonable estimates with fractions;
▲ compute with fractions; and
▲ apply fractions to a variety of problem-solving situations that come from real-world contexts and from other areas of the mathematics curriculum.

This book is meant to be an extension of *Lessons for Introducing Fractions, Grades 4–5*. The lessons in this book assume that students have a foundation of the understanding and skills that were the focus of the first book. Specifically, this includes strong understanding and skills with the ideas in the list above for fractions that involve halves, fourths, eighths, and sixteenths and also at least beginning understanding and skills with fractions that involve thirds, sixths, and twelfths. The three introductory chapters in this book are reliable indicators about whether the lessons in this book are appropriate for your students or whether you should consider introducing them to the lessons in the previous book.

In the area of computation, the lessons in this book address addition and subtraction, but not multiplication and division. It was actually my initial intent to include multiplication and division in this book, but after spending several years in classrooms with a focus on helping students make sense of multiplying and dividing, I decided that these operations deserve a book of their own. If you're interested, see the Teaching Arithmetic book *Lessons for Multiplying and Dividing Fractions, Grades 5–6.*

A cautionary note: Even if students are comfortable with basic ideas about fractions, I find that partial understanding and confusion are typical. While students may feel comfortable working with fractions that involve halves, fourths, and eighths, for example, they may be shaky about working with thirds, fifths, and sixths. If their understanding and skills with whole numbers are weak, especially in the areas of multiplication and division, they may have a more difficult time with fractions. And if students' previous experience with fractions involved a major emphasis on following rules and procedures, rather than working to make sense of fractions, they may not have had the opportunity to develop the kind of understanding necessary to be successful.

The Structure of the Lessons

The lessons in this book vary in several ways. Some require one class period; most call for two or three periods, with additional time for repeat experiences or variations; and one lesson, the first in the book, can easily span four days or more of instruction. The lessons include explorations, games, and problem-solving experiences. Some lessons reinforce students' previous learning, giving students opportunities to revisit ideas, while others introduce students to new ideas that extend their learning.

To help you with planning and teaching the lessons in this book, each is organized into the following sections:

Overview To help you decide if the lesson is appropriate for your students, this is a nutshell description of the mathematical goal of the lesson and what the students will be doing.

Materials This section lists the special materials needed along with quantities. Not included in the list are regular classroom supplies such as pencil and paper. Worksheets that you need to duplicate are included in the Blackline Masters section at the back of the book.

Time Generally, the number of class periods is indicated, sometimes with a range that allows for different-length periods. It is also indicated when activities are meant to be repeated from time to time.

Teaching Directions The directions are presented in a step-by-step lesson plan.

Teaching Notes This section addresses mathematical and pedagogical issues underlying the lesson and, when appropriate, indicates the prior experiences or knowledge students need.

The Lesson This is a vignette that describes what actually occurred when the lesson was taught to one or more classes. While the vignette mirrors the plan described in the teaching directions, it elaborates with details that are valuable for preparing and teaching the lesson. Samples of student work are included.

Extensions This section is included for some of the lessons and offers follow-up suggestions.

Questions and Discussion Presented in a question-and-answer format, this section addresses issues that came up during the lesson and/or questions that have been posed by other teachers.

How to Use This Book

Teaching the lessons as described in the fourteen chapters requires at least twenty-six days of instruction, not including time for repeat experiences as recommended for some lessons, or for the twelve individual assessments suggested. While it's possible to spend a continuous stretch of weeks on these lessons, I don't think that is the best decision. In my experience, time is required for students to absorb concepts, and I would rather spend a three-week period and then wait a few months or so before returning for another three-week period, or arrange for three chunks of time, each two weeks or so, spaced throughout the year. When students return to ideas after a break, they bring not only the learning they've done in other areas but also a fresh look that some distance can provide. Also, spending time in between on whole number multiplication and division, on learning about decimals and percents, and on experiences with algebra, measurement, geometry, and probability will strengthen students' learning of fractions.

CHAPTER ONE
DIVIDING BROWNIES

Overview

In this lesson, students explore different ways to divide "brownies" into halves, fourths, and eighths. The brownies are 4-by-4-square grids with the corners of the squares indicated by dots; each brownie has an area of 16 square units. A particular benefit of this exploration is that two approaches are combined in one investigation. Students can divide brownies either by using a spatial approach (focusing on the shapes of the fractional parts) or a numerical approach (calculating the number of square units in the shapes they create). Also, while helping students see relationships among halves, fourths, and eighths, the lesson helps reinforce for students the different ways to represent equivalent fractions.

Materials

- ▲ *Fractions on Grids (4-by-4 Squares)* worksheet, 4 per student (see Blackline Masters)
- ▲ *Large 4-by-4 Grids* worksheet, 1 per pair of students (see Blackline Masters)
- ▲ optional: *Fractions on Grids (6-by-4 Squares)* worksheet, for Extension activity, several per student (see Blackline Masters)
- ▲ optional: *Large 6-by-4 Grids* worksheet, 1 per pair of students (see Blackline Masters)

Time

- ▲ four class periods, plus four additional days for the extension

Teaching Directions

1. Draw six grids (4-by-4 squares) of "brownies" on the chalkboard or on a projected overhead transparency.

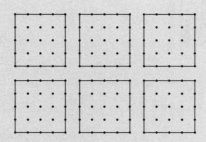

2. Ask students: "How might you divide each of these brownies in half so that two people would each get the same share to eat?" As students explain ways, record them on the grids on the board. Students typically first suggest the following four ways:

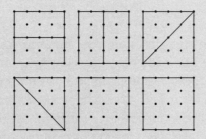

If students don't offer other ways, make a suggestion to push their thinking: "Think of ways that don't use one straight cut but that still cut the brownie into two pieces that are the same size." If this doesn't spark any ideas, have them talk in pairs or small groups. Or you can show the class several examples:

3. Give an individual assignment. Distribute one *Fractions on Grids (4-by-4 Squares)* worksheet to each student. Tell the student to divide each brownie into two equal pieces, dividing each one in half a different way. Also tell them that for each brownie they divide, they should be sure that they can explain how they know that the two pieces really are halves. It's fine for students to talk among themselves as they work, but each should record on his or her own worksheet.

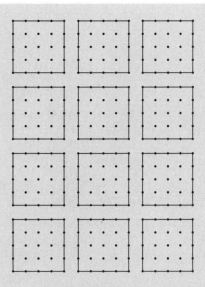

4. Interrupt the class in time to lead a class discussion about the different ways the students divided brownies in halves. Erase the grids on the board or projector and draw six more. Invite students to come to the board or projector, draw one of their examples, and explain to the class why the pieces are halves.

5. On the next day, repeat Steps 1 through 4 for fourths, and then on the following day, repeat again for eighths. For more experienced classes, you may prefer to give the assignment of dividing brownies into fourths and eighths at one time, distributing two worksheets to each student. Or you may assign fourths as a class investigation and then assign eighths to be investigated for homework. Whichever way you choose, don't rush the class discussions about how students divided the brownies.

6. After students have had experience dividing brownies into halves, fourths, and eighths, give each a fresh sheet and say: "On this sheet, you should explore ways to divide each brownie so that it shows a combination of halves, fourths, and eighths. You don't have to show all three fractions on each brownie, but you must show at least two."

7. Initiate a class discussion to talk about fractions larger than one. Pose the problem: *How many brownies would we need to give five people each one-fourth of a brownie?* Model for the class how to record the solution:

$\frac{1}{4} + \frac{1}{4} + \frac{1}{4} + \frac{1}{4} + \frac{1}{4} = \frac{5}{4}$

$\frac{1}{4} + \frac{1}{4} + \frac{1}{4} + \frac{1}{4} + \frac{1}{4} = 1\frac{1}{4}$

Then present other symbolic representations and ask them to discuss why each is true:

$1\frac{1}{4} + \frac{3}{4} = 2$

$2 - \frac{5}{4} = \frac{3}{4}$

$$2 - 1\tfrac{1}{4} = \tfrac{1}{2} + \tfrac{1}{4}$$

$$\tfrac{1}{4} + \tfrac{1}{2} + \tfrac{1}{8} = 1 - \tfrac{1}{8}$$

8. Distribute the *Large 4-by-4 Grids* worksheet, one for each pair of students. Ask each student in each pair to choose one brownie from his or her sheet that shows halves, fourths, and eighths to reproduce on a grid on their *Large 4-by-4 Grids* and then post the sheet. They should color and label sections to make them easily visible.

9. Have students examine the posted grids. Then lead a class discussion that focuses on relationships among wholes, halves, fourths, and eighths. Pose statements and ask students to identify grids that illustrate them. Following are ideas for statements; the particular grids posted may provide you with other ideas:

$\tfrac{5}{8}$ is more than $\tfrac{1}{2}$

$\tfrac{1}{8}$ is $\tfrac{1}{2}$ of $\tfrac{1}{4}$

$\tfrac{1}{2} = \tfrac{4}{8}$

$\tfrac{4}{8}$ is $\tfrac{1}{4} + \tfrac{1}{4}$

$\tfrac{1}{4}$ and $\tfrac{1}{4} = \tfrac{1}{2}$

$\tfrac{1}{8}$ is $\tfrac{1}{4}$ of $\tfrac{1}{2}$

$\tfrac{2}{8} = \tfrac{1}{4}$

10. As an extension, introduce the same activities using the *Fractions on Grids (6-by-4 Squares)* worksheet, with grids that each represent rectangular brownies. These grids allow the students to think about halves, thirds, fourths, sixths, eighths, and twelfths.

Teaching Notes

The fractions the students investigate in this activity—halves, fourths, and eighths— are the fractions they investigated when constructing and using fraction kits. (See *Teaching Arithmetic: Lessons for Introducing Fractions, Grades 4–5*, Chapters 2 and 15, or the booklet, *The Fraction Kit Guide*.) However, because the brownies have a different shape than the strips used in the kits, they give students another way to visualize these fractions and how they relate to one another. Changing the shape of the whole and the context of the problem presents a fresh challenge to students and builds their flexibility in thinking about fractions and the relationships among them.

When students divide the brownies, some focus on the sixteen smaller squares in each, interpreting one-half of a brownie as eight small squares, one-fourth as four squares, and one-eighth as two squares. Other students, however, don't rely on counting the smaller squares but instead focus on how the shapes of the pieces they create relate to the brownie as a whole. Both approaches are fine. While students may have a natural preference for one approach over the other, the activity can help them move beyond their strength and learn to think about fractional parts in another way.

In my experience, I've found that students who focus on counting smaller squares tend to divide brownies into more unusual shapes, more often making noncongruent halves, for example, and verifying that they are halves by calculating their areas. Be careful not to let students think that more complex shapes are better in any way. What's more important is that students understand why shapes illustrate specific fractional parts.

Also, be sure that students making more intricate shapes still focus on them as fractional parts of the whole brownie and understand that halves of the same whole have to be the same size, that is, have the same area. We often hear students say, "Your half is bigger than my half," referring to two shares that aren't really halves. While this language is commonly used in a colloquial sense, students need to understand that in a mathematical sense, halves of the same whole have to be the same size. This activity can help make this distinction clear.

The Lesson

▲▲

DAY 1

Before class began, I drew on the board six 4-by-4 square grids like the ones on the worksheet the students would be using. (To make this easier, you may want to project an overhead transparency of the worksheet onto the board and mark the dots.)

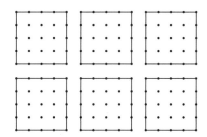

I asked, "Let's see if we can figure out how to divide each of these grids in half in a different way. Think of each as a brownie that you'll cut so that two people would each get the same amount to eat."
Students' hands went up. I called on Daniel.

"Can I come up and do it?" he asked.

"I'd rather you explain your idea and I'll see if I can draw what you're thinking,"

I answered. I chose this way because the experience of explaining their thinking is good practice for students. Also, I wanted to see what geometric vocabulary would emerge from the lesson.

"Just draw a line down the middle from the top to the bottom," Daniel said.

"Do you mean a vertical line like this?" I asked, using the word *vertical* to reinforce this terminology as I drew a line. Daniel nodded to indicate that I had correctly interpreted his idea.

"That's what I was thinking," Ali said.
"Me, too," Sarah added.
"I know another way," Eli said. "Draw the line across the middle."
"Do you mean a horizontal line, like this?" I asked, drawing on the second grid.

Dividing Brownies 5

"That's it," Eli said.

"Another way?" I asked. I called on Katia.

"Make a slanty line," she said.

"Tell me where to start the line," I said.

"In the corner," Katia responded.

"Which corner?" I prodded.

"On the top, over there on the left," Katia said, "and then come down to the bottom on the right."

"Do you mean a diagonal line, like this?" I asked, drawing on the third grid. Katia nodded.

"Another way?" I asked.

Sophia answered next. "Draw a line like Katia's, but in the other direction."

"Can you describe your idea using the word *diagonal*?" I asked Sophia.

"Draw a diagonal line from the top right down to the bottom left," she said. I did so on the fourth grid.

"Another way?" I asked.

The class was silent. Nick raised a hand and then pulled it back down. "No, that's already up there," he said.

I waited a bit more and then said, "Try to think of ways that don't use one straight cut, but that still cut the brownie into two pieces that are the same size. Talk at your tables and see what you can come up with."

The noise level in the class rose as students began to talk. Some got out pencils and paper to sketch. It's typical for a class to get stuck after these first four suggestions, but I find that if I give students time to talk together, they typically come up with other ways that work. I walked around, observing the progress at the

tables. After a few moments, I called the class back to attention. Lots of hands were raised. I called on Andrew.

He said, "This is really hard to explain. Can I come up and draw it?" I decided not to spend the time having students struggle with explaining but to move the lesson forward more quickly by having them come up and draw. Andrew came up to the board, realized that he wasn't sure what to do, went back for his paper, and then drew his idea.

"How do you know for sure that the two pieces are halves?" I asked.

"They both have eight squares in them," Andrew said, dividing the grid into squares to show what he meant. "See, the whole thing is sixteen, so eight is half."

I turned to the class. "Thumbs up if you understand what Andrew said, thumbs down if you're not sure." Carolyn and Lindsay had thumbs down, so Andrew explained again.

"See, there are sixteen small squares," he said, counting them one by one to prove this. "So eight is half because eight plus eight is sixteen." Carolyn and Lindsay were both satisfied.

Emmy added, "You can see they're both the same. One is kind of upside down from the other."

"Oh yeah," Nick commented.

"Yes, I can see how you could rotate one and it would fit exactly on the other," I said and then asked, "Who would like to divide the last brownie into halves in another way?" I called on Maria. She came up with her paper and drew on the last grid.

"I checked like Andrew did," she explained. "They're both eight."

"Thumbs up if you agree, thumbs down if you want to challenge or would like more explanation," I said. Everyone had a thumb up. Maria sat down.

I then asked the class to look again at the brownies cut with diagonal lines, as Katia and Sophia had suggested. "Can you count the squares on these to be sure that each half is worth eight squares?" I asked. I wanted the students to think about counting and combining halves of squares. A buzz broke out in the class and I waited a moment before asking the students for their attention. Then I called on Claudia. She came up to the board and explained her idea, using Katia's brownie.

"See, there are six whole squares," she said, drawing lines and marking Xs to show them on the bottom diagonal half. "Then these two halves make one more, and that's seven, and two more halves make eight." She looked at me.

I looked at the class asked, "Questions?"

"Could you do that again?" Carolyn asked. Carolyn often needed to check to be sure she understood.

"OK," Claudia said and repeated her explanation. Carolyn was satisfied and there were no other questions.

An Individual Assignment

I then told the students what they were to do next. I showed them the worksheet of grids and said, "I'm going to give each of you one of these. Look for ways to divide each brownie on the worksheet in half in a different way. For each brownie you divide, be sure that you can explain how you know that the two pieces really are halves."

"Can we work together?" Melissa wanted to know.

"Yes," I said, "but you each must record on your own paper."

"Can we use the ones on the board?" Eli asked.

"No," I said, "see if you can find others."

"I think it will be hard to fill the sheet," Nick said.

"Just see how many you can find," I said.

The students got to work. As I circulated, I noticed that some students relied on counting squares before drawing while others drew, then counted, and made corrections if necessary. All of the students were involved. As they worked, I erased the brownies we had divided on the board and drew six blank grids for a class discussion. When about ten minutes remained in the period, I called the class to attention. No one had completed the entire page, but they had done enough to make me feel confident that they understood the assignment. In the last few minutes of class, I had six students come to the board, divide one of the blank grids in half, and explain to the class how they knew they had divided the grid into two equal pieces.

DAY 2

I began class by drawing four grids on the board. I then asked the students, "How can we divide these grids into fourths, each in a different way?" After they suggested two ways quickly, there was a pause before students thought of two more ways.

"How many small squares are in each fourth?" I asked. After a moment, all hands were up and I asked the students to say the answer together softly.

"Four," they chorused.

"Who can explain why a fourth of the grid has to be four squares?" I asked.

Antonio answered first. He said, "A fourth is half of a half, so it has to have four squares."

Emmy said, "The whole brownie is sixteen, and if you divide sixteen by four, you get four."

Maria pointed to the first grid divided into four squares and said, "You can see that one is in fourths, and you can count and see that there are four in each corner."

This introduction went more quickly and smoothly than the previous day's introduction, which is typical when students have had previous experience with an activity. I distributed fresh copies of the worksheet and asked the students to explore a different way to divide each grid into fourths. All of the students were engaged. As they worked, I erased the grids on the board and drew six blank grids.

I interrupted the students about twenty minutes before the end of class to have students present their discoveries. I asked three students to come up, divide a grid into fourths, and explain to the class how they knew that the brownie was in four equal pieces. Callie made a mistake in her drawing but quickly correctly it when Mark pointed it out.

I used the three other blank grids to introduce how to divide brownies into eighths. As I did before, I asked students for suggestions and recorded their ideas on the board. I then explained that their homework assignment was to take home a worksheet and divide each of the brownies into eighths.

"We'll begin class tomorrow by having you share your papers at your tables," I said. I often do this with homework. In

this way, students who were absent the day before or who didn't do the assignment have a chance to get caught up as others at their table share and discuss their work.

DAY 3

After the students talked with one another about how they had divided brownies into eighths, I explained what they would do in class today. "I'm going to give you each a new sheet. Today's assignment is a little different. On this sheet, you'll combine fractional parts on each brownie. That is, you need to divide each brownie so that it shows a combination of halves, fourths, and eighths. You don't have to show all three fractions on each brownie, but you must show at least two different-size pieces on each."

As with all new directions, there was some confusion, so I drew an example on the board, dividing a grid to show two-fourths and four-eighths.

"It looks like a butterfly," Ali said.

"Because pieces will be different sizes, you should label each section," I explained. As the students watched, I labeled each section of the brownie. I then asked, "Who can explain why my labels are correct?"

Sarah came up to explain. "The fourths are easy because you can see how four of them fit into the whole brownie. And you chopped each fourth in half, and half of a fourth is an eighth."

"Who has another way to explain?" I asked. I called on Davy.

He said, "Fourths have four squares and eighths have two. You can just count." He came up and showed how to count the squares.

I gave one more direction: "I'll interrupt you in a while and ask you to choose one brownie from your sheet, reproduce it on a larger grid, and post it." I showed them the paper they would use for this and where they should post it. "On the larger grid, you should color and label the sections so that everyone can see them easily. Also, please choose a brownie that shows halves, fourths, and eighths. Each page has two grids on it, so two people can share each sheet."

I gave one final reminder. "Remember to have at least two different-size fractional pieces on each brownie, and remember to label the parts."

I circulated as the students worked and was pleased that the students were working well, chatting with one another in a relaxed manner as they divided their grids. I checked on the few students who needed some support.

A Class Discussion

When I noticed that a few students were finishing dividing the last grid, I interrupted the class. I said, "In just a moment, it will be time for you to choose a brownie with a half, a fourth, and an eighth on it and record it on a larger grid. But first I'd like all of you to put down your pencils and give me your attention."

I waited a moment until I could see all of the students' eyes facing me. Then I asked them to watch as I drew on the board. I drew the dots to make a brownie grid, then I drew a line vertically to divide it into two rectangular halves. "So, if I cut the brownie this way, there are two halves, right?" All of the students nodded in agreement.

"Say this half is mine," I said, pointing to the rectangular region on the right. "And this half is yours," I added, turning to Delia, who was sitting near the front. She nodded.

"I don't feel like eating all of my half right now," I continued. "I think that I'll eat only half of my piece." I drew a line across my half so it was now two squares, saying as I did so, "So I'm going to eat just half of my half." I shaded in the top piece to show what I would eat.

"How much of the whole brownie is the piece I'll eat?" I asked.

Most hands shot up immediately and I waited until every student had a hand raised. "Let's answer together quietly," I said.

"One-fourth," they said in unison.

"Who can explain why the piece I'm planning to eat, the piece that I shaded in, is one-fourth of the whole brownie?" I asked. "How would you convince someone that you're right?"

Delia said, "You can see that if I cut my half into two pieces like you did, then there would be four pieces all the same, so they're all one-fourth."

Jack, next to Delia, said, "Two-fourths make a half, so half of a half is a fourth."

Robin said, "See, your half of the brownie has eight squares, so if you eat half of them, there are four squares."

"I agree that the piece I was going to eat has four small squares in it," I said, "but how does that tell me for sure that it's one-fourth of the whole brownie?" I traced around the whole brownie with my finger to emphasize that I was looking at the whole.

"I know," Claudia said. "Can I come up and show?" I agreed.

Claudia came to the board, pointed to the piece I was going to eat, and said, "You have four squares here." She then pointed to the part of my half that I wasn't going to eat and said, "You have four squares here." Finally she pointed to Delia's half and said, "And there are four squares here and here. That makes four pieces like that, so they're fourths."

Nick added, "Yeah, they're fourths. There are four of them."

"If I eat just half of my half, and Delia eats all of her half," I said, shading in Delia's half, "how much of the brownie will be left over?"

Most of the students answered together, "One-fourth."

"So, how much of this brownie would have been eaten up?" I asked. "Raise a hand when you've figured this out." I waited for everyone to raise a hand and again had them answer quietly together.

"Three-fourths," they said.

"Look," Sophia explained, "this half has two-fourths and one more fourth makes three-fourths." The others seemed satisfied.

"Is three-fourths more or less than one-half?" I asked.

"More," everyone answered with certainty. I was keeping my questions simple to allow every student to stay engaged with the discussion.

"What if I gave everyone at Delia's table one-fourth of a brownie to eat?" I asked. "There are five students at her

table, so I'd need five-fourths. How many brownies would I need?" I chose Delia's table because there were five students and I wanted to talk with the students about fractions larger than one. If there hadn't been a table with five students, I would have named five students and then presented the problem.

"I don't get it," Carolyn said.

"I know," Matthew said. "You need two brownies."

"No, you need one brownie and only one-fourth of another," Jack added.

"I knew that," Matthew said, "but you have to cut into two brownies to get a fourth for each person."

"I get it now," Carolyn said.

I then drew two squares on the board without dots in them. "Can you divide each of these into fourths?" I asked Carolyn. She nodded, came up, and correctly divided each into four squares.

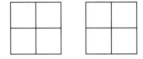

"Write the fraction for one-fourth inside each section to show that you think they're all fourths," I said. She did so and then sat down, pleased to have been successful.

"So if I gave each student at Delia's table one-fourth of a brownie, how much brownie would I use up?" I asked.

"One and a fourth," Jack answered.

"And how much would be left for me?" I grinned.

The students had several answers. "A half and a fourth." "Three-fourths." "You'd get more."

"Here's a math sentence that describes what we've been talking about," I said. "See if this makes sense." I wrote underneath the two squares divided into fourths:

$$\tfrac{1}{4} + \tfrac{1}{4} + \tfrac{1}{4} + \tfrac{1}{4} + \tfrac{1}{4} = \tfrac{5}{4}$$

They nodded their agreement. I wrote another sentence and asked, "How about this? Is this sentence true?"

$$\tfrac{1}{4} + \tfrac{1}{4} + \tfrac{1}{4} + \tfrac{1}{4} + \tfrac{1}{4} = 1\tfrac{1}{4}$$

They agreed again. "Who can explain?" I asked.

Andrew said, "Five-fourths is the same as one whole brownie and one-fourth of another brownie."

Emmy added, "You can put four fourths together to make one whole brownie, and then you have one more fourth left over, so it's one whole and one-fourth."

"What about this sentence?" I asked, writing on the board:

$$1\tfrac{1}{4} + \tfrac{3}{4} = 2$$

Maria volunteered to explain. "If you give one and a fourth brownies to Delia's table, then there is three-fourths of a brownie left. And if you take the three-fourths for yourself, then you use up two whole brownies."

I continued in this way with other sentences, asking students to explain why each made sense in terms of dividing brownies. Referring to the context of brownies gives students a concrete way to think about fractional relationships like these.

$$2 - \tfrac{5}{4} = \tfrac{3}{4}$$

$$2 - 1\tfrac{1}{4} = \tfrac{1}{2} + \tfrac{1}{4}$$

$$\tfrac{1}{4} + \tfrac{1}{2} + \tfrac{1}{8} = 1 - \tfrac{1}{8}$$

I then gave the students time to prepare their larger grids and post them. "If you finish before the end of class, look at the others that are posted. Then you can have some time for quiet reading." I ended class by reminding those who hadn't finished their large grids to be sure to post them before math class the next day.

DAY 4

I began class by giving the students a few minutes to look over the grids that had been posted. It was a colorful display. Then I initiated a class discussion to focus on recording fractional relationships. To begin, I wrote on the board:

$\tfrac{5}{8}$ *is more than* $\tfrac{1}{2}$.

$$\tfrac{5}{8} > \tfrac{1}{2}$$

Some students nodded. I said, "These both say the same thing, that five-eighths is more than one-half. Who can explain why this is true? If it helps, you can use one of the grids posted to explain your reasoning." I called on Michael.

He said, "Eight-eighths make a whole, and four of those eighths is half. And four-eighths and one-eighth is more than half, and you need one more eighth on four-eighths to get five-eighths. So five-eighths has to be more than one-half." As Michael spoke, I recorded on the board, checking with Michael after I wrote each sentence to see that I was representing his thinking accurately:

$\tfrac{8}{8} = 1$ *whole*

$\tfrac{4}{8} + \tfrac{1}{8}$ *is more than one-half*

$$\tfrac{4}{8} + \tfrac{1}{8} = \tfrac{5}{8}$$

When I do this sort of modeling how to record, I often use a mix of words and symbols for operations—*is more than* for >, *one-half* for $\tfrac{1}{2}$, and so on. It seems that when I use words, the translation is easier, at least at first.

"Does anyone have a different way to explain why five-eighths is more than one-half?" I asked. I called on Emmy.

She said, "Four-eighths is the same as one-half because four is half of eight, so there are half of them. And five-eighths is more than four-eighths. So five-eighths has to be more than half. Besides, five is more than half of eight." I recorded on the board:

$$\frac{4}{8} = \frac{1}{2}$$

$$\frac{5}{8} \text{ is more than } \frac{4}{8}$$

$$\frac{5}{8} > \frac{1}{2}$$

"Does anyone have another way to explain?" I continued. I called on Nick.

He said, "Because five times eight is forty, and four times eight is twenty-four, and forty is more than twenty-four." I didn't correct Nick's multiplication error but instead focused on his logic of multiplying the numerators and denominators of the fractions to compare them. When students offer erroneous reasoning, as Nick did, I try to present them with a contradiction that will help them see that their logic is faulty. In this case, I wrote two fractions on the board:

$$\frac{1}{4} \qquad \frac{1}{2}$$

"Which of these fractions is larger?" I asked.

"One-half," Nick answered quickly.

"But one times four is four, and that's more than one times two, which is two," I said.

Nick thought for a moment and then grinned good-naturedly. "It doesn't work for everything, so I guess you can't do that," he said.

I continued with other fraction sentences, having students explain and writing on the board to record their thinking mathematically. Following are the sentences we discussed:

$$\frac{1}{8} \text{ is } \frac{1}{2} \text{ of } \frac{1}{4}$$

$$\frac{2}{2} = 1 \text{ whole}$$

$$\frac{2}{2} \text{ is } \frac{8}{8}$$

$$\frac{4}{8} \text{ is } \frac{1}{4} + \frac{1}{4}$$

$$\frac{1}{4} + \frac{1}{4} = \frac{1}{2}$$

$$\frac{1}{8} \text{ is } \frac{1}{4} \text{ of } \frac{1}{2}$$

$$\frac{2}{8} = \frac{1}{4}$$

While the context of brownies is real and accessible to children, students may not understand that their ideas translate to other situations. To end the discussion, I brought the children's attention to all that I had written on the board.

"These are a lot of ideas about fractions that relate to thinking about brownies," I said. "Suppose we leave all of the sentences on the board to look at again tomorrow. But instead of thinking about brownies to prove that they are true, suppose we use pies. Do you think that all of the sentences will still be true for dividing pies? Show a thumb up if you think they'll all be true for sure, a thumb down if you think that they won't all be true, and a thumb sideways if you're not sure." More than half of the students put their thumbs up, four students held their thumbs down, and six students held their thumbs sideways. I've learned that partial and fragile understanding is part of the learning process, and I knew that for some students there was still much to be done to develop their understanding.

EXTENSION

Introduce the same activities with grids that are 6-by-4 squares each to represent rectangular brownies. These allow you to ask the students to think about halves, thirds, fourths, sixths, eighths, and twelfths. However, wait a week or more before doing this; the students will most likely have had their fill of this activity for a while.

Questions and Discussion

▲▲▲

▲ How are you sure that a student who says that half a brownie is worth eight squares really understands the idea of halves?

I had the same question when I first started using this activity with students. However, I've come to realize that if confusion exists, it's an opportunity to help students stretch their understanding. For example, I remember when Matthew showed me a grid he had correctly divided into noncongruent halves.

I asked Matthew, "How do you know that the two pieces of the brownie are halves?" "Because they're both eight squares," he responded quickly.

I then asked, "If you cut a brownie into two pieces this way, and I took one piece and you took the other, would we both have the same amount of brownie to eat?" My question stopped Matthew cold. I waited a moment and rephrased my question to be sure that he understood what I was asking. "Does it matter which piece you would choose if you really liked brownie and wanted as much as possible?" I asked.

"That one looks bigger," Matthew replied, pointing to the section on the left that touched all four sides, "but I'm not sure."

I used Matthew's shape for a class discussion. Some students were instantly clear that both shapes had to be the same size. "Eight small squares are eight small squares," Sophia said with a tone of impatience. Sarah tried to help Matthew understand why. She drew Matthew's halves on another grid, cut them out, then showed how she could cut one of his halves and make it fit exactly on the other. "What a mess of crumbs you'll have!" Robbie commented.

▲ Is it necessary to refer to the grids as brownies? Can't the students just think of them as squares?

It seems to make the issue of fractions clearer when there's a familiar context for children to refer to and visualize as they think and explain their ideas. Referring to the squares as brownies works well, I've found. But I've learned that using just one context or one model can limit children's thinking. Because something holds true with the square model of a brownie, children do not necessarily think it's true for the circular model of a pie or for the rectangular model of a candy bar. I think that it's valuable to use real-world contexts that are familiar to students and help them think concretely about abstract ideas.

▲ Why did you choose to introduce sentences with adding and subtracting fractions in an activity that had the students exploring fractional parts?

Adding and subtracting fractions emerge naturally when students think about combining parts of brownies and equivalent shares. In this instance, I was building on the fractional relationships the students had explored, so it seemed appropriate. Also, I like to ask students to think about adding and subtracting fractions without resorting to rules about least common multiples and common denominators but by relying on what they know about the fractional relationships instead.

CHAPTER TWO
IN SIZE ORDER

Overview

This two-part lesson gives students experience with comparing and ordering fractions. The first part involves the students in a whole-class discussion in which they generate a set of eight fractions between zero and one, four of which are less than one-half and four that are greater than one-half. The students then order the fractions they've generated from smallest to largest. In the second part of the lesson, students work in pairs and use the same criteria to generate and order another set of eight fractions; pairs then exchange and order each other's fractions.

Materials

▲ 8 4-by-6-inch index cards
▲ 3-by-5-inch index cards cut in half, 8 halves per pair of students

Time

▲ two class periods

Teaching Directions

1. Ask the students to raise their hands when they have thought of a fraction that is greater than one-half and less than one whole. Wait until all hands are raised and then call on someone to report. Have him or her also explain why the fraction is greater than one-half and less than one whole. Record the fraction on the board.

2. Ask the students for another fraction that is greater than one-half and less than one whole with a denominator that is different from the denominator in the first fraction. Record.

3. Repeat for a third fraction.

4. Repeat for a fourth fraction, asking this time for a fraction with the denominator of 100. (If one of the fractions you already recorded has 100 for its denominator, do not impose this stipulation.)

5. Now ask the students for four more fractions that are less than one-half, greater than zero, one with the denominator of 100, and the other three with denominators different from any of those already used.

6. Write the fractions on eight 4-by-6-inch index cards. Turn the cards facedown, shuffle them, and place the top card on the chalkboard tray so that the students can see the fraction. Then turn over the other cards, one by one, and have students place each on the chalkboard tray so that the fractions go from smallest on the left to largest on the right. When a student places a card, he or she should also explain his or her reasoning.

7. Give the directions for an assignment on which students will work with partners. Each pair makes up a set of eight fractions following the same criteria used for the eight fractions the class just sorted and records them on a sheet of paper. The pair then rewrites the fractions from smallest to largest and, underneath, explains its reasoning for placing three of the fractions. It helps to write the directions on the board as a reference for the students.

1. *Write four fractions $> \frac{1}{2}$ and < 1.*
   Use different denominators.
   One denominator has to be 100.
   Do not use equivalent fractions.
2. *Repeat Step 1 for four fractions $< \frac{1}{2}$ and > 0.*
3. *Write the fractions on a sheet of paper.*
4. *Put the fractions in order and then write them on your paper again.*
5. *Write explanations about how you placed three of the fractions.*

8. When you've checked that partners correctly completed the assignment, give them eight halves of 3-by-5-inch index cards on which to write their fractions. Have them write their names on the back of each card and give them a rubber band to help keep them together. Then have pairs exchange cards and order and record each other's fractions. Students should check each other's work.

Teaching Notes

The inspiration for this lesson came from the *Put in Order* activity that appears in Chapter 13 of the Teaching Arithmetic book *Lessons for Introducing Fractions, Grades 4–5*. When teaching a class that had experienced the *Put in Order* activity the year before, I created this extension to review comparing and ordering fractions with the class and also to give the students a more challenging experience than the original activity provided. In this new activity, instead of ordering fractions that I identified, the students generated fractions and then put them in order. This removed the careful control I had imposed by choosing fractions that I knew the students could compare. The new activity went well. If you think your class would benefit from an easier entry into ordering fractions, however, then you might try the original lesson in *Lessons for Introducing Fractions*.

During the discussion in the first part of this lesson, Alan, one of the fifth graders, gave a reason for why he thought that three-eighths was larger than two-sevenths. He made the conjecture that if you add one to both the numerator and denominator of a fraction (in this case, two-sevenths), then the new fraction (three-eighths) is always larger. Sandro then shared that he had been thinking about the same idea. Alan's and Sandro's ideas inspired Chapter 7, "Fraction Sequences," a lesson that is appropriate whether or not a student in your class comes up with the same idea.

The Lesson

▲▲

DAY 1

"Raise your hand when you've thought of a fraction that's more than one-half and less than one whole," I said to begin the lesson. About six hands shot up immediately, and I waited. As more hands were raised, the stragglers realized that I was expecting everyone to participate. Soon, everyone had raised a hand. I called on Manuel.

"Three-fourths," he said. I wrote on the board:

$$\frac{3}{4}$$

"How do you know that three-fourths is more than one-half and less than one whole?" I asked.

"Easy," he said. "Two-fourths is half and three-fourths is more than that, and I know it's less than one because you need four-fourths to make a whole." I nodded my acceptance of his answer.

"Who can think of a fraction with a different denominator that is also more than a half and less than a whole and that isn't equivalent to three-fourths?" I then asked. I called on Sadie.

"Five-sixths," she said and then explained, "because it's one-sixth less than a whole and it's more than three-sixths." I

recorded $\frac{5}{6}$ on the board next to $\frac{3}{4}$:

$$\frac{3}{4} \quad \frac{5}{6}$$

"And another fraction with a different denominator that is a different value than three-fourths and five-sixths?" I asked. I called on Carlotta.

"Two-thirds," she said. "One-third is less than half, so two-thirds has to be more." I added $\frac{2}{3}$ to the board:

$$\frac{3}{4} \quad \frac{5}{6} \quad \frac{2}{3}$$

I then said to Carlotta, "You're correct that two-thirds is more than one-half, but your reason isn't convincing. For example, I know that one-fourth is less than one-half, but two-fourths isn't more than one-half." When students offer incorrect or partially correct ideas, I try to present contradictions that will push them to revisit their reasoning.

"But two-thirds *is* more than half," Carlotta defended.

"Yes, I agree," I said, "but how could you convince someone?" I waited a bit, but Carlotta couldn't think of a way to explain.

"Would you like someone to help?" I asked. Carlotta nodded. She looked around the class at the raised hands and called on Barton.

Barton explained, "If you had

something divided into thirds and you wanted half of the something, you'd have to have one-third and then a half of another third, and that's less than two-thirds."

Hope had another way to explain. "When we used pattern blocks, the blue block was one-third of the hexagon, and two blues covered more than half. If you want to cover half, you have to use a blue and a green."

Alan had a third way. "Two-thirds of a dollar is more than fifty cents," he said.

"How much is two-thirds of a dollar?" I asked.

Alan thought for a moment and then said, "One-third is thirty-three cents, so two-thirds is like sixty-six cents."

No other student volunteered to share an idea, so I asked for another fraction. This time I specified the denominator. "What's another fraction that is more than one-half, less than one whole, and has a denominator of one hundred?" I asked. I had planned to suggest one hundred because of the reference of money even before Alan had responded with his reasoning. I called on Tamika.

She said, with a grin, "Seventy-two hundredths. That's more than fifty-hundredths and less than a whole." I added $\frac{72}{100}$ to the board:

$$\frac{3}{4} \quad \frac{5}{6} \quad \frac{2}{3} \quad \frac{72}{100}$$

I then changed the question. "Now I'd like fractions that are less than one-half and more than zero. One of them should have a denominator of one hundred and the others should have denominators we haven't used yet," I said.

Machiko offered two-fifths. She explained, "You'd need two and a half–fifths to make a half, so two-fifths is smaller." I recorded $\frac{2}{5}$ on the board:

$$\frac{3}{4} \quad \frac{5}{6} \quad \frac{2}{3} \quad \frac{72}{100} \quad \frac{2}{5}$$

Pia, Lynnea, and Kalil offered three more fractions:

$$\frac{3}{4} \quad \frac{5}{6} \quad \frac{2}{3} \quad \frac{72}{100} \quad \frac{2}{5} \quad \frac{2}{100} \quad \frac{2}{7} \quad \frac{3}{8}$$

Using the Fractions for an Activity

I then took eight 4-by-6-inch index cards and, as the students watched, I wrote one of the fractions on each. I shuffled the cards facedown, turned over the top card, and placed it on the chalkboard tray. It was $\frac{2}{3}$.

"It's *Put in Order*!" Carlotta said. She remembered the activity from the previous year.

"Yes," I responded and reviewed the procedure. "If you take a turn, you'll pick one of the cards without looking and then place it on the chalkboard tray so that the fractions go from smallest on the left to largest on the right." Almost all of the students had then hands up, willing to draw and place a card.

Before calling on anyone, I said, "If I call on you, after you place the card on the chalkboard tray, you have to explain to the class why you placed it where you did."

Mike's hand was raised. Because Mike didn't often volunteer, I took this opportunity to give him a chance to contribute. He came up, drew $\frac{2}{5}$, and placed it to the left of $\frac{2}{3}$. Then he turned to the class and explained, "The numbers on the top tell that there are the same number of pieces, and the fifths are smaller pieces than thirds, so I know that two-fifths is less."

I asked Mike a question to model using the terminology of *numerator* and *denominator*. "So since the numerators were the same, you let the denominators tell you which is larger?" Mike nodded, pleased, and sat down. I planned to ask the students later to write explanations for placing fractions, and I know writing on the board provides models for them. Therefore, before calling on another student, I recorded Mike's idea on the board:

$\frac{2}{5} < \frac{2}{3}$ because the numerators tell that there are the same number of pieces, but fifths are smaller pieces than thirds.

I called on Libby to choose and place the next card. She showed the class the fraction: $\frac{2}{7}$. Libby placed $\frac{2}{7}$ in the first position:

$$\frac{2}{7} \quad \frac{2}{5} \quad \frac{2}{3}$$

"It's like Mike said," Libby explained. "There are two pieces, but sevenths are smaller." She sat down. I recorded on the board:

$\frac{2}{7} < \frac{2}{5}$ because there are two pieces in both, but sevenths are smaller than fifths.

Tomas came up to draw the next card. It was $\frac{3}{4}$. "Three-fourths is bigger than two-thirds," Tomas said and placed the card in the last position:

$$\frac{2}{7} \quad \frac{2}{5} \quad \frac{2}{3} \quad \frac{3}{4}$$

He then turned to the class to explain. "I know that if you have three-fourths, then there's one piece left," he began. But then he got flustered and couldn't explain further. He stood for a bit, his face reddening. He asked if he could sit down.

"Tell me what you were thinking about when you said there was one piece left if you had three-fourths," I prodded.

Tomas stood quietly for a moment. "I can't remember," he said.

"Can you draw something to show me what you meant?" I asked.

"Can I?" Tomas said, brightening a bit. I nodded. He drew a circle on the board and said, "This is a pizza." Then he divided it into fourths, shaded in three of them, and pointed to the unshaded section. "See, this extra piece is left."

"How does that tell you to put the three-fourths after the two-thirds?" I asked.

"Oh, yeah," Tomas said. Next to the first circle, he drew another, divided it into thirds, and shaded in two of them. "This has one piece left, but it's a bigger piece, so it has to be smaller."

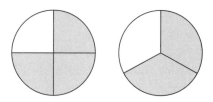

"What has to be smaller?" I asked.

"The two-thirds," he said.

"OK, explain it once more," I said. "Your reasoning made sense to me, but I think it could help you to explain it again." Tomas now gave a clear and uninterrupted explanation. Having students persist with making sense of an idea often helps cement their understanding. It's worth pushing as long as a student isn't too flustered to persevere. I wrote on the board:

$\frac{3}{4} > \frac{2}{3}$ because $\frac{3}{4}$ needs a $\frac{1}{4}$ piece to make a whole, and $\frac{2}{3}$ needs a $\frac{1}{3}$ piece to make a whole, which is a bigger piece than the $\frac{1}{4}$ piece, so $\frac{2}{3}$ has to be smaller.

Kendra came up next and drew the card with $\frac{5}{6}$ on it. She placed it after $\frac{3}{4}$.

$$\frac{2}{7} \quad \frac{2}{5} \quad \frac{2}{3} \quad \frac{3}{4} \quad \frac{5}{6}$$

To explain, she used the same reasoning that Tomas did. First she drew a circle, divided it into six pieces, and shaded five of them.

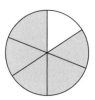

She then said, "There's only a one-sixth piece left over in a whole, and that's smaller than the one-fourth piece." I recorded:

$\frac{5}{6} > \frac{3}{4}$ because there's only $\frac{1}{6}$ left to make a whole, and $\frac{3}{4}$ needs $\frac{1}{4}$ to make a whole, and $\frac{1}{6} < \frac{1}{4}$.

Jake next drew $\frac{2}{100}$ and explained why it went first. "Two-hundredths is smaller than two-sevenths because hundredths are smaller than sevenths."

$$\frac{2}{100} \quad \frac{2}{7} \quad \frac{2}{5} \quad \frac{2}{3} \quad \frac{3}{4} \quad \frac{5}{6}$$

For the sake of time, I didn't record Jake's explanation since it was the same as the explanations that Mike and Libby had given. I called on Patrick to try the next fraction. He turned over the card to reveal $\frac{72}{100}$. Several students commented, "Oh no!" "It's a hard one." "We won't be able to figure this out." Patrick was stuck and looked to me for help.

I said to him, "How about if you all talk at your tables about where seventy-two–hundredths belongs?" Patrick nodded, relieved, and rejoined his table. A buzz broke out in the room as students began to talk. After a few moments, I called the class to attention. Jimmy was waving his hand, eager to share his idea.

"I got it!" he exclaimed. "It's easy with money."

I turned to Patrick. "Would you like to place the fraction?" I asked.

"It's OK if Jimmy does it," Patrick said.

"Jimmy, do you want to place the fraction?" I asked.

Jimmy responded, "Yes. No. Wait." I waited. Then he said, "Yes!" and came up to the board. He put the fraction just before $\frac{3}{4}$.

$$\frac{2}{100} \quad \frac{2}{7} \quad \frac{2}{5} \quad \frac{2}{3} \quad \frac{72}{100} \quad \frac{3}{4} \quad \frac{5}{6}$$

"I know that three-quarters is the same as seventy-five cents," he explained. "And seventy-two–hundredths is the same as seventy-two cents, so it has to be less than three-quarters." Some of the other students congratulated him. I recorded:

$\frac{3}{4} > \frac{72}{100}$ because $\frac{3}{4}$ of $1.00 is 75¢, and $\frac{72}{100}$ of $1.00 is 72¢.

"That explains why seventy-two–hundredths belongs before three-fourths," I said and then added, "but how do you know that seventy-two–hundredths is more than two-thirds?"

"Because it's so close to three-fourths," Jimmy responded.

"It's only three-hundredths away," Alan commented.

"That's like three cents," Tamika added.

"And two-thirds is less than seventy-two cents," Sadie said.

"How much is two-thirds of a dollar?" I asked. "Raise a hand if you know." Even though this had come up earlier in the lesson, I was curious about who knew this. I've learned that just because information is made public in the classroom, such as when Alan said that two-thirds of a dollar is about sixty-six cents, I can't assume that it makes sense to all of the students or that they will be able to recall it later.

"Talk at your table about this," I said. After a moment, I called the class to attention and asked students to raise their hands if they were willing to explain. Practically all of the students raised their hands, and I called on Machiko.

She said, "There are one hundred cents in a dollar, and you can't really make three even piles, but almost—thirty-three plus thirty-three plus thirty-three is ninety-nine cents. So, one-third is thirty-three and two-thirds is sixty-six. And, like Sadie said, that's less than seventy-two cents." I recorded on the board:

$\frac{72}{100} > \frac{2}{3}$ because $\frac{72}{100}$ of $1.00 is 72¢, and $\frac{2}{3}$ of $1.00 is 66¢.

Placing the Last Fraction

The last fraction, $\frac{3}{8}$, gave the class the most difficulty. Barton volunteered, and when he came up, he said, "I know it goes before the two-thirds because three-eighths is less than half, but I'm not sure if it goes before or after the two-fifths." No one else in the class had advice to offer him. Finally, Alan had an idea.

"I think it's more than two-sevenths," he said, "because if you look at two-thirds and three-fourths, you know three-fourths is more, and you get three-fourths from adding one to the two numbers in two-thirds. So I think that if you add one to the numerator and the denominator, the new fraction is bigger."

"Hey, that makes sense," Sandro said. "I was thinking the other day about counting in fractions—one-half, two-thirds, three-fourths, four-fifths, like that. Whenever you make both numbers one bigger, the fraction gets bigger." I didn't comment on Sandro's idea about "counting in fractions," but I wrote on the board the sequence that he reported:

$$\frac{1}{2}, \frac{2}{3}, \frac{3}{4}, \frac{4}{5}, \dots$$

"It works with five-sixths," Pia said. "If you add one to the four and one to the five in four-fifths, you get five-sixths, and it's bigger. It's only one-sixth from one whole, and that makes it closer."

"Look, it works with one-third and two-fourths!" Barton said. "You add one to the one and one to the three, and you get two-fourths, and that's the same as one-half, so it's bigger than one-third."

"Does this really work?" Tamika asked with some skepticism. "Can we do that?"

I responded, "You know, I've never thought about this before. It's very interesting and seems to work. Let's talk about it some more at another time, but first let's try to think of another way to compare two-sevenths and three-eighths to be sure that three-eighths is larger." I wrote these two fractions on the board to the side of the others to help focus the students' attention on them:

$$\frac{2}{7} \qquad \frac{3}{8}$$

Jake, whose head had been lowered as he worked with pencil and paper, raised his hand. "I got it," he said. "I made fifty-sixes." He came up and showed what he did. Jake really meant fifty-sixths, not fifty-sixes. He showed how he changed three-eighths to twenty-one–fifty-sixths and two-sevenths to sixteen–fifty-sixths. "So three-eighths *is* bigger," he said.

Sandro now had another idea. He came up to the board and drew two circles. He divided the first one into eighths, shaded in three of them, and said, "This has five-eighths left." Then he had difficulty dividing the other circle into sevenths, but did so after a few attempts. He shaded in two-sevenths and said, "This has five-sevenths left."

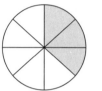

But then Sandro lost his train of thought and couldn't find his way. I was tempted to prompt him to think about which fraction was closer to a whole—$\frac{3}{8}$ is $\frac{5}{8}$ from 1, and $\frac{2}{7}$ is $\frac{5}{7}$ from 1. Since $\frac{5}{7}$ is larger than $\frac{5}{8}$, $\frac{2}{7}$ is farther from 1 and, therefore, $\frac{3}{8}$ has to be larger than $\frac{2}{7}$. But other hands were raised, so I held my thought to see what would emerge.

Sadie next explained why three-eighths is less than two-fifths. She said, "I think that three-eighths is smaller than two-fifths. I did kind of what Jake did, but I changed them to fortieths." She came to the board and wrote:

$$\frac{3}{8} = \frac{15}{40}$$

$$\frac{2}{5} = \frac{16}{40}$$

"Wow, they're pretty close," Tomas said.

I then asked students how they felt about placing $\frac{3}{8}$. "Show a thumb up if you're sure you know where it goes, show a thumb down if you don't know, and show a thumb sideways if you have an idea but you're not totally sure about it." About half of the students showed thumbs up, two showed thumbs down, and the rest showed thumbs sideways. Rather than keep discussing this problem, I decided to move the lesson forward to an assignment that I knew would give students additional experience with comparing fractions like these.

An Assignment for Partners

I gave the students directions about how they would repeat the activity with partners, thinking of eight fractions as we had done before and ordering them. Also, they would describe in writing how they decided to place some of their fractions. I knew that they wouldn't have time to complete this assignment, but they would have time to get started. Then I could take their papers home, see what help they needed, and have them continue the next day. "You'll each work with a partner now and you'll record together on one paper," I said. "Together, you'll make up your own set of eight fractions and then put them in order." I wrote the directions on the board:

1. *Write four fractions* $> \frac{1}{2}$ *and* < 1.
   Use different denominators.
   One denominator has to be 100.
   Do not use equivalent fractions.
2. *Repeat Step 1 for four fractions* $< \frac{1}{2}$ *and* > 0.
3. *Write the fractions on a sheet of paper.*
4. *Put the fractions in order and then write them on your paper again.*
5. *Write explanations about how you placed three of the fractions.*

I used the fractions we had just discussed to review the directions and show them how they were to organize their papers. I drew a sample paper on the board and titled it *Ordering Fractions*. I

drew lines to indicate where they should write their names. Then I wrote the eight fractions twice, once in the order they gave them to me and then in order from smallest to largest. Beneath I indicated where they were to record their three explanations. I pointed to how I had recorded on the board the explanations from Mike, Libby, Tomas, Kendra, Jimmy, and Machiko. "These are examples of the kinds of explanations you are to write," I told the class.

Ordering Fractions

$\frac{3}{4}$ $\frac{5}{6}$ $\frac{2}{3}$ $\frac{72}{100}$ $\frac{2}{5}$ $\frac{2}{100}$ $\frac{2}{7}$ $\frac{3}{8}$

$\frac{2}{100}$ $\frac{2}{7}$ $\frac{3}{8}$ $\frac{2}{5}$ $\frac{2}{3}$ $\frac{72}{100}$ $\frac{3}{4}$ $\frac{5}{6}$

1. _____
2. _____
3. _____

"What if our fractions are too hard?" Hope asked.

"You can either ask me for help or choose fractions that you can figure out," I responded.

"Can we do more than one set?" Lynnea asked.

"Yes, if you have time, you can make a second set," I said.

There were no more questions, so I assigned partners and asked them to begin working. I circulated and observed. There was the typical confusion that exists whenever students do something new, and I was busy answering questions and giving help as needed. At the end of the period, I collected the students' papers.

No one had completed the assignment, and when I read their papers, I made comments on Post-it Notes when I noticed errors. For example, several papers had a fraction out of order. For these, I wrote on the note: *One fraction is out of order. Try to find it.* On Jake and Tomas's paper, I also wrote a hint: *The fraction in the wrong place is greater than* $\frac{1}{2}$. I gave the boys this hint because I knew that they were often impatient and were easily frustrated. I didn't give a hint for students who I didn't think needed it, or if the error was more obvious and easy to correct. A few students had fractions with the same denominators, and I asked them to correct this. Also, Jimmy and Libby had included in their eight fractions both two-thirds and eight-twelfths and I wrote on their Post-it: $\frac{2}{3} = \frac{8}{12}$, *so please change one of them so that no fractions are equivalent.*

DAY 2

Before returning the students' papers to them, I told them about the Post-it Notes on some of their papers. "I read your papers last night, and if I noticed that you had a fraction out of order, I wrote

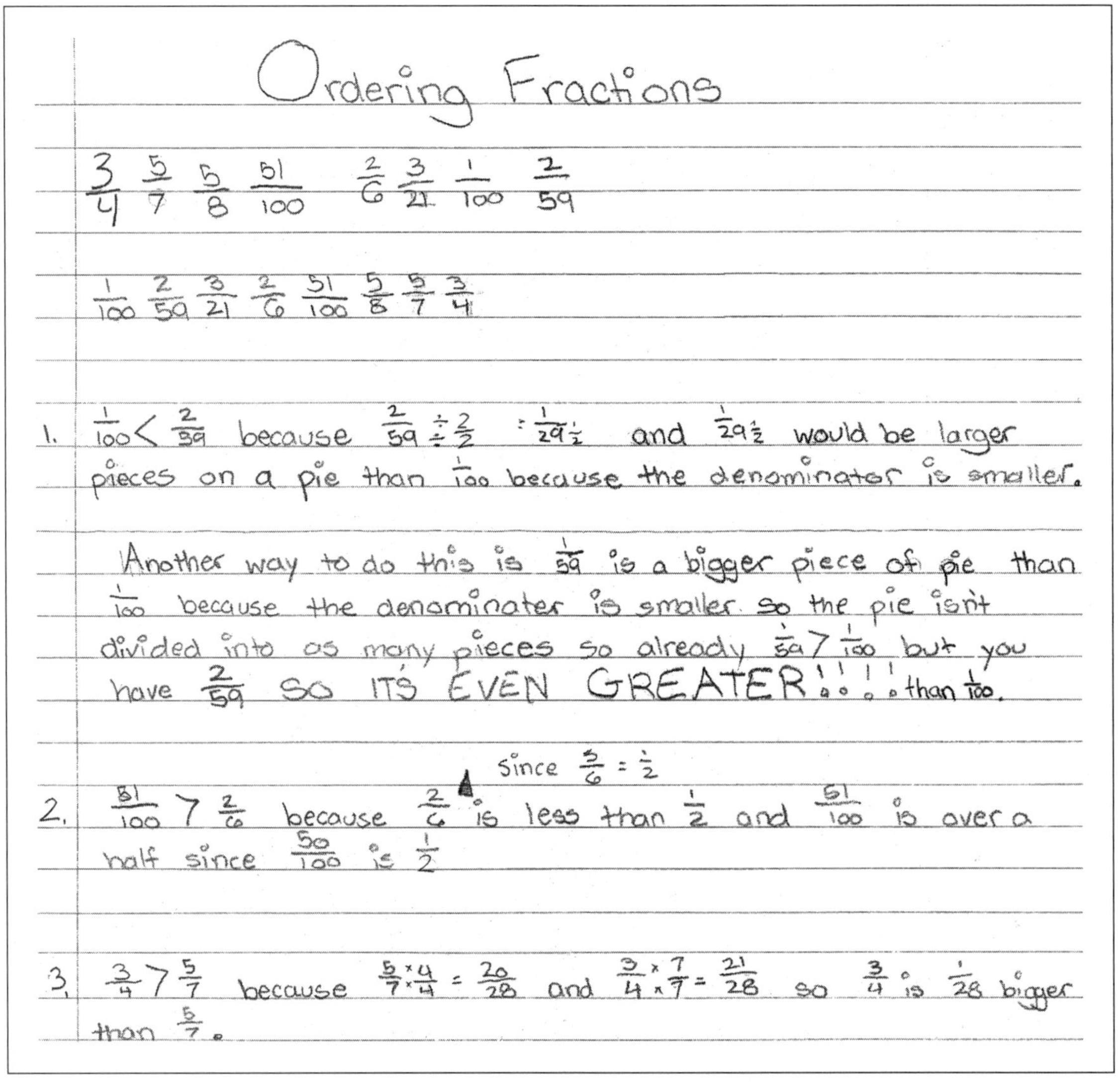

Ordering Fractions

$\frac{3}{4}$ $\frac{5}{7}$ $\frac{5}{8}$ $\frac{51}{100}$ $\frac{2}{6}$ $\frac{3}{21}$ $\frac{1}{100}$ $\frac{2}{59}$

$\frac{1}{100}$ $\frac{2}{59}$ $\frac{3}{21}$ $\frac{2}{6}$ $\frac{51}{100}$ $\frac{5}{8}$ $\frac{5}{7}$ $\frac{3}{4}$

1. $\frac{1}{100} < \frac{2}{59}$ because $\frac{2}{59} \div \frac{2}{2} = \frac{1}{29\frac{1}{2}}$ and $29\frac{1}{2}$ would be larger pieces on a pie than $\frac{1}{100}$ because the denominator is smaller.

Another way to do this is $\frac{1}{59}$ is a bigger piece of pie than $\frac{1}{100}$ because the denominater is smaller so the pie isn't divided into as many pieces so already $\frac{1}{59} > \frac{1}{100}$ but you have $\frac{2}{59}$ SO ITS EVEN GREATER!!!!! than $\frac{1}{100}$.

2. $\frac{51}{100} > \frac{2}{6}$ because $\frac{2}{6}$ is less than $\frac{1}{2}$ since $\frac{3}{6} = \frac{1}{2}$ and $\frac{51}{100}$ is over a half since $\frac{50}{100}$ is $\frac{1}{2}$

3. $\frac{3}{4} > \frac{5}{7}$ because $\frac{5 \times 4}{7 \times 4} = \frac{20}{28}$ and $\frac{3 \times 7}{4 \times 7} = \frac{21}{28}$ so $\frac{3}{4}$ is $\frac{1}{28}$ bigger than $\frac{5}{7}$.

Figure 2–1 *Sadie and Machiko gave two explanations for why* $\frac{1}{100}$ *is less than* $\frac{2}{59}$, *both using the context of pieces of pie.*

that on a Post-it Note. Or if I noticed any other problem that you need to pay attention to, I wrote that as well. If you don't have a Post-it on your paper, then I didn't find any errors. Also, remember to write your three explanations." I then returned the papers and students got to work on them. (See Figures 2–1 through 2–4.)

As pairs completed their papers, I checked them over and then gave them eight cards made from 3-by-5-inch index cards cut in half and a rubber band, asking them to record their fractions, write their names on the back of each card, and put the rubber band around the set of cards. I began matching pairs who had completed their cards. For each, I gave the same direction. "Exchange cards with each other. Put the fractions in order and record them on a separate sheet of paper. When you've both finished, check each other's answers."

At the end of class, I had the students place their sets of cards in a box. I planned to use them as an option for choice time.

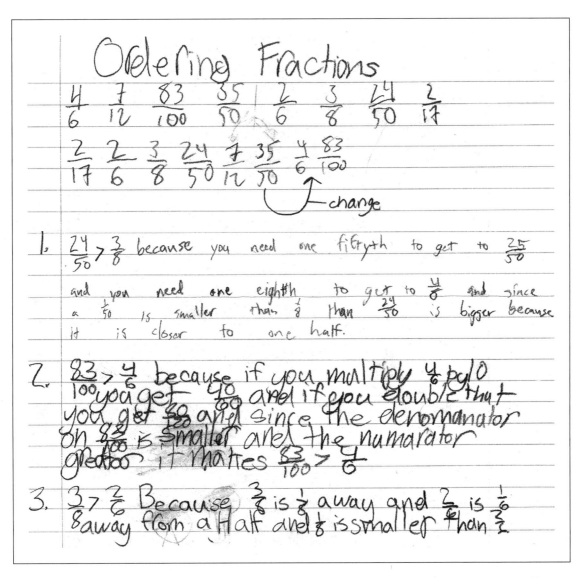

▲▲▲▲▲▲Figure 2–2 *Jake and Tomas corrected the error they had made in ordering $\frac{35}{50}$ and $\frac{4}{6}$. They gave an unusual but correct explanation for why $\frac{83}{100}$ is greater than $\frac{4}{6}$.*

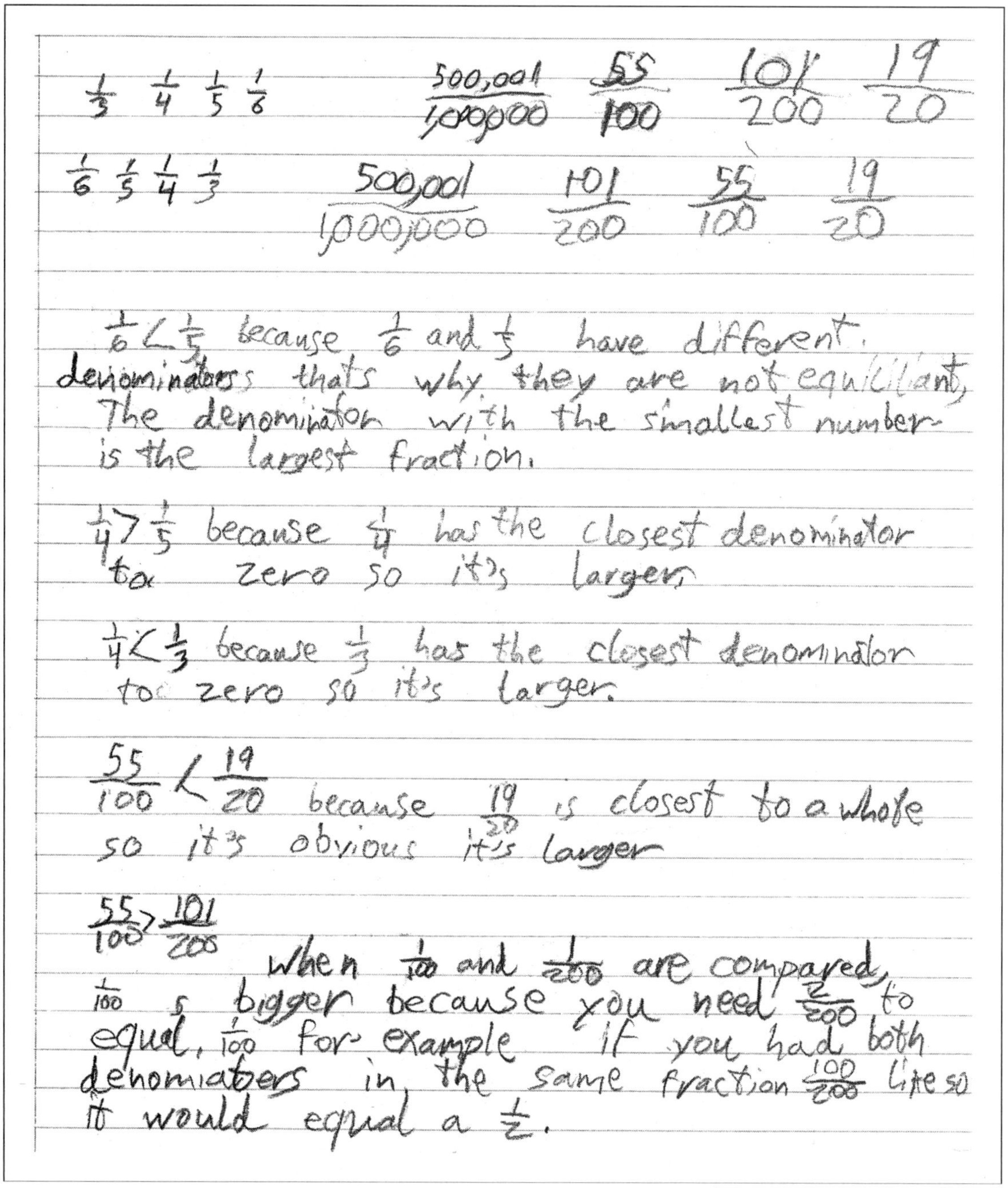

$\frac{1}{3}$ $\frac{1}{4}$ $\frac{1}{5}$ $\frac{1}{6}$ $\frac{500,001}{1,000,000}$ $\frac{55}{100}$ $\frac{101}{200}$ $\frac{19}{20}$

$\frac{1}{6}$ $\frac{1}{5}$ $\frac{1}{4}$ $\frac{1}{3}$ $\frac{500,001}{1,000,000}$ $\frac{101}{200}$ $\frac{55}{100}$ $\frac{19}{20}$

$\frac{1}{6} < \frac{1}{5}$ because $\frac{1}{6}$ and $\frac{1}{5}$ have different denominators that's why they are not equivilant. The denominator with the smallest number is the largest fraction.

$\frac{1}{4} > \frac{1}{5}$ because $\frac{1}{4}$ has the closest denominator to zero so it's larger.

$\frac{1}{4} < \frac{1}{3}$ because $\frac{1}{3}$ has the closest denominator to zero so it's larger.

$\frac{55}{100} < \frac{19}{20}$ because $\frac{19}{20}$ is closest to a whole so it's obvious it's larger

$\frac{55}{100} > \frac{101}{200}$ when $\frac{}{100}$ and $\frac{}{200}$ are compared, $\frac{}{100}$ is bigger because you need $\frac{2}{200}$ to equal $\frac{}{100}$ for example if you had both denomiators in the same fraction $\frac{100}{200}$ like so it would equal a $\frac{1}{2}$.

▲▲▲▲▲▲**Figure 2–3** *After Barton and Mike completed their three explanations, I asked them to write two more with fractions that were more complicated than the ones they initially chose: $\frac{1}{6}$, $\frac{1}{5}$, $\frac{1}{4}$, and $\frac{1}{3}$.*

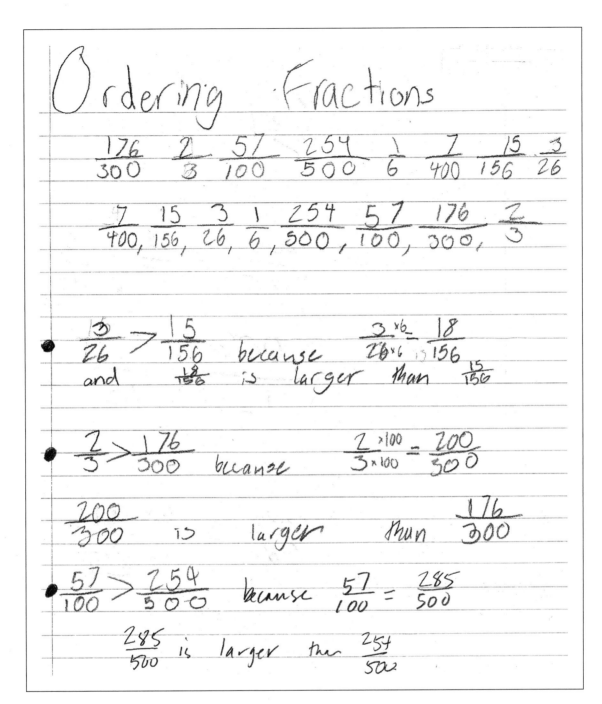

Ordering Fractions

$$\frac{176}{300} \quad \frac{2}{3} \quad \frac{57}{100} \quad \frac{254}{500} \quad \frac{1}{6} \quad \frac{7}{400} \quad \frac{15}{156} \quad \frac{3}{26}$$

$$\frac{7}{400}, \frac{15}{156}, \frac{3}{26}, \frac{1}{6}, \frac{254}{500}, \frac{57}{100}, \frac{176}{300}, \frac{2}{3}$$

• $\frac{3}{26} > \frac{15}{156}$ because $\frac{3 \times 6}{26 \times 6}$ is $\frac{18}{156}$

and $\frac{18}{156}$ is larger than $\frac{15}{156}$

• $\frac{2}{3} > \frac{176}{300}$ because $\frac{2 \times 100}{3 \times 100} = \frac{200}{500}$

$\frac{200}{300}$ is larger than $\frac{176}{300}$

• $\frac{57}{100} > \frac{254}{500}$ because $\frac{57}{100} = \frac{285}{500}$

$\frac{285}{500}$ is larger than $\frac{254}{500}$

▲▲▲▲▲▲Figure 2–4   *Sandro and Hope used the same method for each of their explanations—converting fractions so that they had the same denominators.*

Questions and Discussion

▲▲

▲ *Why did you have students work in pairs to generate their own fractions? I think that if they had worked on their own, it would have been a better assessment of what they knew.*

When students work in pairs, they have the chance to talk about their thinking with each other, and I feel that this talking supports their learning and helps them formulate, cement, and extend their understanding. Also, while they are working on creating and ordering their fractions, I have the opportunity to circulate and observe, which allows me to listen to their ideas, ask questions, and informally assess their understanding. However, having students work alone to generate their own set of eight fractions would be fine and could serve as a useful assessment of your students.

▲ *I worry that there will be too much chaos when students exchange cards. Do you have any management tips?*

The class was active, for sure, and somewhat noisy, but the students were engaged with the mathematics of ordering fractions and the task of checking each other's papers. The noise was productive. This wasn't the first time the students had been given this sort of freedom in a class, however, so they were aware of my expectations. When I first use an activity like this, I talk with the students about what their responsibilities are and what I'll be looking for. I tell them that I expect them to engage with the activity, not to get off task, and to keep their voices as low as possible. I ask them what sorts of things I might notice that would indicate that they are behaving appropriately. Then I ask them what I might notice that would indicate that they are behaving inappropriately. The first time, I let an activity go for only five or ten minutes. Then I interrupt them to talk about the experience and problem solve difficulties, if any. Making this effort at the beginning of the year pays off for making choice time and active involvement successful throughout the year. There are always a few students who need more monitoring, but I think it's important to help develop in students the kind of independence and responsibility that makes them autonomous learners.

▲ *When Tamika asked if it was OK to add one to the numerator and denominator, you responded that you weren't sure. Was this true, or were you trying to keep the issue open for the class?*

I really wasn't sure at this time. There have been times over the years when an idea or problem has come up in a class that I haven't yet thought about or am not sure about. In those instances, I answer honestly. Then I seek out the help of a colleague and get back to the students. In this situation, once I understood the mathematics involved, I used my understanding to generate another lesson. (See Chapter 7, "Fraction Sequences.")

It think that it's important and valuable to let students know that I don't always have the answer, but that I'm willing to work on a problem or idea that is new to me. I tell the students that not all math problems are solved instantly and that, at times, mathematicians work for months or years on one particular problem.

There are times in class, however, when I do understand a new idea or am sure about a problem, but I don't want to reveal what I know to the students. Rather, I want the students to have the chance to think for themselves. In these instances, I also answer honestly, telling the students that I have already thought about this, but I don't want to reveal the conclusion until they have time to think about it on their own.

CHAPTER THREE
BALLOONS AND BROWNIES

Overview

This lesson gives students experience thinking about fractions as parts of wholes and as parts of sets. The contexts of balloons and brownies present students with situations where objects can and cannot be divided into smaller parts. While it makes sense to divide a brownie in half, it doesn't make sense to divide a balloon in half. The lesson helps students see the relationship between fractions and division of whole numbers and encourages students to think about factors and multiples.

Materials

▲ *Balloons and Brownies* worksheet, at least 2 per student (see Blackline masters)
▲ optional: beans, 1 small cupful per table

Time

▲ two class periods; lesson can be repeated multiple times

Teaching Directions

1. On the board, draw three columns. In the first column, list the fractions $\frac{1}{2}, \frac{1}{3}, \frac{1}{4}, \frac{1}{5}, \frac{1}{6}, \frac{1}{8}, \frac{1}{10}$, and $\frac{1}{12}$. Title the second column *Balloons* and the third column *Brownies*. Above the chart, draw a box large enough to write in it a two-digit number.

	Balloons	Brownies
$\frac{1}{2}$		
$\frac{1}{3}$		
$\frac{1}{4}$		
$\frac{1}{5}$		
$\frac{1}{6}$		
$\frac{1}{8}$		
$\frac{1}{10}$		
$\frac{1}{12}$		

2. Ask the students: "What do you notice about the fractions I listed?" Have all who are interested share their ideas.

3. Tell the class that fractions with a numerator of one are called "unit fractions." Then explain that you'll write a number in the box and then they'll find the fractional part of that number for each fraction listed. Ask for suggestions for a friendly number. Their suggestions will reveal their understanding or intuition about finding fractional parts. Twelve is a good number for a first experience. If no student suggests it, tell them that you think it's a number that is friendly for this activity and ask them to see if they can figure out why. Write *12* in the box.

4. Start with $\frac{1}{2}$, the first fraction on the list, and ask: "If you had a bunch of twelve balloons, how many would half of them be?" Ask students to explain their reasoning. Record the answer next to $\frac{1}{2}$ in the Balloons column: $\frac{1}{2}$ *of 12 = 6.* Then ask: "How many brownies are half of twelve brownies?" Again, have students explain their reasoning and record the answer: $\frac{1}{2}$ *of 12 = 6.*

5. Continue with the other fractions on the list. When you get to $\frac{1}{5}$, discuss that the difference between sharing balloons and brownies is that a brownie can be divided into smaller parts, but a balloon can't. Model how to represent the answer in each case. In the Balloons column next to $\frac{1}{5}$, either write an *X* to indicate that you can't share them equally or record: $\frac{1}{5}$ *of 12 = 2 R2.* In the Brownies column, record: $\frac{1}{5}$ *of 12 = $2\frac{2}{5}$.* Continue for the remaining four fractions, being particularly sure that the students understand that you *can't* have one-eighth or one-tenth of twelve balloons and that they *can* figure one-eighth and one-tenth of twelve brownies.

6. Distribute two *Balloons and Brownies* worksheets to each student. Ask them to complete both, one for the number twenty-four and the other for a number of their choosing. Collect their papers at the end of the period. (Most won't have time to complete them both.)

7. On Day 2, begin class with a discussion of the different ways students solved the problems on the sheet for twenty-four. Then return the unfinished papers and have the students continue their work.

Teaching Notes

Finding fractional parts of balloons and brownies gives students the chance to think about fractions in situations where objects can and cannot be divided into smaller parts. For example, thinking about finding $\frac{1}{3}$ of 10 brownies calls for dividing 1 of the brownies into thirds to get the answer of $3\frac{1}{3}$. With 10 balloons, however, it doesn't make sense to have $\frac{1}{3}$ of a balloon. This real-world connection can help build students' understanding of fractions.

The relationship between division of whole numbers and finding fractional parts is revealed naturally in the lesson. It seems obvious to students that to find $\frac{1}{3}$ of 10 calls for dividing 10 by 3. While the students typically arrive at the answer of $3\frac{1}{3}$ when finding $\frac{1}{3}$ of 10 brownies, $\frac{10}{3}$ is also a mathematically correct representation, although "ten-thirds" isn't how we colloquially describe the result of taking $\frac{1}{3}$ of 10 brownies. Not only is $\frac{10}{3}$ mathematically equivalent to $3\frac{1}{3}$, but $\frac{10}{3}$ also means the same as $10 \div 3$. It's not always evident to students that fractions are actually representations of division, that a fraction like $\frac{1}{2}$ can be interpreted as $1 \div 2$. This lesson provides a foundation on which to build this understanding of the connection between division and fractions.

The lesson asks students to focus only on unit fractions—one-half, one-third, one-fourth, and so on. With all problems, keep the emphasis of class discussions on finding answers, representing them with fractions, explaining why they make sense, and listening to others' strategies.

The Lesson

▲▲

DAY 1

I began the lesson by ruling three columns on the board, making a replica of the *Balloons and Brownies* worksheet. In the left-hand column, I listed the fractions $\frac{1}{2}$, $\frac{1}{3}$, $\frac{1}{4}$, $\frac{1}{5}$, $\frac{1}{6}$, $\frac{1}{8}$, $\frac{1}{10}$, and $\frac{1}{12}$. I titled the second column *Balloons* and the third *Brownies*. Above the chart I drew a box large enough to write a number inside.

"What do you notice about the fractions I listed?" I asked.

"They all have a one on top," Anisa answered.

"The denominators are different," Elliot added.

	Balloons	Brownies
$\frac{1}{2}$		
$\frac{1}{3}$		
$\frac{1}{4}$		
$\frac{1}{5}$		
$\frac{1}{6}$		
$\frac{1}{8}$		
$\frac{1}{10}$		
$\frac{1}{12}$		

"You skipped seven, nine, and eleven," Alexa observed.

"You're all right," I replied. "Fractions that have a numerator of one are called 'unit fractions,' and we'll begin this activity by thinking about the particular fractions I wrote on the board. I skipped the unit fractions with seven, nine, and eleven in the denominator because they're less common than the ones I included."

"Why did you write 'Balloons' and 'Brownies'?" Niko wanted to know.

"Let's try the activity and you'll see why," I answered. "In the box, we'll write a number, and then we'll find the fractional parts of the number for all the fractions I listed. What numbers do you think would be 'friendly' to use?"

Tillie raised her hand. "I think two," she said.

"I think twelve," Sonia offered. I recorded both of their suggestions on the board.

Elizabeth said, "How about four hundred eighty? It will work for all of them." Elizabeth had a remarkable mathematical mind that made her both a challenge and a joy to teach. In this instance, she figured out that 480 was a multiple of all of the denominators in the fractions I had listed. No one else seemed to make this connection, however. I didn't respond in any special way but merely recorded *480* on the board under 2 and 12.

"What other numbers do you think would be friendly to use?" I asked.

"Maybe twenty-four," Pedro said. I recorded *24*.

There were no other suggestions. "Let's see," I said, "I'll choose one of these and write it in the box." I chose 12. If 12 hadn't been suggested, I would have suggested it. It's an easy number to use to introduce the activity.

I then asked, "If you had a bunch of twelve balloons, how many would half of them be?"

"Six," the students chorused. Next to $\frac{1}{2}$ on the chart in the Balloons column, I wrote: $\frac{1}{2}$ *of 12 = 6*.

"How do you know?" I asked.

"Easy," Letitia said, "because twelve divided by two is six."

"Did anyone think of it in a different way?" I asked.

"I did six plus six is twelve," Dario said.

"I know six times two is twelve," Midori added.

"Or two times six is twelve," Booth said.

"I know three and three make six, and six and six makes twelve," Niko said. I wasn't sure that Niko was relating to the problem as much as telling me another way to get to twelve, but I didn't comment.

"What about brownies?" I asked. "How many brownies are half of twelve brownies?"

Several students responded. "There are six." "It's the same." "It's still six." "That's easy." I recorded in the Brownies column: $\frac{1}{2}$ *of 12 = 6*.

"Let's try one-third," I said. "How many balloons would there be in one-third of a bunch of twelve balloons?" It was obvious to several children immediately that the answer was four; others had to think for a moment. Again, I had them report the ways they thought about the problem. And again, they knew the answer was the same for brownies. I recorded in each column: $\frac{1}{3}$ *of 12 = 4*.

"Why do you make us do it for balloons and brownies?" Dario asked.

"I think you'll see why in just a bit," I responded.

Figuring one-fourth of twelve, for both balloons and brownies, went smoothly. I recorded in both columns: $\frac{1}{4}$ *of 12 = 3*.

Abby made an observation. "It's easy to figure one-fourth if you look at one-half," she said.

"Why is that so?" I responded. Abby wasn't able to explain why. She had an intuitive feeling that this was so, but she couldn't find the words to substantiate her idea. Sonia volunteered to help.

"It's because one-fourth is half of one-half," she said. "That's what makes it easy."

"Uh oh!" Booth said. "Now I see what happens next with balloons and brownies. Look at one-fifth!" There were some groans as the students realized that twelve couldn't be evenly divided by five.

"There's two left over," Kalila said. "If you divide twelve by five, you get two with two left over."

"So, if I wanted to share a bunch of twelve balloons among five of you so you each got one-fifth of the bunch, how many balloons would you each get?" I asked.

"It doesn't work," Midori said.

"Oh, I know," Dario said. "We'd get two, but we'd have to pop the extra two balloons."

"Or you could cut them in pieces and divide them up," Elliot added.

"Then they would be useless," Sonia pointed out, always practical.

"What about with brownies?" I asked. "If your share was one-fifth of a dozen brownies, how many would you get?"

"It's the same," Sahara said. "It's two with two left over."

"You can divide up the extras," Letitia said. "Divide each of them into fifths. Then you get one-fifth of each. So you'd get two whole brownies and two-fifths more."

"Oh yeah," Dario said. Several expressed their agreement, but others weren't so sure. I made a sketch on the board, first drawing twelve circles to represent twelve balloons, then circling groups of two balloons to make five equal groups, leaving two extras.

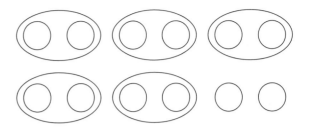

Then I drew twelve squares to represent brownies, again circling groups of two to make five equal groups. I then divided each of the two extras into fifths, explaining as I did so, "I can cut the two extra brownies into fifths as Letitia suggested. Then each of the five people would get one-fifth of each of the two leftover brownies." This seemed to help others. I recorded in the Brownies column: $\frac{1}{5}$ of $12 = 2\frac{2}{5}$.

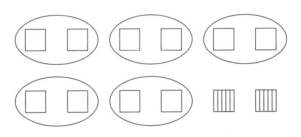

"We can't divide twelve balloons into fifths because twelve isn't divisible by five," I said.

"What's divisible?" Niko asked.

"It means that five doesn't go into twelve evenly," Elizabeth answered.

"And you can't cut up balloons like you can brownies," Sonia added. I drew an X in the Balloons column next to $\frac{1}{5}$ to indicate that it wasn't possible to divide twelve balloons into fifths. Also, to give the students another way to record, I wrote: $\frac{1}{5}$ of $12 = 2$ R2.

"I'm glad we're going on to one-sixth," Kalila said. "That will be much easier."

We continued discussing the rest of the problems. It was obvious to the students that they couldn't share twelve balloons equally among eight or ten people, so we merely needed to record an X in the Balloons column next to $\frac{1}{8}$ and $\frac{1}{10}$. But it wasn't obvious to all of the students how to share eight and ten brownies among twelve people. For each, I drew twelve squares on the board and had volunteers come to the board and demonstrate how to divide them equally.

Midori came to the board to show how to share twelve brownies among eight people. First she drew a circle around each of eight brownies and explained, "There are enough so everyone gets one. Then there are four more to divide up." She turned back to the board and divided each of the remaining four brownies in half. "See, everyone gets half more."

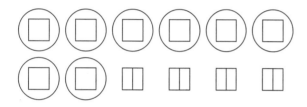

To help students who still might be unsure, I asked Midori, "Suppose you were one of the eight people sharing the brownies. Can you shade in what you would get to eat?" Midori nodded. She shaded in the first brownie and then half of one she had divided.

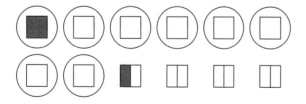

"And how much is your share?" I asked.
"One brownie and a half," she replied.
"Can you write your share as a number?" I asked. Midori wrote on the board: $1 + \frac{1}{2}$.

"That's one way to tell how much you would get," I agreed. "But you can also

write your share as a mixed number. That's a whole number and fraction side by side, without the plus sign." I wrote on the board: $1\frac{1}{2}$.

I repeated this process for sharing twelve brownies among ten people, again drawing twelve squares to represent the brownies. Elliot came to the board, circled ten of the squares, then divided each of the last two into tenths. He made vertical lines and had difficulty squeezing them all in, but he finally managed to do so to his satisfaction. He shaded in one person's share and wrote: $1\frac{2}{10}$.

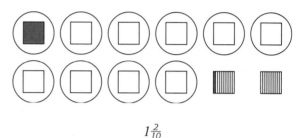

$$1\frac{2}{10}$$

Sharing twelve brownies among twelve people was easy for all of the students, and I completed the chart on the board.

12		
	Balloons	Brownies
$\frac{1}{2}$	$\frac{1}{2}$ of 12 = 6	$\frac{1}{2}$ of 12 = 6
$\frac{1}{3}$	$\frac{1}{3}$ of 12 = 4	$\frac{1}{3}$ of 12 = 4
$\frac{1}{4}$	$\frac{1}{4}$ of 12 = 3	$\frac{1}{4}$ of 12 = 3
$\frac{1}{5}$	X	$\frac{1}{5}$ of 12 = $2\frac{2}{5}$
$\frac{1}{6}$	$\frac{1}{6}$ of 12 = 2	$\frac{1}{6}$ of 12 = 2
$\frac{1}{8}$	X	$\frac{1}{8}$ of 12 = $1\frac{1}{2}$
$\frac{1}{10}$	X	$\frac{1}{10}$ of 12 = $1\frac{2}{10}$
$\frac{1}{12}$	$\frac{1}{12}$ of 12 = 1	$\frac{1}{12}$ of 12 = 1

An Individual Assignment

I then explained that I was going to give each of them two blank *Balloons and*

Brownies worksheets that were like the chart that I had drawn on the board. "To start, write the number twenty-four in the box on one of the worksheets," I explained. "Then fill in the chart just as I did on the board for twelve. I'll set a cup of beans at each table. You may want to use them as balloons or brownies to help, or you may want to draw balloons and brownies as we did on the board. For the second sheet, you can write any number you'd like in the box."

I distributed the worksheets and beans and gave one last direction. "When you finish the first sheet, with twenty-four in the box, bring it to me to check. Then you can start the second sheet with any number you'd like."

"Can we work together?" Alexa asked.

"Yes, you can talk with the person next to you," I said, "but I want you each to complete your own paper."

Observing the Students

Since finding one-half of twenty-four was simple for the students, all of them were able to get started on the assignment. It wasn't until they reached one-fifth that some students started to have difficulty.

When Sahara, for example, was working to figure out one-fifth of twenty-four brownies, she drew twenty-four squares in four rows with six in each. She then circled the first five columns of squares, which told her that each person would get four brownies and there were four brownies left over. Then she divided each of the four extras into halves, carefully drawing arrows to connect each half of a brownie with a whole brownie. That used up two and a half of the extra brownies, leaving three halves remaining. Sahara divided each of these halves in half, making six quarters. Using arrows again, she gave each share a quarter and then realized that she was still left with one-fourth of a brownie.

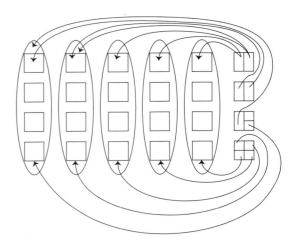

Sahara brought her paper to me. "Now what?" she asked, confused and a little frustrated.

"You could divide that last fourth into five pieces," I suggested.

"Okay," she said and did so. "But what do I write?"

"How much do you think those little pieces are each worth?" I asked.

Sahara thought for a moment and then said, "They're each a fifth of one-fourth. How do I write that?"

"You could write it just as you said it," I answered and wrote on her paper: $\frac{1}{5}$ *of* $\frac{1}{4}$.

"I don't get it," she said.

"If I were one of the five people, can you shade in what would be my share?" I asked. Sahara did so.

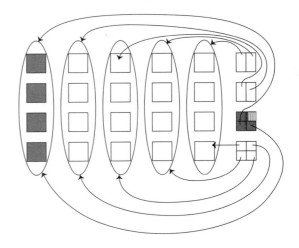

"So I would get four whole brownies, then half of a brownie, then a quarter of a brownie, and then one of these little pieces, which is one-fifth of a quarter," I said, recording as I identified the pieces: $4 + \frac{1}{2} + \frac{1}{4} + \frac{1}{5}$ of $\frac{1}{4}$.

"Is that what I write?" Sahara asked.

"Well, I could tidy it up a bit," I said. "How much is one-half and one-fourth together?"

"Three-fourths," Sahara answered.

"So I could write this," I said and wrote: $4\frac{3}{4} + \frac{1}{5}$ of $\frac{1}{4}$.

Sahara said, "I just don't get that last part, the one-fifth of one-fourth."

"Well, let's look at the problem another way. Here's another suggestion," I said. "Why not go back to where you had four whole leftover brownies. Instead of dividing each of the four brownies in half, divide each of them into fifths, the way we did with twelve brownies before."

Sahara's face brightened. "Oh yeah,"

she said and went to work. When I checked later, she had written: $\frac{1}{5}$ of $24 = 4\frac{4}{5}$.

Soon afterward, Magda came to me with the same problem. "How would you feel about having Sahara help you?" I asked. "She has already worked on that problem, and it would help her to explain it to you." Magda agreed, so she and I went over to Sahara's desk.

"Can you explain to Magda how you figured out one-fifth of twenty-four?" I asked Sahara.

"Sure," she said, seeming pleased to share her knowledge.

Students had different ways to show how they figured. Some used addition. Niko, for example, wrote: $\frac{1}{6}$ of 24 is 4 becuse $4 + 4 + 4 + 4 + 4 + 4 = 24$. Dario also used addition (see Figure 3–1).

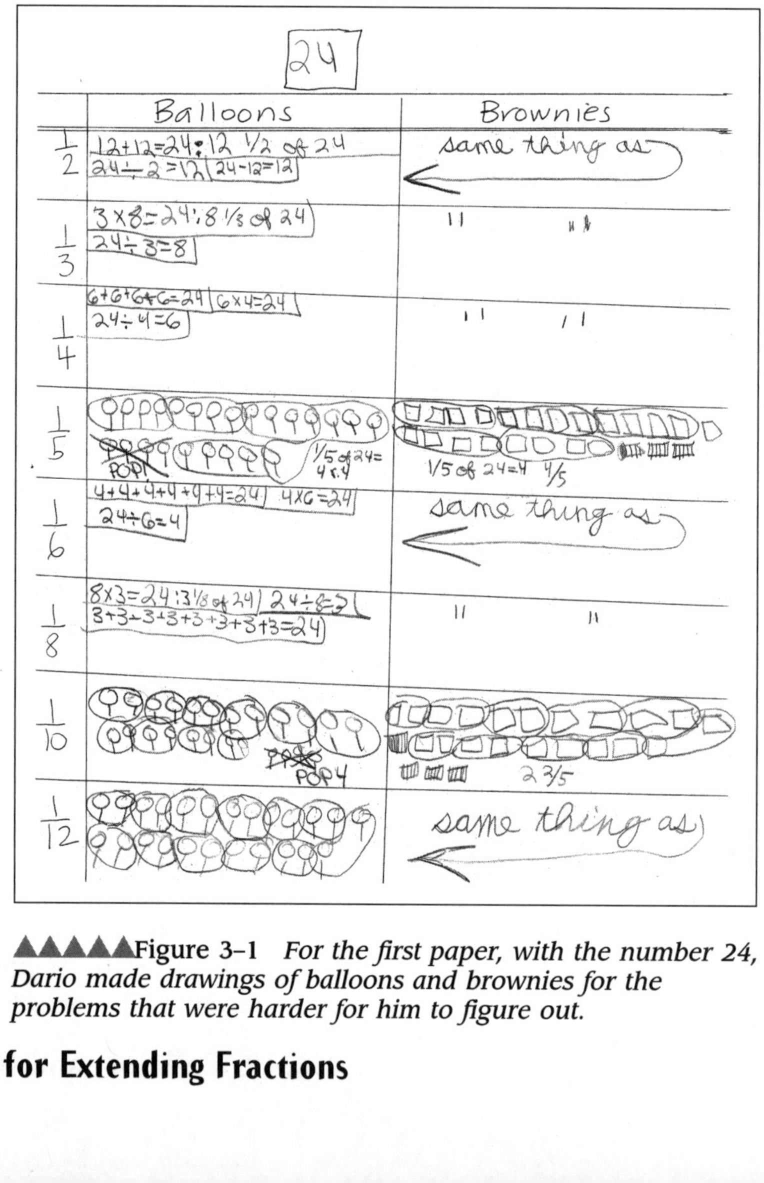

▲▲▲▲▲▲Figure 3–1 *For the first paper, with the number 24, Dario made drawings of balloons and brownies for the problems that were harder for him to figure out.*

Sonia wrote: $\frac{1}{6}$ of 24 = 4 because 24 ÷ 6 = 4. (See Figure 3–2.)

Kalila explained in two ways. She wrote: $\frac{1}{6}$ of 24 = 4, 6 × 4 = 24, 24 ÷ 6 = 4.

The students' choices of numbers for the second sheet varied. Some wanted a big number challenge. Booth, for example, picked one thousand (see Figure 3–3). Others wanted a challenge, but not with such a large number. Emma, for example, picked thirty-four; Geoff picked one hundred; Sahara and Tillie picked fourteen (see Figure 3–4). Niko picked ten because he thought it would be easy.

Alexa and Sonia chose fourty-eight. "It's a little bigger, but we thought we could do it," Sonia explained.

Kalila and Letitia worked together on 480 to find out why Elizabeth had said earlier that it would "work for all of them." "She was right," Kalila said later. "It's really friendly. They're all coming out even." They seemed impressed that Elizabeth knew that. (See Figure 3–5.)

Elizabeth, always looking for a math challenge, decided to skip the first assignment for the number twenty-four (with my agreement) to try to find the fractional parts of fifteen-sixteenths.

"I'll do it, too," I said, "and we can compare answers." I was always searching for ways to meet Elizabeth's needs, which were formidable. (See Figure 3–6.)

By the end of the period, all of the students had finished their first sheet, but only ten students had begun another. I collected all of the students' papers and planned to have them continue their work the next day.

	Balloons	Brownies
$\frac{1}{2}$	$\frac{1}{2}$ of 24=12 because 24÷2=12	$\frac{1}{2}$ of 24=12 because ....
$\frac{1}{3}$	$\frac{1}{3}$ of 24=8 because 24÷3=8	$\frac{1}{3}$ of 24=8 because ....
$\frac{1}{4}$	$\frac{1}{4}$ of 24=6 because 24÷4=6	$\frac{1}{4}$ of 24=6 because ....
$\frac{1}{5}$	$\frac{1}{5}$ of 24 = 4 with 4 left over because 24÷5=4 R4	$\frac{1}{5}$ of 24=4$\frac{4}{5}$ because—I can't explain it, but I know what it is.
$\frac{1}{6}$	$\frac{1}{6}$ of 24=4 because 24÷6=4	$\frac{1}{6}$ of 24=4 because ......
$\frac{1}{8}$	$\frac{1}{8}$ of 24=3 because 24÷8=3	$\frac{1}{8}$ of 24=3 because ....
$\frac{1}{10}$	$\frac{1}{10}$ of 24=2 and 4 left over because 24÷10=2 R4	$\frac{1}{10}$ of 24=2$\frac{2}{5}$ because—I can't explain it, but I know what it is.
$\frac{1}{12}$	$\frac{1}{12}$ of 24=2 because 24÷12=2	$\frac{1}{12}$ of 24=12 because ......

▲▲▲▲▲▲**Figure 3–2** *Sonia reasoned numerically to solve all of the problems for 24 balloons and brownies.*

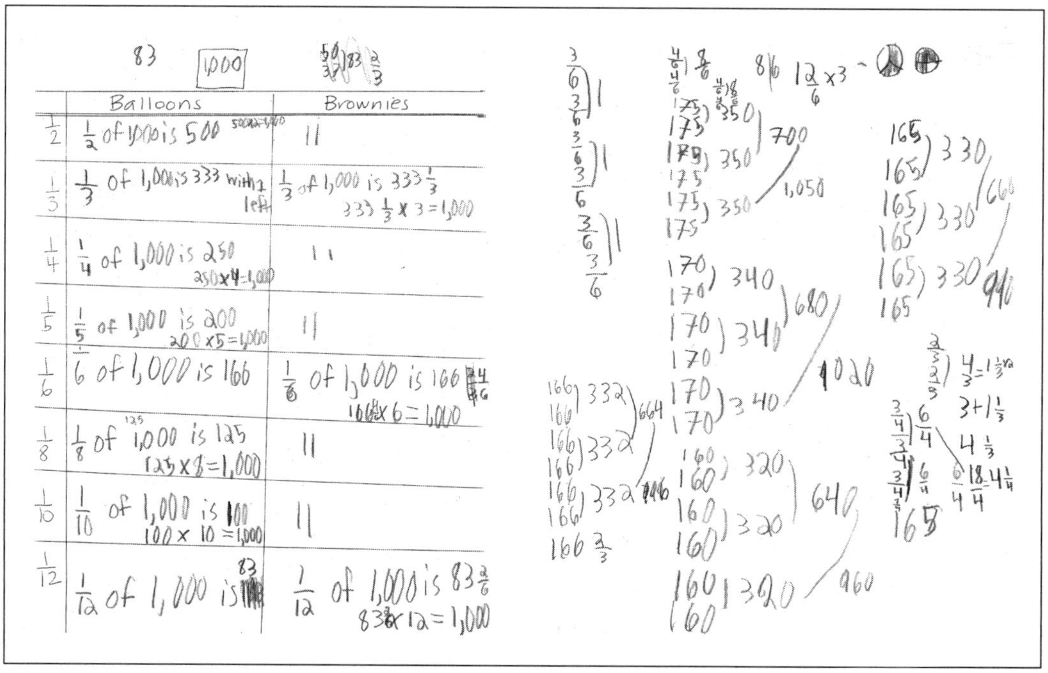

Figure 3–3 table (top):

83 |1,000| 50/.../83...

	Balloons	Brownies
$\frac{1}{2}$	$\frac{1}{2}$ of 1,000 is 500 500×...	11
$\frac{1}{3}$	$\frac{1}{3}$ of 1,000 is 333 with 2 left	$\frac{1}{3}$ of 1,000 is $333\frac{1}{3}$ $333\frac{1}{3} \times 3 = 1,000$
$\frac{1}{4}$	$\frac{1}{4}$ of 1,000 is 250 250×4=1,000	11
$\frac{1}{5}$	$\frac{1}{5}$ of 1,000 is 200 200×5=1,000	11
$\frac{1}{6}$	$\frac{1}{6}$ of 1,000 is 166	$\frac{1}{6}$ of 1,000 is $166\frac{4}{6}$ 166×6=1,000
$\frac{1}{8}$	$\frac{1}{8}$ of 1,000 is 125 125×8=1,000	11
$\frac{1}{10}$	$\frac{1}{10}$ of 1,000 is 100 100×10=1,000	11
$\frac{1}{12}$	$\frac{1}{12}$ of 1,000 is 83	$\frac{1}{12}$ of 1,000 is $83\frac{2}{6}$ $83\frac{2}{6} \times 12 = 1,000$

▲▲▲▲▲▲Figure 3–3 *Booth was interested in exploring the fractional parts of a large number and chose 1000. He did a good deal of figuring on the back of his paper.*

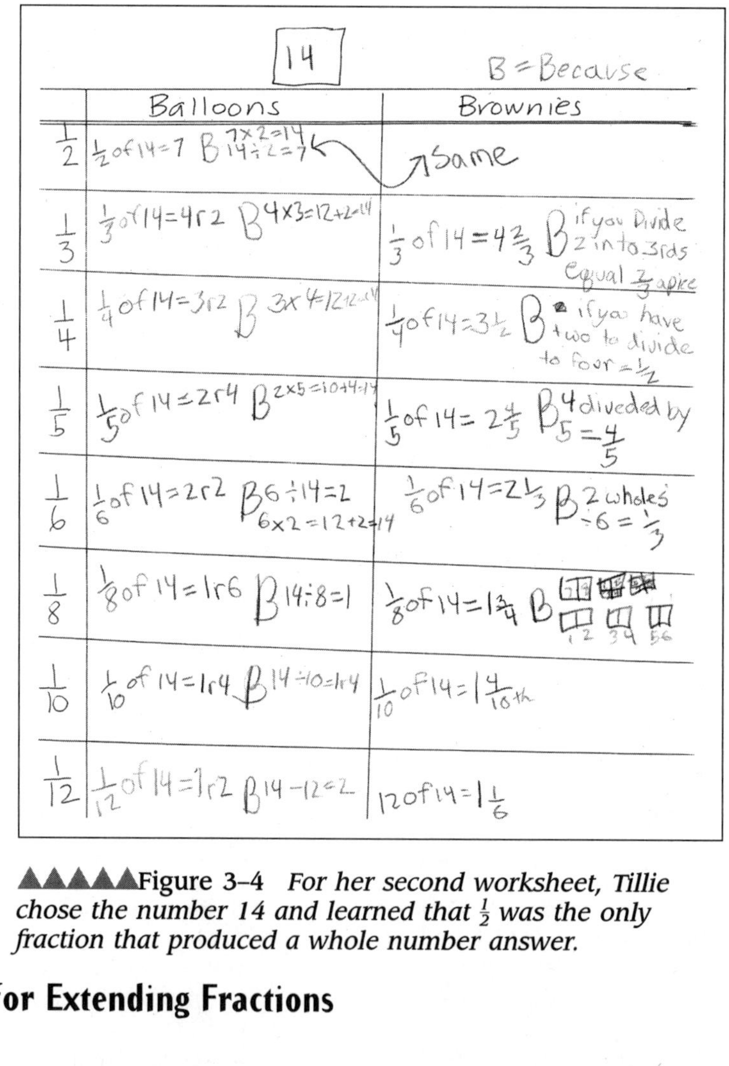

Figure 3–4 table (bottom):

|14| B = Because

	Balloons	Brownies
$\frac{1}{2}$	$\frac{1}{2}$ of 14 = 7 B $7\times2=14$ $14\div2=7$	Same
$\frac{1}{3}$	$\frac{1}{3}$ of 14 = 4 r 2 B $4\times3=12+2=14$	$\frac{1}{3}$ of 14 = $4\frac{2}{3}$ B if you divide 2 into 3rds equal $\frac{2}{3}$ apiece
$\frac{1}{4}$	$\frac{1}{4}$ of 14 = 3 r 2 B $3\times4=12+2=14$	$\frac{1}{4}$ of 14 = $3\frac{1}{2}$ B if you have two to divide to four = $\frac{1}{2}$
$\frac{1}{5}$	$\frac{1}{5}$ of 14 = 2 r 4 B $2\times5=10+4=14$	$\frac{1}{5}$ of 14 = $2\frac{4}{5}$ B 4 divided by 5 = $\frac{4}{5}$
$\frac{1}{6}$	$\frac{1}{6}$ of 14 = 2 r 2 B $6\div14=2$ $6\times2=12+2=14$	$\frac{1}{6}$ of 14 = $2\frac{1}{3}$ B 2 wholes ÷6 = $\frac{1}{3}$
$\frac{1}{8}$	$\frac{1}{8}$ of 14 = 1 r 6 B $14\div8=1$	$\frac{1}{8}$ of 14 = $1\frac{3}{4}$ B 1 2 3 4 5 6
$\frac{1}{10}$	$\frac{1}{10}$ of 14 = 1 r 4 B $14\div10=1$ r 4	$\frac{1}{10}$ of 14 = $1\frac{4}{10}$th
$\frac{1}{12}$	$\frac{1}{12}$ of 14 = 1 r 2 B $14-12=2$	$\frac{1}{12}$ of 14 = $1\frac{1}{6}$

▲▲▲▲▲▲Figure 3–4 *For her second worksheet, Tillie chose the number 14 and learned that $\frac{1}{2}$ was the only fraction that produced a whole number answer.*

36   Lessons for Extending Fractions

	Balloons	Brownies
$\frac{1}{2}$	$\frac{1}{2}$ of 480=240 because $240 \times 2=480$	→same
$\frac{1}{3}$	$\frac{1}{3}$ of 480=160 because $3\times160=480$	→same
$\frac{1}{4}$	$\frac{1}{4}$ of 480=120 because $120\times4=480$	→same
$\frac{1}{5}$	$\frac{1}{5}$ of 480=96 because $5\times96=480$	→same
$\frac{1}{6}$	$\frac{1}{6}$ of 480=80 because $80\times6=480$	→same
$\frac{1}{8}$	$\frac{1}{8}$ of 480=60 because $60\times8=480$	→same
$\frac{1}{10}$	$\frac{1}{10}$ of 480=48 because $\begin{smallmatrix}48\\\times10\end{smallmatrix}$	→same
$\frac{1}{12}$	$\frac{1}{12}$ of 480=40 $40\times12=480$ because $\begin{smallmatrix}40\\\times12\\\hline 80\\40\\\hline 480\end{smallmatrix}$	→same

▲▲▲▲▲▲Figure 3–5 *Letitia and Kalia chose 480, the number that Elizabeth had earlier identified as one that would "work for all of them." Letitia was impressed that Elizabeth was right.*

	Balloons	Brownies
$\frac{1}{2}$	$\frac{15}{16} \div 2 = \frac{15}{32}$	$\frac{15}{16} \cdot \frac{1}{2} = \frac{15}{32}$
$\frac{1}{3}$	$\frac{15}{16} \div 3 = \frac{15}{48}$	
$\frac{1}{4}$	$\frac{15}{16} \div 4 = \frac{15}{64}$	
$\frac{1}{5}$	$\frac{15}{16} \div 5 = \frac{15}{80}$	
$\frac{1}{6}$	$\frac{15}{16} \div 6 = \frac{15}{96}$	
$\frac{1}{8}$	$\frac{15}{16} \div 8 = \frac{15}{128}$	
$\frac{1}{10}$	$\frac{15}{16} \div 10 = \frac{15}{160}$	
$\frac{1}{12}$	$\frac{15}{16} \div 12 = \frac{15}{192}$	

▲▲▲▲▲▲Figure 3–6 *Elizabeth, a gifted math student, chose the number $\frac{15}{16}$. She ignored the context of balloons and brownies and showed her understanding of the relationship between figuring fractional parts and division.*

DAY 2

I began class by talking with the students about the different ways they had solved some of the problems with twenty-four, beginning with Niko's, Sonia's, and Kalila's explanations for finding one-sixth of twenty-four, then discussing some of the other problems. Following this, I gave directions about what they were to do.

"You each need to complete your two papers today, one for twenty-four and the other for any number of your choice. In a moment, I'll hand back the papers I collected yesterday. Remember, when you complete your first paper, bring it to me. If you finish both papers before the end of the period, then find a partner and play one of the games on our choice list." I know that students work at different paces and that I need to provide ways to keep students purposefully engaged when they complete work more quickly than others. The list of choices included fraction games and activities that I had been teaching the class for just this purpose.

I returned the partially completed papers and the students got to work. As before, I circulated, talked with students requesting help, and discussed their papers as they finished them. I asked students who finished early either to do another sheet or to pick one of the math choices available to them.

Questions and Discussion

▲▲

▲ *Don't the students get confused between thinking about division and thinking about taking fractional parts?*

Students bring their understanding of division to these problems. The connection seems natural to them, and the problems help make the link apparent. Also, the problems are a way to introduce the idea of representing remainders to division problems as fractions.

▲ *Why did you allow the students to choose the numbers they were to use for their second worksheet? Wouldn't it have been better for a class discussion if they had all used the same numbers?*

Giving them a choice is a way for me to see how much they're willing to challenge themselves. It's a useful way for me to assess their skill and comfort. Besides, they all had the experience of working on twelve and twenty-four before they had the option to choose their own numbers.

▲ *Why do you record the students' ideas on the board? What purpose does this serve?*

I do this regularly for several reasons. One is to model for students how to represent their ideas mathematically. Another is to check that I am correctly interpreting students' thinking. A third is that we then have a reference for our discussion that's useful for revisiting students' ideas.

CHAPTER FOUR
FRACTIONS AND VENN DIAGRAMS

Overview

This lesson uses Venn diagrams to provide students experience with comparing fractions. Students sort fractions into two intersecting sets that have labels such as "greater than one-half," "less than one," "greater than one-fourth," and so on. First, in a whole-class lesson, students place fractions on Venn diagrams and explain their reasoning. Individual assignments then provide additional practice and also engage students in creating Venn diagrams for others to examine.

Materials

▲ 20 4-by-6-inch index cards, each with a fraction written on it—$\frac{1}{8}$, $\frac{1}{4}$, $\frac{1}{3}$, $\frac{1}{2}$, $\frac{2}{8}$, $\frac{2}{5}$, $\frac{2}{3}$, $\frac{3}{10}$, $\frac{3}{8}$, $\frac{3}{6}$, $\frac{3}{5}$, $\frac{3}{4}$, $\frac{4}{4}$, $\frac{5}{12}$, $\frac{5}{4}$, $\frac{7}{2}$, $\frac{8}{8}$, $\frac{11}{12}$, $\frac{49}{100}$, $\frac{70}{100}$

▲ *Fractions and Venn Diagrams* worksheet, 1 per student (see Blackline Masters)

Time

▲ two class periods, plus additional fifteen-minute sessions to present student work

Teaching Directions

1. Introduce or review Venn diagrams using a nonfraction context. Draw two intersecting circles on the board, label them *I am a girl* and *My shoes have laces*, and ask students where their names belong. Repeat with labels *< 25* and *Odd*.

2. For convenience of discussion, label the four sections of two intersecting sets as shown.

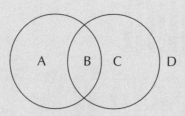

3. Draw two intersecting circles and label them $> \frac{1}{2}$ and < 1. Show the class the fraction cards, one by one, and ask a volunteer to write each fraction where it belongs on the Venn diagram. Discuss each.

4. Repeat for two other labels: $> \frac{1}{4}$ and $< \frac{3}{4}$.

5. Distribute the Venn diagram worksheets for students to do individually.

6. Begin the next day's class with another experience, this time for a Venn diagram with labels $> \frac{1}{2}$ and > 1.

7. Next, draw on the board a Venn diagram that contains fractions but has incomplete labels. (Use the diagram shown below or create one of your own.) Give students time to talk in pairs about what the labels might be and what other fractions you could have written in the sections. Then discuss.

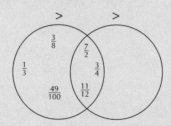

8. Give directions for an individual assignment; write them on the board:

1. *Draw intersecting circles.*
2. *Pick labels.*
3. *Write fractions, at least three in each section that's possible.*
4. *Have a partner check your fractions.*

9. Over the next week or so, copy the Venn diagrams from students' papers onto the board for the class to discuss. (Check with students that this is OK with them and also be careful about protecting their anonymity.)

Teaching Notes

Sorting fractions into Venn diagrams provides another context in which students can apply their understanding about comparing fractions. On Venn diagrams, fractions aren't placed in order of magnitude as they are on number lines, but instead are grouped into sets by particular attributes. Venn diagrams provide pictorial representations of sets and the relationships between them.

Sometimes sets are disjoint; that is, they have no elements in common. The set of fractions greater than one-half, for example, doesn't overlap at all with the set of fractions less than one-half. However, when sorting fractions into sets that are greater than one-half and less than one, there are fractions that fit in both—two-thirds, three-fourths, and nine-tenths, for example. Sorting fractions into two sets on Venn diagrams presents students with the task of identifying fractions that belong in each set, those that belong in both sets, and those that belong in neither.

It's important for this lesson that students understand how Venn diagrams are used. Even if they have learned about them previously, it may help to provide a review to eliminate possible confusion. The vignette that follows offers one way to do this.

The Lesson

▲▲▲

DAY 1

Before asking the students to place fractions on a Venn diagram, I used a different context to introduce the idea of using a Venn diagram to classify information. I drew two intersecting circles on the board and labeled them *I am a girl* and *My shoes have laces.*

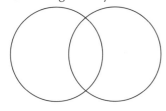

I said to the class, "Think about where you'd write your name so it's in the correct place. Raise your hand when you've decided." Some hands shot up immediately, but I waited to give others a chance to think. When about two-thirds of the students had their hands raised, I called on Aimee.

"In the middle," she said.

"Here?" I asked, pointing to the intersection of the circles. Aimee nodded.

"Who can explain why Aimee's name belongs here?" I asked. Hands shot up and I called on Jerry.

"She's a girl and her shoes have laces," he answered.

I wrote *Aimee* in the correct place and said to the class, "The middle section is

the intersection of the two circles. Drawing circles like this and using them to sort information is called making a Venn diagram." I wrote *intersection* and *Venn diagram* on the board.

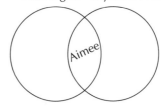

I then called on Kenny to tell me where to write his name. "In the laces circle," he said.

"Aimee is written in the laces circle," I said. "Shall I write your name in the same place?"

"No," Kenny said, "mine goes in the right part of the circle, not in the middle."

To emphasize the correct terminology of *intersection* instead of *middle*, I said, "Yes, your name doesn't belong in the intersection because you're a boy." I wrote *Kenny* in the correct place.

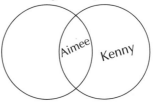

Fractions and Venn Diagrams　**41**

Others students' hands were waving and I called on several more students to tell where their names belonged, prompting them to use *intersection* instead of *middle*. Learning new language best occurs from using it in the context of an activity. After reminding several students, I no longer had to do so.

Jabir raised his hand. "What if you don't fit in either circle?" he wanted to know.

I replied, "Then you'd write your name outside both circles. Where does your name belong?"

"In the right circle with the other boys," he said.

"You can only be outside if you're a boy and your shoes don't have laces," Ruana said. We checked, and all of the boys' shoes had laces, so no one's name belonged outside the circles.

A Second Venn Diagram
I then erased the circles, redrew them, and wrote new labels: *< 25* and *Odd*.

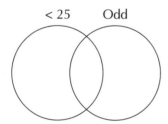

"For this Venn diagram, think about placing numbers in the circles," I said.

"What does 'L twenty-five' mean?" Nickie wanted to know. She wasn't familiar with the mathematical symbol I had written and saw it as the letter L. I wrote *less than 25* above < 25 and, as a review for the class, I wrote on the board:

$<$ *is less than*
$=$ *is equal to*
$>$ *is greater than*

I then gave the class further directions. "In a moment, I'll ask for volunteers to tell me where to write a

number. Each time I write one, the rest of you should indicate that you agree with thumbs up, disagree with thumbs down, or you're not sure with your thumb sideways. That way I can get a sense of what you understand and what's confusing you."

"I don't get it," Keira said.

"Who can explain to Keira what you're to do with your thumbs?" I said, surprised at her question since this was standard classroom procedure.

"That's not what I don't get," Keira responded, helping me realize that I had misinterpreted her question. "I don't know what you mean about writing numbers."

"Let's have someone tell me where to write a number," I said. "Then you can show by holding up your thumb sideways if you don't understand." Other students were waving hands to offer a number. I called on Colton.

"My number is ten and it goes only in the left circle," he said.

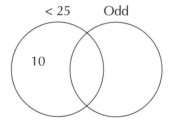

Not all of the students held up a thumb. I reminded them to do so and waited. Most agreed with Colton, but a few showed thumbs down or sideways.

"As long as I see different thumbs, we need an explanation," I said. "Colton, can you explain why ten belongs in the left-hand circle?"

"It's less than twenty-five but it's even, so it only goes in one circle," he said.

To clarify for the few who still seemed confused, I traced the left-hand circle with my finger. "Everything in this circle should be less than twenty-five, so ten fits here."

I traced around the right-hand circle and said, "The numbers that belong in here must be odd, but ten isn't odd. That's why it can't go in this circle. So it goes in the part of the left-hand circle that doesn't intersect with the other circle." This seemed to help. Several students said, "Oh yeah!" or "I get it now."

I called on Stella next. "I'm nine and it goes in the intersection. It's in both." Again there were a few thumbs that weren't up, so I again explained as I did with ten, tracing each circle with my finger and explaining that the number nine belonged in both.

No more hands were raised to volunteer a number. I was surprised until Ruana told me that they were all nine or ten years old. It seems that the personalizing of gender and laces on shoes implied that the numbers were supposed to be personal as well. "Ah," I said, "you thought I meant your ages. No, you can use any numbers you'd like." Hands shot up and I called on Lily.

"I think you should write the number thirteen in the intersection," she said. Others laughed. The class knew that thirteen was Lily's favorite number and that she used it whenever she could. All thumbs were up. Monica volunteered twenty-one for the intersection and, again, all thumbs were up.

Marcel went next. "I think that you should write fifty outside both circles." A buzz broke out in the room and there was a mixture of thumb responses. (If Marcel or someone else hadn't suggested a number that wasn't in either set, I would have done so.)

"Marcel, can you explain?" I asked.

He did so with a grin. "It's not less than twenty-five and it's not odd, so it can't go in either of them."

"Can you write numbers outside the circles?" Inez asked.

"Remember, she said we could," Ruana responded.

"Does it make sense for fifty to be outside?" I asked Inez. She nodded.

"It's the only place that makes sense," I confirmed, "and it's fine." Marcel's contribution sparked a flurry of numbers outside both sets. Steven suggested one hundred, then Joseph suggested one thousand, and then Jared suggested one million. To stop the escalating suggestions, I gave another direction, "Let's continue placing numbers in this Venn diagram until we have three numbers in each area." I drew another Venn diagram and labeled the areas A, B, C, and D to make it easier to refer to them.

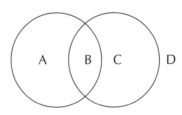

"We don't need any more numbers in Section B, the intersection, or in Section D, outside both circles," I continued. "But we need two more numbers in A and three in C." Genevieve and Kenny gave numbers for Section A—twenty and two. Khalil, Genevieve, and Amanda gave numbers for Section C—fifty-five, ninety-nine, and twenty-seven.

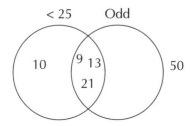

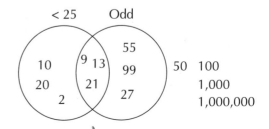

Sorting Fractions

The students seemed to understand how to sort numbers in a Venn diagram, so I erased what we had done and shifted the lesson into fractions. I drew and labeled two new circles: $> \frac{1}{2}$ and < 1.

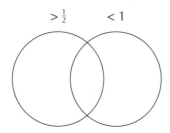

"Nothing will work," Aimee blurted out. I didn't respond to her but reviewed the symbols for greater than and less than and then showed the class the set of 4-by-6-inch fraction cards I had made. "I'll show you these fractions one by one and we'll talk about where each belongs."

I held up the card with $\frac{1}{3}$ on it and asked, "Who would like to come up and write the fraction where it goes on the Venn diagram?" I called on Inez and she wrote $\frac{1}{3}$ in the intersection of the two circles.

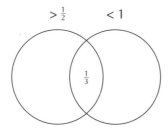

"Show a thumb up, down, or sideways," I reminded the class. There was a smattering of each.

"Ah, I see that there's some disagreement," I said. "Inez, can you explain?"

Inez began, "One-half is one whole split into two pieces and . . . ." She faltered and then said, "Oh, I don't know how to explain."

"Would it help to make a drawing?" I suggested. Inez nodded. She came to the board, drew a circle, divided it in half, and wrote $\frac{1}{2}$ in one section. Then she drew another circle, divided it into thirds, and labeled one section with $\frac{1}{3}$.

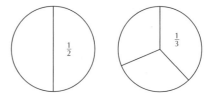

"What does the drawing tell you?" I asked.

"One-third is less than one-half because you have more pieces," Inez said with confidence.

"I agree," I confirmed. "So now explain why you wrote one-third in the intersection of the two circles."

"Well, it's less than one," she began. "You can see that. And it's more than . . . no, it's less than one-half. Hey, that's not right." Inez erased the $\frac{1}{3}$ and stood there, perplexed. "There's no place it can go," she said.

"Yes, there is," Kenny called out.

"Please let Inez think," I said to Kenny. "You'll have a turn soon."

Inez pointed to the right-hand circle and said, "If it's less than one, it has to go in this circle. But it can't go in the other. Oh, I get it, it goes here." She wrote $\frac{1}{3}$ in Section C.

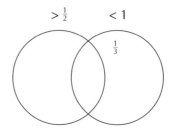

"Am I right?" she asked me. I nodded. She let out a big sigh, went back to her desk, and flopped into her seat.

"Thinking about fractions can be hard," I said, "and thinking about fractions in front of the class can be even harder. You did really fine, Inez. Who wants to try the next fraction?"

I held up $\frac{1}{4}$ and called on Jerry. He came to the board and wrote $\frac{1}{4}$ next to $\frac{1}{3}$.

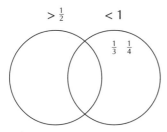

Then he turned to the class and said, "Thumbs?" I think that Jerry's confidence influenced some children who weren't really sure to put their thumbs up, but Keira's and Marcel's thumbs were clearly sideways. "It's the same as one-third," Jerry explained. "It's less than one but it's not more than one-half." Keira and Marcel nodded. Their nodding didn't convince me that they understood, but I didn't want to probe them more at this time. Instead, I opted to see what would happen with more experience.

Next I held up $\frac{2}{3}$. "Talk to the person next to you about where two-thirds belongs. Then raise your hand if you'd like to come to the board." Asking students to confer with a classmate gives them a chance to try out their ideas in a safer and less formal way. After a moment almost half of the students had raised their hands. I called on Nickie. She came up and wrote the fraction in the intersection.

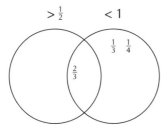

All thumbs were up except for Keira's. "I kind of get it," Keira said, "but I better hear more." I complimented her on her

judgment about her needs and asked Ruana to explain.

"It's in between one-half and one, so it goes in the middle," she said.

"You mean the intersection," Inez corrected, now recovered from her ordeal at the front of the room.

"Are you convinced?" I asked Keira. She nodded "yes."

Next Lily came up to write $\frac{3}{5}$. She placed it in the intersection and offered an explanation without checking thumbs. "It's easy to decide that it's less than one, and I know it's more than one-half because two plus three makes five and three is more than two."

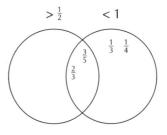

"Now I really don't get that!" Keira said.

Lily explained more. "Well, if you have three-fifths, there are only two-fifths left, and that's less than three-fifths, so three-fifths has to be more than half." Keira didn't seem reassured.

"How many fifths make one-half?" I asked the class.

"You can't do it," Kenny blurted out. "It's not even."

"Yes, you can," Jerry said. "Half of five is two and a half."

"What kind of fraction is that?" Colton said. I wrote on the board: $\frac{2\frac{1}{2}}{5}$.

"Wow!" Colton said, "Can you do that?"

"Well, I just did," I answered. "We haven't seen any fractions yet with a fraction for the numerator or denominator, but you'll encounter them in high school. They're called 'complex fractions.' And this complex fraction is equal to one-half because the numerator is half of the denominator. So I know that three-fifths is more than half." I glanced at Keira. She seemed to be hanging in there. I wasn't so sure about Joseph or Marcel, but I pressed on. I know that thinking about fractions is difficult for some students, but I also know that given time and opportunities, their understanding will grow and strengthen.

Jabir came up next and wrote $\frac{5}{12}$, then Genevieve wrote $\frac{3}{8}$. These seemed OK for the class. Steven volunteered for $\frac{7}{2}$ but became confused at the board.

"It's the same as three and a half, isn't it?" he asked me.

"How did you figure that?" I asked.

Steven drew a square and divided it in half. "Here's a brownie in two halves," he said. He continued drawing and dividing squares until he had shown seven halves. "See, it takes three squares and a half more."

"So where will you write the fraction?" I asked. Steven wrote it outside both circles. There was a mixed reaction from the class, followed by a lively discussion.

"It's more than one so it has to be outside this circle," Steven said.

"But it's more than one-half, so it should be inside the other circle," Lily countered.

"It's too big for that circle," Aimee said.

"No it's not," Jared said. "Anything bigger than one-half belongs in that circle." Steven realized his error and moved the fraction.

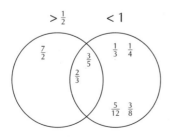

"Oh yeah," Aimee said. Others murmured their agreement.

Kenny came up and wrote $\frac{11}{12}$ next. "It's less than one because twelve-twelfths is one," he explained. "It's one-twelfth less than a whole, and it's also greater than one-half."

Joseph came up to write $\frac{4}{4}$. "It's one whole so it's not less than one," he thought aloud. But then he was stuck.

"Can anyone help?" I asked. Joseph called on Stella.

Stella said, "I look at four-fourths and then I look just at the right circle and ask myself: 'Is it less than one?' The answer is no. Then I look at the left circle and ask myself: 'Is it more than one-half?' The answer is yes. So it goes just in the left circle."

"Here?" Joseph asked, pointing to Section A. Stella nodded "yes." Joseph looked more relieved than confident.

Keira smiled. "I get that one," she said.

I continued with more fractions—$\frac{49}{100}$, $\frac{8}{8}$ (which Keira volunteered for and did correctly), $\frac{3}{4}$, $\frac{1}{2}$, $\frac{2}{8}$, $\frac{3}{6}$ (which showed me Marcel's fragile understanding), and $\frac{1}{8}$.

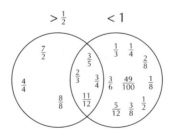

Keira then asked, "Does anything go outside both circles? I can't think of anything." Even though Keira lacked mathematical confidence, she continued to push herself to think.

"I don't think there are any," I said. "A number line helps me see why all the numbers are covered." I drew a number line to show how I was thinking.

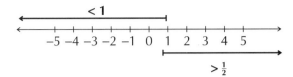

Another Venn Diagram

I then erased the circles and drew two more on the board with new labels: $> \frac{1}{4}$ and $< \frac{3}{4}$. I held up $\frac{1}{2}$. Ruana wrote it in the intersection and explained, with confidence, "The only thing greater than one-fourth and less than three-fourths is two-fourths, and that's the same as one-half, so it goes here."

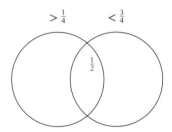

No one commented on Ruana's reasoning. I held up $\frac{3}{5}$, curious to see what they would do with another fraction that also belonged in the intersection. Colton came up.

"It's way more than one-fourth because it's more than one-half," he began. "And I think it has to be less than three-fourths because if you have five pieces, they're smaller than if you have four pieces, so three-fifths is less than three-fourths. I think it goes in the intersection." Ruana looked momentarily startled, then she grinned.

Nickie then placed $\frac{2}{2}$. "It can't be less than three-fourths because it's a whole," she said, "so it has to go in Section A."

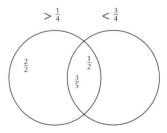

An Individual Assignment

I then gave the class an assignment to do individually. I had prepared a worksheet with two intersecting circles, one labeled $> \frac{1}{4}$ and the other labeled < 1. I reviewed the directions I had written on it: *Write at least three fractions in each section of the Venn diagram. Choose one fraction from each section and explain below how you know it's in the correct place.* Ruana pointed out that no fractions could go outside the circles; I and others agreed.

The students seemed to know what was expected of them. But once they began to work, a good deal of confusion broke out, even among the students who had shown confidence and understanding during the lesson. I've learned that individual assignments are essential for getting a true picture of what students understand and can do.

Lily, for example, who was eager and confident throughout the lesson, and Keira, who had had difficulty, were both stumped on how to find fractions that belonged only in section A, that were greater than one-fourth but not less than one.

"What about the number three and one-half?" I asked. "Where would you put it?"

"It's not a fraction," Lily said and then corrected herself. "Well, it's got a fraction in it, but I thought we had to write fractions."

I acknowledged that my directions called for writing fractions. "And three and one-half is a mixed number since it has both a whole number and a fraction in it. Can you write three and one-half as a fraction?" I asked.

The girls were stumped and remained quiet, which was interesting to me because Lily had been vocal when Steven had been at the board, working with the $\frac{7}{2}$ card. Lulu, sitting nearby, jumped into the conversation. "Remember what Steven did with the brownies?" Lulu asked.

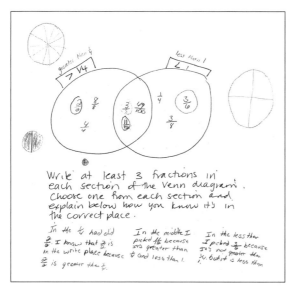

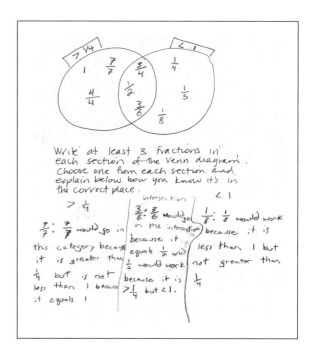

▲▲▲▲▲▲Figure 4–1 *Marcel's paper revealed his confusion with comparing $\frac{1}{4}$ and $\frac{3}{6}$.*

Lily came to life. "Oh, I get it!" she said, and wrote $\frac{7}{2}$ on her paper. Keira followed her lead. I wasn't sure what they were thinking, but I left them so I could attend to other students.

When I reviewed the girls' papers later, I saw that both had placed fractions correctly but didn't have time to write explanations. Almost a third of the class

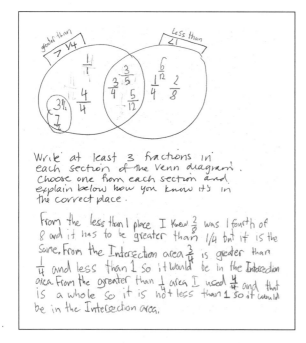

▲▲▲▲▲▲Figure 4–2 *Except for $\frac{6}{12}$, Jerry placed fractions correctly.*

▲▲▲▲▲▲Figure 4–3 *Ruana's fractions and explanations were correct.*

didn't have time to write explanations, but the rest completed the assignment. Rather than asking the students to finish their papers for homework, I chose to collect what they had done and use their work to help me plan the next day's lesson. (See Figures 4–1 through 4–3.)

DAY 2

I began the lesson by telling the students what I had learned from looking at their papers from the day before. "Parts of the assignment were easy for some of you and parts were more difficult. I noticed that thinking about fractions that are greater than one seems to be giving some of you difficulty. This reminded me that math is hard sometimes. I'll try to give you more experiences to help you."

My plan for this day was to give them more time to work individually. But first I started with a whole-class experience to review what we had done the day before and to help them understand their new assignment.

I drew two intersecting circles and labeled them $> \frac{1}{2}$ and > 1. As I had done the day before, I held up fraction cards, asking students to talk among themselves first and then asking volunteers to write them in the correct place on the Venn diagram. I had chosen the labels because they resulted in an empty region—Section C. The fractions I selected for them to place were $\frac{11}{12}$, $\frac{3}{4}$, $\frac{8}{8}$, $\frac{49}{100}$, $\frac{5}{4}$, $\frac{1}{8}$, and $\frac{7}{2}$. The last fraction, $\frac{7}{2}$, raised some questions.

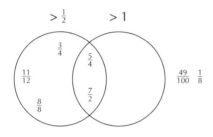

"I get how eleven-twelfths is eleven out of twelve pieces," Genevieve said, "but I don't get how seven-halves is seven out of two pieces." I wasn't sure how to respond to Genevieve's comment.

"Let's see what we know about these two fractions," I said, feeling my way. "Who has something to offer?"

"Twelve pieces are smaller than two pieces," Kenny said.

"When the top number is bigger than the bottom number, it has to be bigger than a whole," Colton added. "So seven-halves is more than one."

"The bottom number tells you how many pieces you divide it into and the top number tells you how many pieces," Ruana said.

"A bigger denominator means smaller pieces," Lily said.

"I think that seven-halves is three brownies and a half of a brownie, like Steven did," Inez said, referring to what Steven had drawn on the board the day before.

"Do these ideas make sense to you, Genevieve?" I asked. She nodded.

I added, "Saying 'eleven out of twelve pieces' makes sense if you're thinking

about a dozen pieces, and saying 'eleven-twelfths' makes sense if you're thinking about dividing up one whole. But with seven-halves, the only way to describe what it means, I think, is to say 'seven halves,' which is three wholes and one more half." I'm not sure this was adequate, but it was all I could think of to say in response to Genevieve.

Presenting a Puzzle

I then erased the circles, drew two new ones, labeled both of them only with greater than signs and wrote six fractions, three in Section A and three in Section B.

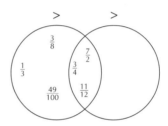

"I didn't include fractions in the labels," I pointed out. "That's because this way I've made the Venn diagram into a puzzle for you to figure out. Talk in your groups about what you think the fractions in the labels might be. Also, think about where you might place other fractions."

I gave the students several minutes to talk. After several raised their hands, ready to report, I brought the class back to attention. I pointed to Section A and asked, "Who knows another fraction that belongs here?" I waited a moment while some hands went down and others went up. I called on Jerry.

"Two-fourths," he said.

"I agree," I said. I wrote $\frac{2}{4}$ in the Venn diagram, then pointed to Section B, the intersection, and asked again, "Who knows another fraction that belongs here?" Asking students for fractions to place in the sections rather than asking for fractions for the labels gave me a chance to check on the understanding of students who reported while also allowing more time for others to think about what the labels might be.

"Four-fifths," Jared offered. I nodded and wrote $\frac{4}{5}$ in the intersection.

"What about a fraction here?" I asked, pointing to Section D, the outside.

Inez answered, "One-fifth. I think everything in the left circle is more than one-fourth, and one-fifth is smaller than one-fourth, so it has to be outside both circles."

"So what can the labels be?" I asked. About half the students raised their hands. I called on Nickie.

"The left one is greater than one-fourth," she said.

Genevieve added, "The right one is greater than one-half because all the fractions in the intersection are more than one-half." There were murmurs of agreement from other students about what Nickie and Genevieve had said. I wrote the labels on the Venn diagram. Other correct labels were also possible, but these worked, so I didn't push further.

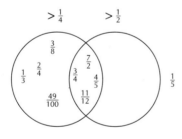

I then asked, "Where does one-fourth belong?"

"Outside," several students answered in unison.

"I don't get that!" Keira said, but then added, "Oh yeah, it's not greater than one-fourth or one-half."

"What about one-half?" I asked. After a few comments, there was consensus that it belonged in Section A.

An Individual Assignment

I gave the students directions for what they were to do next. "Now you'll put fractions in sets again, but this time you can pick the labels you want to use. Watch as I do another example." I drew two circles on the board, labeled them $> \frac{1}{4}$ and $< \frac{3}{4}$, and then reasoned aloud as I entered several fractions.

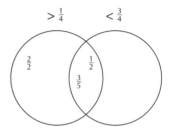

"In a moment you'll each do this," I said, writing directions on the board:

1. *Draw intersecting circles.*
2. *Pick labels.*
3. *Write fractions, at least three in each section that's possible.*

Some of the students began to reach for paper, but I stopped them and asked them to listen to the last direction. "Please listen. There's one more part to the assignment," I said. "Once you do the first three parts, have a partner check that your fractions are correct." I wrote the remaining direction on the board:

4. *Have a partner check your fractions.*

The students dove into their work. As is typical with lessons, students are more successful after a second experience. Also, giving students a chance to choose their own fractions allows them to level the activity for themselves, which gives me insights into their confidence and ability. While Keira, for example, chose labels of $> \frac{2}{4}$ and < 1, Khalil chose the more challenging labels of $< \frac{3}{5}$ and $< \frac{6}{4}$.

Some students had difficulty finding fractions for the labels they chose. Lily, for example, chose $> \frac{1}{3}$ and $< \frac{3}{6}$ and told me, after thinking for a while, that she couldn't write any fractions in the intersection. "Nothing's in between," she said.

I mused aloud. "Let's see, three-sixths is the same as one-half." Lily nodded her agreement.

"Do you know how many twelfths one-half is?" I asked her.

She answered easily, "Six-twelfths."

"Do you know how many twelfths one-third is?" I then asked. Lily thought for a moment, then answered, "Four-twelfths."

"Aha!" I said. "So five-twelfths is in between."

"Oh, good," Lily said and went back to her desk. She returned shortly with $\frac{5}{12}$ written in the intersection and handed her paper back to me.

"You need to find two more fractions for the intersection," I said. Lily was surprised that I thought there were other possibilities. Again she was puzzled. With all the activity going on in class, I couldn't take the time to talk with her at length, but I tried another approach. "How about forty-nine–hundredths?" I asked.

"It's less than three-sixths," Lily said. "Just one–one hundredth less." She giggled; this seemed to amuse her.

"Well, since it's only a teeny bit less than one-half, I think it's more than one-third. Besides, I know that one-third is about thirty-three–hundredths, so that convinces me," I said.

"It works!" Lily agreed. When she returned, she had written $\frac{49}{100}$ in the intersection next to $\frac{5}{12}$ and had also written two other fractions—$\frac{149}{200}$ and $\frac{249}{300}$. I glanced at the paper and was pleased that she had completed the assignment. I didn't think about the other fractions she had written, however, and merely accepted her paper.

It wasn't until later when I was home and looked again at Lily's paper that I realized her error, that she had arrived at the two additional fractions in the intersection merely by adding one hundred and then two hundred to the numerator and denominator of forty-nine–hundredths (see Figure 4–4). It's easy to miss something like this in the thick of teaching; the bustle of classroom activity can make it hard to think when you're managing all that's going on. This reminded me of the importance of assigning individual work that has the potential to reveal children's understanding and confusion.

I realized from looking at the class set of papers that other students had also made errors. Some seemed like minor, careless errors while others seemed more substantive. After checking all of their papers, I pulled out those with serious mistakes and decided to deal individually with those children. Also, with students' permission and preserving their anonymity, I planned to copy students' Venn diagrams onto the board for the class to examine, discuss whether there were errors, and offer corrections. I chose papers with and without errors and discussed one or two a day on and off for the next few weeks. (See Figures 4–5 and 4–6.)

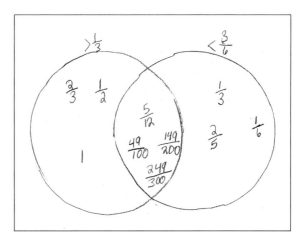

▲▲▲▲▲▲Figure 4–4 *Lily's paper showed her confusion about comparing fractions to $\frac{1}{2}$.*

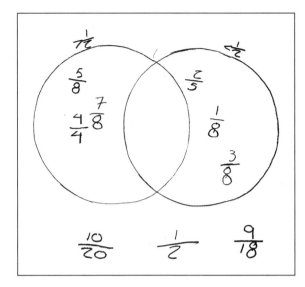

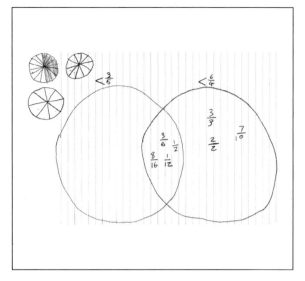

▲▲▲▲▲Figure 4–5 *Aimee was pleased to choose labels that didn't allow fractions in the intersection.*

▲▲▲▲▲Figure 4–6 *For Khalil's Venn diagram, fractions weren't possible in one of the sections.*

Questions and Discussion

▲▲

▲ *Why are they called Venn diagrams?*

They're named for John Venn, an English mathematician who lived from 1834 until 1923 and who did work in statistics, probability, and logic.

▲ *I notice on the Venn diagrams that the numbers are all in a jumble, not in order. Doesn't this confuse the students?*

It's true that the fractions on Venn diagrams aren't in order as they are on a number line. This was confusing initially to some of the students, but after some experience, they were able to stay focused on how the fractions were sorted according to the labels on the sets.

▲ *How did you resolve Lily's error?*

Lily's error in thinking is common for children learning about equivalent fractions. They often rely on their experience with addition, when thinking about fractions requires that they rely on multiplication. With Lily, I thought that it probably wouldn't be hard for her to realize and understand why the fractions she wrote were greater than one-half. But I thought that helping her think about other fractions for the intersection was a larger challenge. And helping her reevaluate and understand the error of her strategy of adding the same number to the numerator and denominator was yet another challenge.

I decided that I'd just tell her that I disagreed with $\frac{149}{300}$ and $\frac{249}{300}$ and ask her to think about why, giving her the choice to work alone or with anyone else. I did this the next day, and it worked. Then I asked her permission to ask the class for help with her puzzle. She agreed and it led to a fruitful discussion that gave Lily a chance to think further about the situation.

CHAPTER FIVE
THE COMPARING GAME

Overview

The *Comparing Game* is a two-person game that provides students practice representing and comparing fractions. Relying on both luck and strategy, the game is appropriate for students still learning to use fractional notation and compare fractions and also engages the interest of students who already are comfortable doing so. The game can be played with either a 1–6 die or a 1–10 die or spinner. Also, the game can be varied so that the winner either has the larger fraction, the smaller fraction, the fraction closer to one-half, or the fraction closer to one.

Materials

▲ 1–6 dice *or* 1–10 dice or spinners, 1 per pair of students
▲ optional: the *Comparing Game* rules, 1 per pair of students (see Blackline Masters)

Time

▲ three class periods, plus additional time for playing

Teaching Directions

1. Tell the students that you'll teach them how to play the *Comparing Game*. Write the name of the game on the board and draw a game board for two players:

2. Ask for a volunteer to come up and model the game with you. Introduce the rules as you play (begin with Version 1). You may want to post the rules for a class reference or distribute individual copies.

The Comparing Game Rules

You need:
  a partner
  a die, a 1-10 spinner, or a bag with slips of paper numbered 1 to 10

Rules

1. Each player draws a game board as shown.
2. Players take turns rolling the die (or spinning the spinner, or drawing a number from the bag) and writing the number in one of the spaces on the game board. Once a number is written, it cannot be changed. The boxes to the side are reject boxes for numbers you don't want to use in your fraction.
3. When you have written a number, pass the die, spinner, or bag of numbers to the other player.
4. Play until both players have recorded a fraction. (One or both of your reject boxes may be empty if you used your rolls to complete your fraction.)
5. Compare fractions to see whose is larger. Make drawings to show the fractions, first agreeing on the shape to use for the whole.
6. Write a math sentence to show whose fraction is larger (for example, $\frac{3}{4} > \frac{2}{3}$).
7. Play at least three rounds.

Version 1: The larger fraction wins.
Version 2: The smaller fraction wins.
Version 3: The fraction closer to one-half wins.
Version 4: The fraction closer to one wins.

3. Have the students play the game with partners for the rest of the period. Then give the homework assignment for them to play with someone at home. Instead of dice or spinners, students can play at home by numbering slips of paper 1 to 6 (or 1 to 10), placing them in a bag, and drawing out a slip to get a number to play.

4. The following day, discuss their experiences playing at home. Then have them play again in class for about fifteen minutes. Circulate and observe. Interrupt the class for a discussion about how to compare two fractions, for example, nine-eighths and nine-fifths, or two fractions that you noticed gave students difficulty. Then have them play some more, changing the rules so that the smaller fraction wins. Give the same homework assignment for them to play with someone at home.

5. On Day 3, again discuss their experience playing at home. Then introduce two more versions of the game and have students play the new versions at least once. It's helpful to write all four versions on the board or, if you posted them, on the directions for the game.

Version 1: The larger fraction wins.
Version 2: The smaller fraction wins.
Version 3: The fraction closer to one-half wins.
Version 4: The fraction closer to one wins.

6. Give a homework assignment and ask students to respond to the following.
1. Which is your favorite version of the game? Describe why.
2. Pick one version of the game and describe the strategies you use to try to win.
3. What other version do you think would be good to play?

Teaching Notes

It's important to provide students practice with comparing fractions, and it's much more enjoyable for students to do so in a game format than merely with a set of exercises. This game also gives students the opportunity to use their logical reasoning ability as they strategize how to place their numbers. Along with comparing fractions, the game provides practice with representing fractions pictorially in some way and also with recording mathematical sentences to report the results of what occurred. In addition, the game gives the students experience thinking about fractions that are larger than one, an important idea that dispels the misconception that some students have that fractions are all smaller than one.

Once students learn how to play the game, it's a useful choice activity for independent work, ideal when some students complete assignments before others. The game also can initiate whole-class discussions. In the class described in the vignette, for example, one of the actual situations that came up when students were playing the game was useful for helping students talk about nine-fifths and nine-eighths.

The Lesson

▲▲

DAY 1

I wrote on the board *The Comparing Game* and drew a game board for each of two players.

"This is a game for two people," I said. "Who would like to volunteer to play with me to help everyone learn the rules?" Hands flew up and I invited Sahara to join me at the chalkboard. I then introduced the rules to the class. "To play this game, we'll use a regular die. We each roll the die four times, taking turns. Each time we roll, we write the number that comes up in one of our boxes. Once you write a number in a box, you can't move it. When we're done, we'll each have a fraction and we may also have extra numbers."

"Do we both write the same numbers?" Sonia wanted to know.

"No," I clarified, "you each roll and write your own numbers."

"What are the two extras for?" Kurt asked.

"They're reject boxes," I answered. "They're places where you can write numbers that you don't want to use for your fraction."

"How do you win?" Miguel asked.

I answered, "When you've each written your numbers, you compare your fractions. The larger fraction wins."

There were no more questions, so I said to Sahara, "Would you like to go first or second?"

"I'll go first," she said. She rolled the die and a 2 came up. Sahara hesitated, not sure where to write the number.

Other students called out suggestions. "Put it on top."

"No, stick it in one of the extra boxes."

"I'd put it on the bottom."

"Yeah, the bottom is much better."

I quieted the class and then said, "It's hard to think when you're up at the board and doing something new. Let's give Sahara a chance to think for herself." I then turned to Sahara and said, "Don't worry too much about making the best move. This is only a trial game to teach the rules. After you play a few times, you'll have some ideas about the best place to play a number."

Sahara, still uncertain, finally decided to write 2 in the numerator.

"Now you pass the die to me and I'll take my turn," I said. I rolled the die. A 3 came up and I wrote it in one of the reject boxes.

Sahara and I continued taking turns. After we each had rolled four numbers, the results were as follows:

Sahara   *Ms. Burns*

$$\frac{2}{3} \quad \boxed{1} \quad \boxed{6} \qquad \frac{5}{2} \quad \boxed{3} \quad \boxed{4}$$

"You lost, Sahara," Midori said. Sahara shrugged, grinning.

"By a lot," Dario added.

Some students weren't as sure about the outcome. There was a large spread of understanding about fractions among the students.

"Let me explain the next part of the game," I said. "When you've both completed your rolls, then you each make a drawing to represent your fraction. Because you want to compare your fractions, you first have to agree on what you'll use for the whole—a circle, a rectangle, or something else that's the same shape and size. That way, you'll be able to compare fractional parts of the same amount."

I turned to Sahara. "What should we draw?" I asked.

"Circles," she said.

"You go first," I said. Sahara drew a circle, divided it into thirds, and shaded in two of them.

As I drew, I talked aloud to explain what I was doing. "My fraction says 'five-halves.' If I draw one circle and divide it into halves, that shows two halves. Another circle gives two more halves." I shaded in all four halves. "I still need one more half." I drew a third circle and shaded in just half of it.

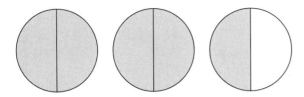

"You win!" Abby said.

"There's one more part to playing the game," I said. "You have to write a math sentence that compares the two fractions." I modeled two ways to do this:

$$\frac{2}{3} < \frac{5}{2}$$
$$\frac{5}{2} > \frac{2}{3}$$

I told Sahara that she could return to her seat, and then I wrote an abbreviated version of the rules on the chalkboard:

1. *Roll four times and write the numbers.*
2. *Each make a drawing.*
3. *Write a math sentence.*

I then said to the students, "I know another way to write a math sentence to compare these two fractions. Instead of writing 'five-halves' I could count the whole circles I shaded in and then count the extra part. That gives me two whole circles and half of another." I wrote two more math sentences on the board to show the children how to write the mixed number:

$$\frac{2}{3} < 2\frac{1}{2}$$
$$2\frac{1}{2} > \frac{2}{3}$$

"Who can explain why two and one-half is worth the same as five-halves?" I asked. I waited to see who would raise their hands and called on Letitia.

"See, it takes two halves to make a whole circle," she said, pointing to one of the circles I had drawn. "So another circle is two more, and that's four, and there's one more half." Letitia delivered her explanation confidently.

"I have another way to show it," Paul said. He came up to the board, drew five circles, and divided each one in half. Then

he explained how you could put halves together to make wholes. "These two make one whole, and these two make another, and you still have one left over," he said.

I reminded the students once more that there were three parts to playing the game. Then I organized them into pairs. As the students played, I circulated, reminding some of them about choosing the same shape for their drawings, reminding others to write the sentences, helping a few remember which way to draw the greater than or less than sign, and keeping some students on task. By the end of the class, everyone seemed to understand how to play. For homework, I asked the students to play the game with someone at home. For those who didn't have dice available, I showed them how to number six slips of paper from 1 through 6, put them in a bag, and take turns drawing one, being sure to replace it after recording the number.

DAY 2

At the beginning of class the next day, I asked what they had learned from playing the game at home. Several students were eager to report.

"I have a strategy for winning," Elliot said. "Put big numbers on top and little numbers on the bottom."

"It didn't always work," his partner, Booth, said, "but it did most of the time."

"I beat my mom every time," Emma said.

"Not me," Kalila said. "She won every game but one."

"I'm going to give you time to play the game again," I said, "but this time you'll use spinners that have the numbers from one to ten on them. That will give you new fractions to compare. Also, I'm going to interrupt you in about fifteen minutes for a class discussion."

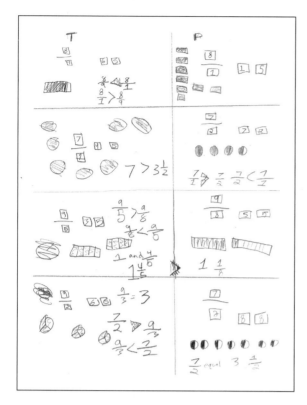

▲▲▲▲▲▲**Figure 5–1** *Tiana and Pedro weren't sure how to compare $\frac{9}{5}$ and $\frac{9}{8}$, the results of their third round. This was a good problem for a class discussion.*

I circulated and observed while the students played, looking to see if there were any fractions that gave students difficulty that I could use for a class discussion. Tiana and Pedro were having difficulty resolving which of them had the larger fraction (see Figure 5–1). When I interrupted the class, I wrote their fractions on the board.

Tiana   Pedro

$\frac{9}{5}$ $\frac{9}{8}$

"Talk with the person next to you about which fraction is greater," I said. "Then I'll have a volunteer come to the board and explain."

After a few moments, I called the students back to attention and asked for a volunteer to explain. I called on Niko. He came to the board and drew four rectangles, two side by side and two underneath them. He divided each of the top two rectangles into fifths, struggling to get the parts the same size. "It's hard to make five pieces equal," he said, erasing lines several times before he was satisfied. He shaded in nine-fifths and then divided each of the two rectangles underneath into eight parts, first dividing each in halves, then fourths, and finally eighths. He shaded in nine of the eighths.

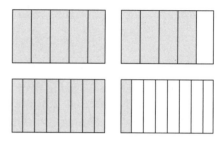

"See," Niko said, pleased with what he had drawn, "they're both more than one rectangle, but you have more with nine-fifths because that's almost two of them."

Sonia then came up and showed the fractions with circles. Her reasoning was similar to Niko's.

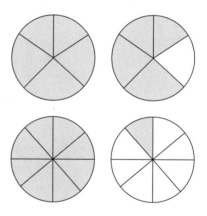

Abby said that she didn't really need to draw rectangles or circles. "I know that ten-fifths would be two wholes, so nine-fifths is just a little less than two. But nine-eighths is just a little more than one."

"That mixes me up," Anisa said, referring to Abby's explanation.

"Me, too," Monique said.

Abby came to the board and showed what she meant with the rectangles and

58   Lessons for Extending Fractions

the circles that Niko and Sonia had drawn. "See, nine-fifths is just one-fifth away from two rectangles, but nine-eighths is seven-eighths away from two rectangles." This satisfied Anisa, but Monique still didn't understand.

Jonah said, "It's hard to draw sometimes, but I know that eighths are smaller than fifths. Do you get that, Monique?" Monique nodded "yes."

"So if you have nine pieces on both fractions, then the nine-fifths has to be more because the pieces are bigger," Jonah said.

"But I don't get why the numbers on top are bigger," Monique persisted. I then realized that Monique's confusion came, in part, because the numerators of the fractions were larger than the denominators. She hadn't had experience with fractions like these. Jonah looked to me for help.

Elliot entered the conversation. "When the number on top is bigger, the fraction is more than one whole thing. That's why it's good to put the big numbers up on top."

After sitting quietly for a moment, Monique said, "Oh, OK." I wasn't sure that Monique was really clear about comparing nine-fifths and nine-eighths, but I didn't push her further in this setting. I knew that I needed to find time to work with her individually.

Dario raised a hand. "Can I come up and write the sentence?" he asked. I agreed, and Dario wrote two versions, using the greater than sign in both:

$$\frac{9}{5} > \frac{9}{8}$$
$$1\frac{4}{5} > 1\frac{1}{8}$$

Kalila then came up and wrote two sentences using the less than sign:

$$\frac{9}{8} < \frac{9}{5}$$
$$1\frac{1}{8} < 1\frac{4}{5}$$

I then told the students that they could continue playing for the rest of the period. "For the rest of your games," I said, "the winner will be the player who winds up with the smaller fraction." Some students groaned.

"It's no big deal," Elizabeth said. "Just do whatever you were doing backwards."

For homework, the students' assignment was to play the new version of the game with someone at home.

DAY 3

The next day, after students reported about playing the game at home, I introduced two additional versions of the game. I wrote on the board:

Version 1: The larger fraction wins.

Version 2: The smaller fraction wins.

Version 3: The fraction closer to one-half wins.

Version 4: The fraction closer to one wins.

"Try Versions Three and Four today," I said. "Later we'll talk about which you like best and the different strategies you used."

"Do we use the dice or the spinner?" Abby wanted to know.

"Your choice," I said. "Or rotate back and forth so you can see which you think makes for a better game." I let the students play for the entire period.

I didn't devote additional class lessons to playing the game but added it to the class list of options for students to play when they finished assignments early. Figure 5–2 and 5–3 show the results of two pairs' games.

EXTENSIONS

To make the game more challenging, ask students to figure out how much larger or smaller one player's fraction is than the other's. Or, for Version 3 or 4, ask them to figure out how far each fraction is from one-half or one.

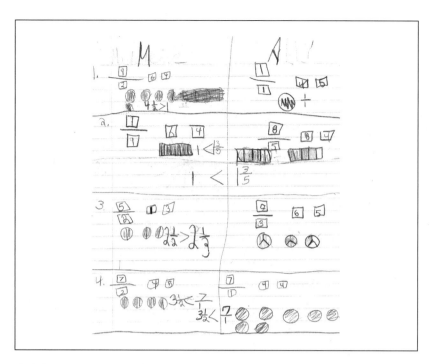

▲▲▲▲▲▲Figure 5–2 *Madeleine and Abby used circles to show their fractions for three of their four rounds.*

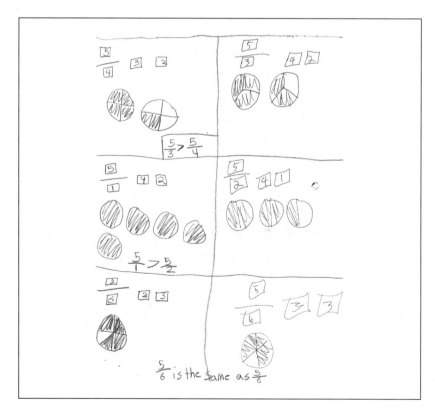

▲▲▲▲▲▲Figure 5–3 *Sahara and Kalila each won a round and then tied in their third round.*

Questions and Discussion

▲▲

▲ *Why did you start with dice and then switch to spinners?*

Either one works fine, but I thought that showing the two choices would give teachers more options for playing the game. You also could use 1–10 dice if you have them. Also, I like making the choices available to students to encourage them to see if the different equipment calls for using different strategies.

▲ *What if students didn't have difficulty, as Tiana and Pedro did?*

Most of the time I've found that some students have difficulty. However, when this doesn't happen, I interrupt the class and initiate a discussion by presenting two fractions for the students to compare. The fractions with which Tiana and Pedro were struggling are particularly good for initiating a discussion about fractions that are greater than one.

▲ *What do you do for students like Monique who seem confused?*

I've learned with Monique, and with other students who seem confused, that when understanding is fragile, students waver back and forth between knowing and not knowing and between being sure and losing confidence. This wavering continues until their understanding is cemented. This requires a good deal more experience for some students than for others, and games like this one can help.

CHAPTER SIX
IN-BETWEEN FRACTIONS

Overview

This lesson calls on the same understanding and skills that students draw on to compare and order fractions but presents a different problem-solving experience. Rather than put fractions in order or tell if one fraction is greater or less than another, this lesson presents students with three fractions—one-half, one-third, and one-fourth—and poses two problems: *Is $\frac{1}{3}$ in between $\frac{1}{2}$ and $\frac{1}{4}$? Name a fraction that is EXACTLY halfway between $\frac{1}{2}$ and $\frac{1}{4}$.* Students think about each problem individually, with partners, and in a whole-class discussion. They then complete a written assignment and participate in a follow-up class discussion.

Materials

▲ *In-Between Fractions* worksheet, 1 per student (see Blackline Masters)

Time

▲ two class periods, plus additional time for repeat experiences

Teaching Directions

1. Write on the board: *In-Between Fractions*. Establish with the class that a fraction is in between two others if it is greater than one and less than the other.

2. Write on the board: *Is $\frac{1}{3}$ in between $\frac{1}{4}$ and $\frac{1}{2}$?* Ask students to think about this quietly by themselves for a moment. Then ask them to turn and talk with a partner about their ideas.

3. Call the students to attention to lead a class discussion about the question. Begin by asking for a show of hands of who thinks that one-third is in between one-fourth and one-half, who thinks it isn't, and who isn't sure.

4. Then ask students to explain their thinking. As each student explains, record his or her idea on the board. Discuss until you feel that students understand that one-third is in between one-fourth and one-half.

5. Pose another problem: *What fraction is EXACTLY halfway between $\frac{1}{4}$ and $\frac{1}{2}$?* As you did before, ask students to think about this quietly by themselves for a moment, and then ask them to turn and talk with a partner.

6. Call the students to attention for a class discussion. Record students' ideas on the board. Help them understand that three-eighths, or any fraction equivalent to it, is exactly halfway between one-fourth and one-half.

7. Give a written assignment and ask students to respond to two problems:

Is $\frac{1}{4}$ in between $\frac{1}{6}$ and $\frac{1}{2}$? Explain.

Name a fraction that is EXACTLY halfway between $\frac{1}{6}$ and $\frac{1}{2}$. Explain.

Either write the questions on the board or duplicate and distribute the *In-Between Fractions* worksheet (see Blackline Masters).

8. After students have completed the assignment, lead a class discussion about their ideas.

Teaching Notes

It's helpful for students to think about the same idea in different ways, and this lesson presents another opportunity for students to compare and order fractions. However, the different context presents a fresh challenge. Approaching the same idea in different ways strengthens students' understanding and helps them develop flexibility in their mathematical thinking.

The emphasis of this lesson should be on the students' reasoning. While all of the students in this class, for example, knew that one-third was in between one-fourth and one-half, their explanations provided valuable information about both their understanding and their misconceptions about fractions.

The lesson is also useful for providing students practice with explaining their reasoning. This is difficult for many students, but with practice and encouragement, students' ability to provide clear and coherent explanations improves. Class discussions are particularly useful for helping students. It's especially important to establish an atmosphere in the class where students know that mistakes in thinking are opportunities for learning. They need to be encouraged to take the risk of offering their ideas because risks can result in learning rewards. These attitudes require reinforcement over time, and this lesson can be helpful.

The Lesson

▲▲▲

DAY 1

As the students were getting settled, I wrote on the board:

In-Between Fractions

I asked the class, "What do you think I mean by 'in-between fractions'?"

About half the students were willing to respond and I called on Gloria. She said, "I think if a fraction is in between, then it's kind of in the middle."

Brendan added, "It's bigger than a certain fraction and smaller than a certain fraction." No one had anything else to add, so I turned to the board and wrote:

Is $\frac{1}{3}$ in between $\frac{1}{4}$ and $\frac{1}{2}$?

As I turned back to the class, some students were already beginning to talk about their ideas. I said, "Think by yourself quietly for a moment about this question." Asking the students to think quietly by themselves gives those who don't think as quickly as others a chance to gather their thoughts. After a moment, I said, "Now talk with the person next to you about your ideas."

After a few moments, I asked for their attention. "Raise your hand if you agree that one-third is in between one-fourth and one-half." Most hands went up.

I then said, "Raise your hand if you disagree." Only Damien raised a hand, looking uncertain when he noticed that he was the only one who held this opinion. Damien had been talking with Eddie, who hadn't raised a hand either time.

"Raise your hand if you're not sure," I said. Eddie, Kensie, and David raised their hands.

"Who would like to explain your thinking?" I asked. I called on Craig.

He said, "Well, the numerators are all the same, they're all ones. But the denominators are different."

"Do you agree or disagree that one-third is between one-fourth and one-half?" I asked.

"Oh yeah," Craig said. "I agree. See, three is in between two and four, and the smaller the denominator, the larger the fraction, so one-third is in between."

"You mentioned that each of the three fractions has a numerator of one," I said. "Does that matter?"

Craig hesitated a moment and then responded, "Kind of, because if the one-fourth was two-fourths, then it wouldn't work."

I turned to the board, saying, "Let me try to record Craig's explanation. Craig, please see if what I write describes your idea." I wrote on the board:

The denominator, 3, is in between 2 and 4, and the smaller the denominator, the larger the fraction. The numerators are all one, so they each have one piece. So $\frac{1}{3}$ is in between $\frac{1}{4}$ and $\frac{1}{2}$.

Craig nodded his agreement. I asked, "How many of you thought the way Craig did?" A few students raised their hands.

"Who has another idea or explanation?" I then asked.

I called on Maggie. She said, "I looked at the fraction kit pieces and you can see that one-third is bigger than one-fourth and smaller than one-half, so I think it's in between." Maggie was referring to the set of fraction kit pieces posted on the board. (These students had previously experienced lessons with fraction kits from Chapters 2 and 15 of the Teaching Arithmetic book *Lessons for Introducing Fractions, Grades 4–5*. [See the booklet, *The Fraction Kit Guide*.] A laminated fraction kit with magnets on the back of each piece was posted so that students had a visual model as a reference.)

1															
$\frac{1}{2}$								$\frac{1}{2}$							
$\frac{1}{3}$					$\frac{1}{3}$					$\frac{1}{3}$					
$\frac{1}{4}$				$\frac{1}{4}$				$\frac{1}{4}$				$\frac{1}{4}$			
$\frac{1}{6}$			$\frac{1}{6}$			$\frac{1}{6}$			$\frac{1}{6}$			$\frac{1}{6}$			$\frac{1}{6}$
$\frac{1}{8}$		$\frac{1}{8}$		$\frac{1}{8}$		$\frac{1}{8}$		$\frac{1}{8}$		$\frac{1}{8}$		$\frac{1}{8}$		$\frac{1}{8}$	
$\frac{1}{12}$	$\frac{1}{12}$	$\frac{1}{12}$	$\frac{1}{12}$	$\frac{1}{12}$	$\frac{1}{12}$	$\frac{1}{12}$	$\frac{1}{12}$	$\frac{1}{12}$	$\frac{1}{12}$	$\frac{1}{12}$	$\frac{1}{12}$				
$\frac{1}{16}$	$\frac{1}{16}$	$\frac{1}{16}$	$\frac{1}{16}$	$\frac{1}{16}$	$\frac{1}{16}$	$\frac{1}{16}$	$\frac{1}{16}$	$\frac{1}{16}$	$\frac{1}{16}$	$\frac{1}{16}$	$\frac{1}{16}$	$\frac{1}{16}$	$\frac{1}{16}$	$\frac{1}{16}$	$\frac{1}{16}$

"Who has another idea to share?" I asked.

Saul said, "I think it's in between, too, because to change one-third to one-half, it would have to be one and a half thirds, and one-fourth would be two-fourths." I wasn't clear about what Saul was explaining, but I'd learned that his reasoning was typically correct, while also often hard to follow. Saul's explanations reminded me that following someone else's thinking can be difficult. It's for this reason that I'm consistent about recording students' ideas on the board and allowing time for others to try to make sense of them. I wrote on the board:

$$\frac{1}{2} = \frac{1\frac{1}{2}}{3}$$

$$\frac{1}{2} = \frac{2}{4}$$

I turned to Saul to make sure that what I recorded was what he meant. Saul nodded and continued his explanation. "So

then one-third has to be less than one-half because one and one-half thirds is equal to one-half. And one-fourth has to be less than one-third because one-third is only one-half of a third away from one-half and one-fourth is a whole fourth away from one-half." I paused for a moment as I worked to understand Saul's thinking. I then tried to record his idea on the board. I wrote:

$$\frac{1}{4} + \frac{1}{4} = \frac{1}{2}$$

$$\frac{1}{3} + \frac{\frac{1}{2}}{3} = \frac{1}{2}$$

I said, "So you're saying that one-fourth is one-fourth away from one-half. I think that means that if you add one-fourth onto one-fourth, then you'll have one-half." Saul nodded his agreement. I continued, "And to make one-third into one-half, you have to add on another half of a third." Saul nodded again.

I pointed to the posted fraction kit pieces to help the others see what Saul was saying. Then I said to Saul, "What I don't understand is how you know that the one-fourth you add onto the one-fourth to get one-half is larger than the half of a third that you add onto the one-third to get one-half." Saul was quiet.

"What is one-half of a third?" I asked the class.

Saul and several other students answered in unison, "One-sixth."

"You can see that on the fraction kit pieces," Clark pointed out.

Several others said, "Oh yeah." "I see it now." "I get it." I added to what I had recorded, circling the $\frac{1}{6}$ and the second $\frac{1}{4}$ in the first sentence:

$$\frac{1}{4} + \boxed{\frac{1}{4}} = \frac{1}{2}$$

$$\frac{1}{3} + \frac{\frac{1}{2}}{3} = \frac{1}{2}$$

$$\frac{1}{3} + \boxed{\frac{1}{6}} = \frac{1}{2}$$

"Is one-fourth larger than one-sixth?" I asked. Many students nodded.

Saul said, "Yes, so one-third has to be closer to one-half than one-fourth is."

I knew that all of the students didn't follow Saul's reasoning. However, I decided not to dwell on his idea anymore and instead asked, "Does anyone have a different way to think about the question?"

Annie shared next. "Well, I thought about it like in pieces," she said. "One-fourth is a smaller piece than one-third because it's like you're sharing with more people. Like if there was a room with three people and then the same room with four people, the people would have less room in the second one." I wrote $\frac{1}{3} > \frac{1}{4}$ on the board. Underneath, I drew two circles and divided and shaded them to represent each of the fractions.

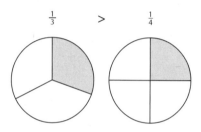

Annie continued, "And then one-half is a bigger piece than one-third, so one-third must be in between." I added $\frac{1}{2}$ to what I had written on the board and illustrated it underneath with a circle with one-half shaded:

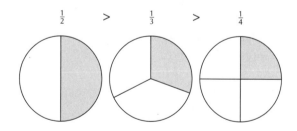

"My sketches may help you compare these fractions," I said, "but remember that sketches aren't exact and you can't always rely on them. In this case, the sizes and the shapes of the pieces are different enough to be convincing, but you still have to be able to give another explanation. Does anyone have another way to explain?"

Clark said, "Well, I changed them all into twelfths. One-half is six-twelfths, one-third is four-twelfths, and one-fourth is three-twelfths. And then I know six-twelfths is the biggest and three-twelfths is the smallest and four-twelfths is in between." I wrote on the board:

$$\frac{1}{2} = \frac{6}{12}$$
$$\frac{1}{3} = \frac{4}{12}$$
$$\frac{1}{4} = \frac{3}{12}$$

Exactly in the Middle

No one else volunteered to share another explanation, so I moved on to what I wanted the students to consider next. I said, "You've presented several different ways to explain why one-third is in between one-fourth and one-half. Listen to my next questions. Is one-third *exactly* halfway between one-fourth and one-half? If you think so, how can you explain why? And if you think that one-third is *not* exactly halfway, then what fraction *is* halfway between? Think quietly on your own for a moment." I turned to the board as the students thought and wrote:

What fraction is EXACTLY halfway between $\frac{1}{4}$ and $\frac{1}{2}$?

When I turned back to the class, I said, "Talk with your neighbor about your thinking." The talking was animated. Many students seemed to have ideas.

After a few moments of talking, I called the class back to attention. "What fractions did you come up with? First I'd like to list all of your possible answers." As students shared, I recorded on the board. Josh offered four and a half–twelfths, Anita suggested three-eighths, and Pierre suggested one-third plus one-sixteenth. I recorded:

$$\frac{4\frac{1}{2}}{12}$$

$$\frac{3}{8}$$

$$\frac{1}{3} + \frac{1}{16}$$

"Who would like to share an idea?" I asked. I called on Hassan.

He said, "If you changed one-fourth to one-sixth, then one-third would be halfway in between, so I know that one-third isn't halfway between one-fourth and one-half." I wrote on the board:

$\frac{1}{3}$ *is exactly halfway between* $\frac{1}{6}$ *and* $\frac{1}{2}$.

I asked Hassan, "How did you figure this out?"

"I made them all sixths," Hassan explained. "One-third is the same as two-sixths, and one-half is the same as three-sixths. Two-sixths is halfway, and that's the same as one-third." I added $\frac{2}{6}$ and $\frac{3}{6}$ to what I had recorded, writing each above its equivalent fraction:

$$\frac{2}{6} \qquad\qquad\qquad \frac{3}{6}$$

$\frac{1}{3}$ *is exactly halfway between* $\frac{1}{6}$ *and* $\frac{1}{2}$.

I then asked, "Who has an idea about what fraction is exactly halfway between one-fourth and one-half?"

Juanita said, "I think that Pierre's idea, one-third plus one-sixteenth, is the same as four and a half–twelfths because if you look at the fraction strips you can tell that they're the same amount." I moved fraction pieces to show Juanita's idea, lining up one-third and one-sixteenth pieces with five one-twelfth pieces.

"But we should only count half of the last twelfth," I said. I knew that Juanita's idea wasn't correct, but the fraction pieces were so close in size that it was difficult to discern this.

$\frac{1}{3}$				$\frac{1}{16}$
$\frac{1}{12}$	$\frac{1}{12}$	$\frac{1}{12}$	$\frac{1}{12}$	$\frac{1}{12}$

Clark, however, disagreed with Juanita. He said, "I don't think that one-third plus one-sixteenth is the same as four and a half–twelfths. Four-twelfths is equal to one-third, but one-sixteenth isn't equal to one-half of a twelfth." Many students nodded, agreeing with Clark, including Juanita. I recorded Juanita's and Clark's ideas on the board:

Juanita $\quad \frac{1}{3} + \frac{1}{16} = \frac{4\frac{1}{2}}{12}$

Clark $\quad \frac{1}{3} = \frac{4}{12}$

$\frac{4\frac{1}{2}}{12} = \frac{4}{12} + \frac{\frac{1}{2}}{12}$

So $\frac{4}{12}$ (or $\frac{1}{3}$) $+ \frac{1}{16}$ can't $= \frac{4}{12} + \frac{\frac{1}{2}}{12}$

I said to the class, "One of the disadvantages of relying on the fraction kit pieces is that because they aren't cut precisely, they can mislead your thinking. That's why we also need an explanation when we show a sketch or the fraction pieces."

Julio reported next. He said, "I have reason to believe that it's four and a half–twelfths. I used a clock." As Julio continued explaining, I turned to the board to record and also to hide my amusement at Julio's choice of words. I drew a circle and made marks for the hours on a clock. Julio said, "One-fourth is at three o'clock, and one-half is at six o'clock, so exactly in the middle would be four thirty, and that's the same as four and a half–twelfths." As I completed my drawing, students said, "Oh, that's right." "I get it." "That's cool."

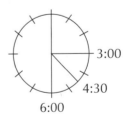

Saul then said, "I think four and a half–twelfths is in the middle because it's one and a half–twelfths away from three-twelfths and one and a half–twelfths away from six-twelfths."

Ally added, "He's right. There are three-twelfths in one-fourth, and six-twelfths in one-half. They're three apart, and half of three-twelfths is one and a half–twelfths."

I pointed to the three possible answers I had recorded on the board and said, "I've heard explanations that convince me that four and a half twelfths is exactly halfway between one-fourth and one-half. What about these other possible answers?"

Pierre said, "Can I change my answer?"

I responded, "Sure. What do you want to change it to, and can you explain why?"

"I think so," Pierre said. "I want to change the 'plus one-sixteenth' to 'plus one–twenty-fourth' because of what Clark said before. I'm not sure it's right, but I think it's right." I made the change to the list of possible answers:

$$\frac{4\frac{1}{2}}{12}$$

$$\frac{3}{8}$$

$$\frac{1}{3} + \frac{1}{24}$$

"Why do you think that one-third plus one–twenty-fourth is right?" I asked.

"I'm not sure, but I think that you only want to add on half of a twelfth from a third, and one–twenty-fourth is the same as half of a twelfth," Pierre said.

"How much is one-third plus one–twenty-fourth?" I asked.

"I think it's the same as four and a half– twelfths," Pierre said, "and I think that's right."

"Hmm, let me think about your idea," I said, and wrote on the board, explaining as I did so:

$\frac{1}{3} + \frac{1}{24}$ *is the same as* $\frac{4}{12} + \frac{1}{24}$

$\frac{1}{24}$ *is the same as* $\frac{\frac{1}{2}}{12}$

$\frac{1}{3} + \frac{1}{24}$ *is the same as* $\frac{4}{12} + \frac{\frac{1}{2}}{12} = \frac{4\frac{1}{2}}{12}$

Pierre nodded his agreement with how I recorded his idea.

"What about the possible answer of three-eighths?" I asked the class.

Kayla's hand shot up. "Oh, I know," she said. "Four-eighths is the same as one-

half, and two-eighths is the same as one-fourth, and halfway between those is three-eighths." I wrote on the board:

$\frac{4}{8} = \frac{1}{2}$

$\frac{2}{8} = \frac{1}{4}$

$\frac{3}{8}$ *is halfway between*

Julio said, "This is really confusing because now both answers seem right."

"Which answers?" I asked.

"Three-eighths seems right now, and so does four and a half–twelfths," he replied.

Craig said, "I think they're both right because they're both the same thing. Can I use the clock to explain it?" I nodded. Craig continued, "If you draw the eighths on the clock, then four and a half is at the same place as the third eighth." I drew a circle, marked the hours, divided the circle into eighths, and then labeled the eighth marks *12; 1:30* and *1½; 3; 4:30* and *4½; 6; 7:30* and *7½; 9;* and *10:30* and *10½.* Some students nodded and others looked confused.

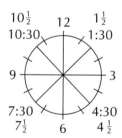

Maria had another explanation. She said, "I changed both of the fractions so that they had the same denominator. Three-eighths is the same thing as nine–twenty-fourths, and then four and a half–twelfths is also the same thing. It's nine–twenty-fourths." I wrote on the board:

$\frac{3}{8} = \frac{9}{24}$

$\frac{4\frac{1}{2}}{12} = \frac{9}{24}$

Francis chimed in, "That's right. Four and a half–twelfths is a third and a twenty-fourth. And a third is eight–twenty-fourths." I recorded:

$$\frac{1}{3} + \frac{1}{24} = \frac{8}{24} + \frac{1}{24} = \frac{9}{24}$$

A Written Assignment

While some of the students were completely engaged in the conversation, others were quiet. It's hard to get feedback during a discussion from students who don't participate very much. Sometimes, however, these quiet students are totally engaged, absorbing ideas and following the discussion. They may be shy or just not eager to talk in front of the class. That's why I'm sure to build partner talk into lessons. Other times, students are quiet because they're confused. An individual assignment can help measure the effectiveness of a class discussion and reveal who needs additional help and whose understanding is strong.

I next asked the students to respond in writing to two questions. I chose a problem that I thought they would all be able to answer correctly. I did this purposely to build their confidence and also to keep the emphasis on writing good explanations:

Is $\frac{1}{4}$ in between $\frac{1}{6}$ and $\frac{1}{2}$? Explain.

Name a fraction that is EXACTLY halfway between $\frac{1}{6}$ and $\frac{1}{2}$. Explain.

"Can we work on this together?" Helene wanted to know.

I responded, "Because I need feedback on the lessons and information about how you're each thinking, please don't work with anyone just yet. I just want you to do the best you can. You'll have a chance to compare ideas later."

"Is it a test?" Craig asked.

"I'm not testing you," I said. "I'm really testing me. I'm trying to find out how well I taught this lesson, and your papers will help me."

"Do we have to write words, or are numbers enough?" Brendan asked.

I answered, "Your paper should be detailed enough to help me understand your thinking. You can use numbers, words, pictures, or any combination of these to explain."

There were no other questions. I distributed the papers I had prepared with the questions on them (see Blackline Masters) and the students got to work.

There wasn't enough time in the class for all of the students to complete the assignment, so I collected their papers at the end of the period. "I'll give you time tomorrow at the beginning of class to complete your work," I told the class. I read the papers that evening. Everyone had answered the first question correctly, but explanations differed. Not everyone had gotten to the second part of the assignment.

DAY 2

I returned the students' papers and let them get back to work. As students finished, I paired them with others who were also finished to compare their explanations. "Talk about how your ideas are alike and how they are different," I explained. "If you want to make any changes to your paper, that's fine."

I circulated and read over students' shoulders. Brendan's paper reflected the most common reasoning that I noticed for explaining why one-fourth is in between one-sixth and one-half. He wrote: *$\frac{1}{4}$ is in the middle of $\frac{1}{6}$ and $\frac{1}{2}$ because if the numerators are all the same the fraction with the smaller denomenator is greater and 4 is in between 6 and 2.*

Three students converted the fractions to fractions with common denominators. Kayla and Craig converted them to twenty-fourths; Clark converted them to twelfths. Clark wrote: *Yes because if you make them all 12ths, $\frac{1}{2} = \frac{6}{12}$, $\frac{1}{4} = \frac{3}{12}$, and $\frac{1}{6} = \frac{2}{12}$ so $\frac{1}{4}$ is between.*

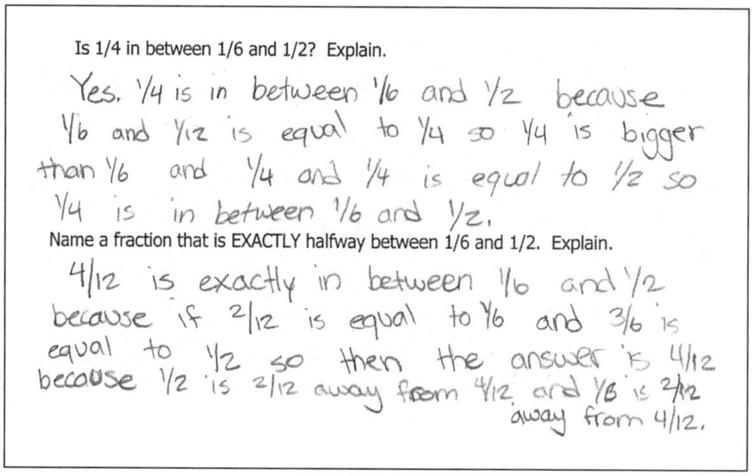

Is 1/4 in between 1/6 and 1/2? Explain.

> Yes. 1/4 is in between 1/6 and 1/2 because 1/6 and 1/12 is equal to 1/4 so 1/4 is bigger than 1/6 and 1/4 and 1/4 is equal to 1/2 so 1/4 is in between 1/6 and 1/2.

Name a fraction that is EXACTLY halfway between 1/6 and 1/2. Explain.

> 4/12 is exactly in between 1/6 and 1/2 because if 2/12 is equal to 1/6 and 3/6 is equal to 1/2 so then the answer is 4/12 because 1/2 is 2/12 away from 4/12 and 1/6 is 2/12 away from 4/12.

▲▲▲▲▲▲**Figure 6–1** *Anita explained why $\frac{4}{12}$ has to be exactly halfway between $\frac{1}{6}$ and $\frac{1}{2}$.*

Anita, Francis, and Sammy compared how far one-sixth and one-fourth were from one-half. Anita, for example, explained: *$\frac{1}{4}$ is in between $\frac{1}{6}$ and $\frac{1}{2}$ because $\frac{1}{6}$ and $\frac{1}{12}$ is equal to $\frac{1}{4}$ so $\frac{1}{4}$ is bigger than $\frac{1}{6}$ and $\frac{1}{4}$ and $\frac{1}{4}$ is equal to $\frac{1}{2}$ so $\frac{1}{4}$ is in between $\frac{1}{6}$ and $\frac{1}{2}$.* (See Figure 6–1.)

Ally, Gloria, and Carla explained why one-sixth is less than one-fourth. Gloria wrote: *Yes, because $\frac{1}{2}$ is $\frac{2}{4}$ which is bigger than $\frac{1}{4}$, and $\frac{1}{6}$ is smaller than $\frac{1}{4}$ because $\frac{1}{6} + \frac{1}{12} = \frac{1}{4}$.*

As he typically did, Clark referred to the pieces in the fraction kit. He wrote: *Yes because if you put the fractions in your fraction kit in order from smallest to biggest it would go like this $\frac{1}{16}, \frac{1}{12}, \frac{1}{6}, \frac{1}{4}, \frac{1}{3}, \frac{1}{2}, \frac{1}{1}$, and imbitween $\frac{1}{2}$ and $\frac{1}{6}$ there is two numbers and the numbers are $\frac{1}{4}$ and $\frac{1}{3}$ so it is in between $\frac{1}{2}$ and $\frac{1}{6}$.*

As I circulated, I stopped and talked with students whose explanations contained errors or were unclear to me or who seemed to be struggling. For example, Saul had written: *Yes, because $\frac{1}{2}$ is the bigger one because you have to add 2 to the 1 in $\frac{1}{6}$ to make it half, and 1 to 1 in $\frac{1}{4}$ to make that half. 2 is bigger than one so $\frac{1}{6}$ is farther away from $\frac{1}{2}$ so $\frac{1}{4}$ is bigger than $\frac{1}{6}$ and $\frac{1}{2}$ is bigger than $\frac{1}{4}$ so $\frac{1}{4}$ is smaller than $\frac{1}{2}$ so yes it is in the middle of $\frac{1}{6}$ and $\frac{1}{2}$.*

I knew that Saul's understanding was strong, but his explanations were often complex and sometimes convoluted. First I asked Saul, "If you add two to one-sixth, don't you get two and one-sixth?"

Saul replied, "I wasn't adding two to one-sixth, I was only adding two to the one in one-sixth."

"So you were adding two more sixths, not two wholes?" I asked.

Saul thought for a moment, then nodded and said, "That's what I meant. Adding two to the one in one-sixth is the same as adding two-*sixths*, and adding one to the one in one-fourth means adding one-*fourth*."

"So one-sixth is two-sixths away from one-half?" I asked. Saul nodded.

"And one-fourth is one-fourth away from one-half?" Saul nodded again.

"Well, the second part of your explanation confuses me," I said. "What do you mean when you write that one-sixth is farther away from one-half so one-fourth is bigger than one-sixth? I agree that one-fourth is bigger than one-sixth, but I don't understand how you're thinking about it."

Saul again thought for a moment and then said, "Well, one-sixth comes first because the pieces are smaller." Saul stopped to think a bit more and then said, "Oh, I know. Two-sixths is the same as one-third, and one-third is bigger than one-fourth." I accepted this response.

I noticed that David's reasoning was incomplete. He wrote: *Yes. Because it is a $\frac{1}{12}$ away from a sixth and a $\frac{1}{4}$ from a half.*

I said to David, "I agree that one-fourth is one-twelfth away from one-sixth and one-fourth away from one-half, but I'm not sure how that tells me why one-fourth is larger than one-sixth and smaller than one-half."

David responded, "Oh, that's easy. Fourths are bigger than sixths and smaller than halves, so one-fourth has to be in between." I had similar conversations with Josh and Sammy.

Eddie struggled with math. He was a persevering student, however, and I'd learned that with enough time and encouragement, Eddie would sort out ideas and make progress. At this point, his understanding was still fragile. He wrote: *yes because $\frac{1}{4}$ is a qurter of $\frac{1}{2}$ and $\frac{1}{6}$ is a $\frac{1}{12}$ away from $\frac{1}{4}$.* When I talked with Eddie, I had him take out his fraction kit. "That's how I figured it out," he said to me. After collecting the pieces in question, he added, "Oops, one-fourth is a quarter of the whole. It's only half of the one-half piece."

"Is one-fourth half of one-half?" I asked him.

Eddie responded, "Yes... no... yes... wait a minute." He referred back to the pieces and then said with confidence, "Two-fourths make a half, so it's half." Then he fiddled with the one-sixth pieces and got excited. "Oh, I see now," he said. "It takes three of the sixths to make a half, so the sixths have to be smaller."

Paul's explanation was unique. He wrote: *Yes, because $\frac{1}{4}$ is a half of a half. So it's less. $\frac{1}{6}$ is less than half of a half.* (See Figure 6–2.) When I asked Paul how he knew that one-sixth was less than half of a half, he responded, "Three-sixths make a half, and half of three-sixths is one and a half–sixths, so one-sixth has to be less."

I could tell from the erasures on her paper that Juanita had been struggling. I was sorry that I hadn't gotten to her earlier so that I could have talked with her about her thinking. I often find saying their ideas aloud helps students face the task of expressing their ideas in writing. Juanita had drawn three circles and divided them into halves, fourths, and sixths. Then, over her erasures, she had written: *Yes because if $\frac{1}{3}$ is exactly half then $\frac{1}{4}$ and $\frac{1}{5}$ is between $\frac{1}{2}$ and $\frac{1}{6}$.*

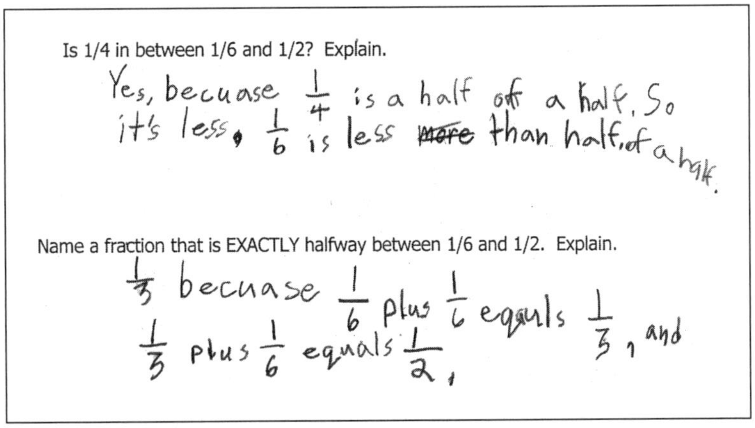

Is 1/4 in between 1/6 and 1/2? Explain.

Yes, becuase $\frac{1}{4}$ is a half off a half, So it's less, $\frac{1}{6}$ is less ~~more~~ than half of a half.

Name a fraction that is EXACTLY halfway between 1/6 and 1/2. Explain.

$\frac{1}{3}$ becuase $\frac{1}{6}$ plus $\frac{1}{6}$ equals $\frac{1}{3}$, and $\frac{1}{3}$ plus $\frac{1}{6}$ equals $\frac{1}{2}$,

▲▲▲▲▲▲Figure 6–2 *Paul gave a unique explanation for the first question and then explained why $\frac{1}{3}$ was exactly halfway between.*

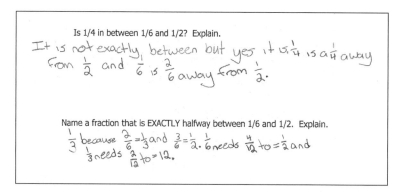

Is 1/4 in between 1/6 and 1/2? Explain.

It is not exactly between but yes it is. 1/4 is a 1/4 away from 1/2 and 1/6 is 2/6 away from 1/2.

Name a fraction that is EXACTLY halfway between 1/6 and 1/2. Explain.

1/3 because 2/6 = 1/3 and 3/6 = 1/2. 1/6 needs 4/12 to = 1/2 and 1/3 needs 2/12 to = 12.

▲▲▲▲▲▲Figure 6–3 Sachi answered both questions correctly.

I asked her, "How do you know that one-third is exactly halfway between one-sixth and one-half?"

Juanita responded, "Two-sixths is equal to one-third, and that's halfway between one-sixth and three-sixths. And I know that three-sixths is equal to one-half."

I then asked, "Can you tell me how you know that one-fourth is in between one-sixth and one-half?"

Juanita said, "Well, if I put the fractions in order, they go one-sixth, one-fifth, one-fourth, one-third, one-half. So one-fifth, one-fourth, and one-third are all in between. Should I write that?"

By this time, most of the others had finished, so I said to Juanita, "No, don't write any more now. I'm going to start a class discussion and I'd rather that you participate than write. I think that the others could benefit from hearing your ideas."

Figure 6–3 shows one student's correct thinking.

A Follow-Up Discussion

I asked the students to come to the rug with their papers for a discussion. I decided to discuss with them how they figured out a fraction that was exactly halfway between one-sixth and one-half. As they were getting settled, I wrote on the board:

Name a fraction that is EXACTLY halfway between $\frac{1}{6}$ and $\frac{1}{2}$.

I then said, "Look at your paper and see what fraction you named. I'd like to begin by listing the answers you came up with, and then we'll discuss them together." I listed the following possible answers:

$$\frac{1}{3}$$

$$\frac{9}{24}$$

$$\frac{1}{4}$$

$$\frac{4}{12}$$

$$\frac{2}{6}$$

For each fraction, I asked students to explain why they thought it was or wasn't exactly halfway. We narrowed the list of correct answers to $\frac{1}{3}$, $\frac{4}{12}$, and $\frac{2}{6}$.

Kayla's reasoning was typical for explaining why two-sixths was exactly halfway between one-sixth and one-half. She wrote: *$\frac{2}{6}$ is $\frac{1}{6}$ greater than $\frac{1}{6}$ and $\frac{2}{6}$ is $\frac{1}{6}$ less than $\frac{1}{2}$ because $\frac{3}{6} = \frac{1}{2}$.*

Carla explained why four-twelfths was exactly halfway. She wrote: *$\frac{4}{12}$ because $\frac{6}{12} = \frac{1}{2}$ and $\frac{2}{12} = \frac{1}{6}$ so whats inbetween that (2, 4, 6) is $\frac{4}{12}$.*

Julio originally thought that one-fourth was correct. He wrote: *Because since there numerator is the same. 4 is also two away from 6 and 2 so it's the same.* (See Figure 6–4.) After some discussion, he revised his answer to four-twelfths. He explained, "If you convert the one-sixth, one-fourth, and one-half to twelfths, they're two-twelfths, three-twelfths, and six-twelfths. So for it to be halfway, it would have to

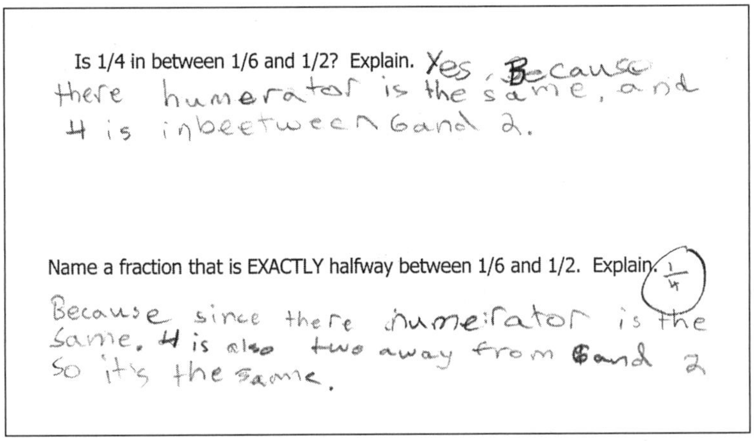

Is 1/4 in between 1/6 and 1/2? Explain. Yes, Because there humerator is the same, and 4 is inbeetween 6 and 2.

Name a fraction that is EXACTLY halfway between 1/6 and 1/2. Explain. 1/4

Because since there numeirator is the same. 4 is also two away from 6 and 2 so it's the saame.

▲▲▲▲▲Figure 6–4 *Julio incorrectly thought that $\frac{1}{4}$ was exactly halfway between $\frac{1}{6}$ and $\frac{1}{2}$. Later, however, he changed his answer.*

be four-twelfths. And that's the same as one-third."

Craig had initially decided that $\frac{9}{24}$ was halfway between. He wrote: $\frac{9}{24}$ *is exactly in between $\frac{1}{6}$ and $\frac{1}{2}$ because the numerator is three down from half and three up from a sixth.* Later he realized that $\frac{1}{6}$ was equal to $\frac{4}{24}$, and $\frac{9}{24}$ is $\frac{5}{24}$ away, not $\frac{3}{24}$.

Questions and Discussion

▲▲▲

▲ *I noticed at the beginning of the lesson, you asked the students to raise their hands to show whether they agreed, disagreed, or were unsure. Won't students with incorrect ideas be embarrassed when they find out that they were wrong? Why do you do this?*

I think it's important to establish a classroom learning environment that encourages risk taking. To do so, students need to understand that errors are opportunities for learning and that learning from our mistakes is important. In order to establish this environment, I reinforce for the students, over and over again from the beginning of the school year, that making mistakes is part of learning and that it's OK to change their mind about any opinion, but that they also have to try to explain why their thinking has shifted. Then I give them a good deal of practice explaining their reasoning. In this way, I put the emphasis of their participation in class lessons on their reasoning. Also, I'm quick to deal with any situation in which a student ridicules another for making an error.

▲ *Sometimes when you ask a question, you call on a volunteer. But other times, you ask students first to think by themselves or talk with a neighbor. How do you decide which protocol to follow?*

If I ask a question that calls for mathematical reasoning, and I suspect that some of the students need more time than others to gather their thoughts, I typically ask for a moment of silent thinking, followed by a chance for them to share their ideas with just one other person. The silent time is also good for the typically fast thinkers who sometimes think more quickly than thoroughly. Sometimes, however, a question that I ask is not particularly mathematically complex or significant. It may be that I'm asking a question more to get their attention, as I did at the beginning of the lesson when I asked what they thought I meant by "in-between fractions." Or it may be that I'm asking a question that I am fairly sure that they all understand; for example, to name a fraction that is less than one-half.

▲ *When you ask students to talk with a neighbor, don't you worry that some students aren't talking about the question you presented? Isn't it hard to monitor what they're doing when everyone is talking at once?*

It does happen, especially at the beginning of the year when I'm establishing norms for classroom behavior, that students do not comply with my expectations for partner talk. Circulating in the room when students are talking is a way to pick up on this sort of behavior. When I notice this happening, I typically join a conversation and ask one or the other of the students to tell me what he or she was thinking. Then I turn to the other and ask the same. Then, before leaving them, I remind them that when I ask them to talk with each other, I expect them to share their thinking without my having to come and monitor them. The next time I use partner talk, I'm careful to check on how they are doing. Doing this consistently with students at the beginning of the year is important, and the payoff is rewarding.

▲ *When a student's paper is incorrect, do you ask him or her to make corrections?*

Sometimes I do and sometimes I don't. If I feel that the exercise of making corrections on their work will further their thinking, then I make the request. Sometimes I'll give them a clean sheet of paper and have them begin again, rather than face their erroneous start. However, if I feel that asking students to do additional writing will result more in frustration than in progress, I don't push them and instead find a way to give them some individual attention. As with many of our instructional decisions, I make decisions in situations like these on a case-by-case basis.

CHAPTER SEVEN
FRACTION SEQUENCES

Overview

In this lesson, students consider the following question: If you add one to the numerator and denominator of a fraction, is the new fraction always greater than the original fraction? The lesson gives students practice with comparing and ordering fractions while also introducing them to the idea of limits. Students investigate the conjecture for several sequences of fractions.

Materials

▲ none

Time

▲ one class period

Teaching Directions

1. Write on the board the following sequence of fractions:

$\frac{1}{2}, \frac{2}{3}, \frac{3}{4}, \frac{4}{5}, \frac{5}{6}, \frac{6}{7}, \frac{7}{8}, \ldots$

You may want to explain to the students that the three dots at the end indicate that the sequence continues. Ask the following questions for a whole-class discussion about the sequence:

▲ A student, Sandro, wrote this sequence of fractions. What pattern do you think Sandro used for the fractions? (The numerator and denominator each increases by one to get the next term, and the numerator is always one less than the denominator.)

▲ Can you continue writing fractions this way forever? (Yes, the sequence can continue forever.)

▲ Does $\frac{99}{100}$ fit the pattern? Explain. $\frac{124}{130}$? Explain. (Continue asking about other fractions, some that do and some that do not follow the pattern that the numerator is always one less than the denominator.)

▲ What other fractions can you think of that also fit the pattern? Explain how you know. (Students may say that the numerator is one less than the denominator, or that the denominator is one more than the numerator.)

2. Tell the class that a student named Alan made a conjecture that if you add one to the numerator and denominaor of a fraction, then the new fraction is always larger. Ask them to talk with a neighbor about whether they think this is true.

3. Then lead a class discussion to help them all realize that the fractions increase in order and get closer and closer to the number one but always are a little bit less. Tell them that the number one is the limit of this sequence, which means that the sequence approaches the number one but never reaches it.

4. Write $\frac{1}{3}$ on the board and ask students to add one to the numerator and denominator. The resulting fraction is $\frac{2}{4}$. Ask: "How can you convince someone that two-fourths is greater than one-third?" Continue the sequence: $\frac{1}{3}, \frac{2}{4}, \frac{3}{5}, \frac{4}{6}, \frac{5}{7}, \ldots$ Have students verify that the fractions get larger.

5. If students are interested, repeat the investigation starting with other fractions. Tell students that these trials aren't definite proof, but it seems that adding one to the numerator and denominator increases the fraction's size.

Teaching Notes

This lesson was inspired when I taught the lesson *In Size Order* (see Chapter 2). During the discussion in the first part of the lesson, Alan, one of the students, gave a reason for why he thought that $\frac{3}{8}$ was larger than $\frac{2}{7}$. He made the conjecture that if you add 1 to both the numerator and denominator of a fraction (in this case, changing $\frac{2}{7}$ to $\frac{3}{8}$), then the second fraction is larger. In response, Sandro, another student, agreed with Alan and explained his fascination with a particular sequence of fractions for which Alan's pattern was true—$\frac{1}{2}, \frac{2}{3}, \frac{3}{4}, \frac{4}{5}, \frac{5}{6}, \frac{6}{7} \ldots$. I've found over the years that other students also come up with Sandro's sequence of fractions. Some report that they see it, in a way, as "counting by fractions" since the numerators and denominators increase by 1 each time. Also, it seems intuitively correct to students that the fractions in the sequence increase in size. However, I had never thought before about how to incorporate Sandro's sequence into a classroom investigation of whether these fractions do, in fact, increase in size. Nor had I ever thought about Alan's generalized conjecture.

I initiated a discussion about Alan's and Sandro's ideas with the class and, since then, have regularly used their ideas for a lesson. With Sandro's sequence, it's possible to compare the fractions by figuring how far each is from 1 whole—$\frac{1}{2}$ is $\frac{1}{2}$ from 1 whole, $\frac{2}{3}$ is $\frac{1}{3}$ from 1 whole, $\frac{3}{4}$ is $\frac{1}{4}$ from 1 whole, $\frac{4}{5}$ is $\frac{1}{5}$ from 1 whole, and so on. Each of these fractions is a unit fraction from 1—$\frac{1}{2}, \frac{1}{3}, \frac{1}{4}, \frac{1}{5}$, and so on. And because students can fairly easily compare unit fractions, they can see how each fraction in Sandro's sequence gets a little closer to 1. The students were fascinated to think about a fraction such as $\frac{999,999}{1,000,000}$ being very, very close to 1 but still smaller than 1. Mathematicians would say that Sandro's sequence approaches the limit of 1; the fractions never reach 1 but keep sneaking up on it.

In the lesson described, Julio applied Alan's idea to $\frac{1}{3}$, adding 1 to the numerator and denominator to get $\frac{2}{4}$. Julio knew that $\frac{2}{4}$ was larger than $\frac{1}{3}$ because $\frac{2}{4}$ is equivalent to $\frac{1}{2}$, which is more than $\frac{1}{3}$. Continuing the pattern produces the sequence $\frac{1}{3}, \frac{2}{4}, \frac{3}{5}, \frac{4}{6}, \frac{5}{7}$, and so on. As with Sandro's sequence, it's possible to verify that these fractions are in increasing order by seeing that the difference from each to 1 is decreasing—$\frac{2}{3}, \frac{2}{4}, \frac{2}{5}, \frac{2}{6}, \frac{2}{7}$, and so on.

Alan's conjecture that adding 1 to the numerator and denominator of any fraction will increase its size can be expressed algebraically: for any fraction $\frac{a}{b}$, is $\frac{a+1}{b+1}$ always greater than $\frac{a}{b}$? What if b is greater than a? Also, what happens when we add any other number, n, to the numerator and denominator—is $\frac{a+n}{b+n}$ always greater than $\frac{a}{b}$ for any number n? Proving these generalized conjectures is out of reach for fifth graders, but raising the questions and discussing them provide the students valuable experience with thinking mathematically.

The Lesson

▲▲

I began the class by writing on the board the following sequence of fractions:

$\frac{1}{2}, \frac{2}{3}, \frac{3}{4}, \frac{4}{5}, \frac{5}{6}, \frac{6}{7}, \frac{7}{8}, \ldots$

I've found over the years that it's common for students to think about this sequence of fractions as a way to "count" in fractions. It's not counting as we do with whole numbers, with the same interval between each successive number—1, 2, 3, 4, and so on—but it does follow a regular pattern of increasing the numerator and denominator in the same way.

I began the discussion by asking, "What do you think the three dots at the end mean?"

"They look like periods," Helene said.

"A period means the end of something," Pierre added.

Kayla knew about this convention. She said, "It means that you can keep going on and on." If no student had given this explanation, I would have done so to introduce the class to this mathematical convention.

I then said, "A student in another class, Sandro, was interested in this sequence and showed it to the class. What pattern do you think Sandro used when writing these fractions? Talk with your neighbor about your ideas." The room got noisy as students talked, many pointing to the fractions on the board. After a few moments, I called them back to attention and asked them to share their ideas.

"They are like counting in the tops and bottoms," Craig offered.

"Can you explain your idea a little more and use fraction terminology?" I responded.

Craig said, "Sure. Look at the numerators. They go one, two, three, four, like that. They're counting. And the same with the denominators."

Celia added, "But the dominators start with two instead of one."

"You add one to the numerator and denominator each time," Eddie said.

"Can we continue writing fractions this way forever?" I asked. Hands shot up.

Clark said, "I think you can go forever because you can always make the numbers bigger and bigger."

Maria added, "They go to infinity."

I wrote on the board:

$$\frac{99}{100}$$

"Is this fraction part of the sequence? Talk at your table about this."

After a few moments, I interrupted the discussions. Everyone agreed that this fraction fit the sequence. David explained, "See, the top is always one less than the bottom, so it works."

"Can you give your idea again using *numerator* and *denominator*?" I asked David.

"The numerator is always one less than the denominator," David said.

"How about this fraction?" I said. I wrote on the board:

$$\frac{124}{130}$$

"No," they chorused.

"Who can explain how you know for sure?" I asked.

Ally answered, "Like David said, the numerator should always be one less."

"But how do you know it will continue like that?" I probed.

"It has to," Ally insisted.

Juanita had another idea. "It's always odd over even, or even over odd," she said, "and your fraction is even over even. I don't think that can be right. Also because of what Ally said."

I continued writing other fractions on the board and asking which belonged to Sandro's sequence, choosing a mixture of fractions that did and did not belong—$\frac{33}{32}$, $\frac{33}{34}$, $\frac{45}{47}$, and so on. There were giggles when I wrote $\frac{999,999}{1,000,000}$, and they all agreed that it fit the pattern.

"Who knows a fraction that fits the pattern?" I asked. Hands shot up and I had several students report. I recorded their fractions on the board.

"Who knows a fraction that doesn't fit the pattern?" I asked. Again, hands shot up and several students reported.

COMPARING THE FRACTIONS

I then said, "Another student, Alan, said that in this sequence of fractions, each fraction is larger than the one that comes before it. Talk to a neighbor about whether you think this is true. Are the fractions getting larger each time?" The room again got noisy as students discussed the question I raised. After a few moments, I asked for their attention and called on students to share their ideas.

Sabrina said, "When you use bigger numbers, they are closer to one whole."

Francis said, "When you use really, really big numbers, the fraction is only a little bit away from one whole. Like with that last one, it's only one-millionth away from one."

"They never will get to one whole," Josh said. "They get close, but they never get there." The students all seemed to be convinced that Sandro's fractions grew larger each time and closer to one whole.

I pointed to the last two fractions I had written in the sequence—$\frac{6}{7}$ and $\frac{7}{8}$. I asked, "Who can explain why seven-eighths is larger than six-sevenths?" About half a dozen students raised their hands. Rather than have one of them explain, I asked the students to talk with their neighbors. This way, more of them would have a chance to voice their ideas. After a few moments, I called the class back to attention. Now almost two-thirds of the students had their hands raised. I called on Pierre.

Pierre said, "It takes one more seventh to get from six-sevenths to one whole. But it takes one more eighth to get from seven-eighths to one whole. One-eighth is less than one-seventh, so seven-eighths is closer to one. So it's bigger." I wrote on the board:

$$\frac{6}{7} + \frac{1}{7} = 1$$

$$\frac{7}{8} + \frac{1}{8} = 1$$

$$\frac{1}{7} > \frac{1}{8}$$

So $\frac{7}{8}$ is closer to 1.

"Did anyone think about this another way?" I asked.

Kayla said, "You can change them both to fifty-sixths."

"Why fifty-sixths?" I asked.

"Because seven and eight both go into fifty-six," Kayla said. As Kayla continued with her explanation, I recorded on the board:

$$\frac{6}{7} = \frac{48}{56}$$

$$\frac{7}{8} = \frac{49}{56}$$

$$\frac{49}{56} > \frac{48}{56}, \text{ so } \frac{7}{8} > \frac{6}{7}.$$

"Wow, they're really close," Clark said.

"They're only one–fifty-sixth apart," Kara said.

No one had another explanation for why seven-eighths is greater than six-sevenths. I then said, "When you have a sequence of fractions like this that are getting closer and closer to one, mathematicians say that the number one is the limit of the sequence. This means that the fractions approach the number one but never quite reach it."

INVESTIGATING ANOTHER SEQUENCE

I posed another problem. I said, "Let's see if the pattern of adding one to the numerator and denominator of a fraction gives a fraction that's larger, even if we don't start with one-half the way that Sandro did in his pattern." I wrote on the board:

$$\frac{1}{3}$$

"What fraction do we get if we add one to the numerator and denominator?" I

asked. I waited a moment and had the class respond in unison. I recorded:

$$\frac{1}{3}, \frac{2}{4}$$

"Is two-fourths greater than one-third?" I asked.

Carla answered, "Two-fourths is half and one-third is less than half."

"What fraction comes next in this sequence?" I asked. Again, I had the class respond in unison and I recorded:

$$\frac{1}{3}, \frac{2}{4}, \frac{3}{5}$$

"Is three-fifths larger than two-fourths?" I asked.

Sabrina answered, "It is because it's more than half."

"And the next fraction?" I asked. The class responded and I recorded:

$$\frac{1}{3}, \frac{2}{4}, \frac{3}{5}, \frac{4}{6}$$

I knew that comparing four-sixths and three-fifths would be harder for some of the students, so I had them discuss first at their tables. Then I asked for their attention and called on Julio.

"This was a little harder," he began. "What we did is change four-sixths to two-thirds. Then we made them both into fifteenths. Two-thirds is ten-fifteenths, and three-fifths is only nine-fifteenths, so it works." I recorded on the board as Julio explained:

$$\frac{4}{6} = \frac{2}{3}$$

$$\frac{2}{3} = \frac{10}{15}$$

$$\frac{3}{5} = \frac{9}{15}$$

Pierre had a different explanation. "I thought about money. First I did what Julio did and changed four-sixths to two-thirds, and I know that's about sixty-six cents. Then I thought about the fifths, and that made me think of twenties— twenty, forty, sixty, eighty, one hundred. So one-fifth is like twenty cents. Then three-fifths is like sixty cents, and that's less than sixty-six cents." I recorded on the board:

$\frac{4}{6} = \frac{2}{3}$

$\frac{2}{3}$ of $1.00 = $.66

$\frac{1}{5}$ of $1.00 = $.20 (20, 40, 60, 80, 100)

$\frac{3}{5}$ of $1.00 = $.60

$.66 is more than $.60, so $\frac{4}{6}$ is more than $\frac{3}{5}$

Celia had another way to explain. She said, "I didn't change four-sixths to two-thirds. I thought that four-sixths is one-sixth away from one-half, because three-sixths is one-half."

"Is four-sixths more or less than one-half?" I asked.

"More," Celia answered. She continued. "And three-fifths is more than one-half, too. Half of five is two and a half, so I didn't know what to do. So I changed three-fifths to six-tenths, and then I knew that it was one-tenth more than one-half. And one-sixth is farther away from one-half." I stopped Celia and recorded on the board:

$\frac{4}{6}$ is $\frac{1}{6}$ more than $\frac{1}{2}$.

$\frac{3}{5} = \frac{6}{10}$ and is $\frac{1}{10}$ more than $\frac{1}{2}$.

$\frac{4}{6}$ is farther away from $\frac{1}{2}$ so $\frac{4}{6}$ is more than $\frac{3}{5}$.

I ended the discussion at this time. I thought that some of the students had

gone as far as they could with it. I said to the class, "It seems that whenever we add one to the numerator and denominator of a fraction, the new fraction is larger than the original fraction. But we can't try this for every possible fraction, so we can't say for sure that it always works. But it seems to do so, and it's something that's interesting to keep thinking about as we study more about fractions."

EXTENSIONS

On other days, investigate other sequences of fractions like these. You can vary the investigations is several ways:

▲ Start with other fractions.
▲ Add 2 to the numerator and denominator each time.
▲ Start with an improper fraction, for example, $\frac{3}{2}$. The sequence would be $\frac{3}{2}, \frac{4}{3}, \frac{5}{4}, \frac{6}{5}, \frac{7}{6}, \ldots$. In this sequence, as for others that begin with fractions greater than 1, the fractions decrease in size, still approaching the limit of 1.
▲ Start with a fraction equivalent to 1, for example, $\frac{2}{2}$. The sequence would be $\frac{2}{2}, \frac{3}{3}, \frac{4}{4}, \frac{5}{5}, \frac{6}{6}, \ldots$. In this sequence, the fractions are all equivalent.

Questions and Discussion

▲▲▲

▲ *How important is it for students to learn about the convention of using three dots to indicate that a sequence continues?*

At some time, all students will encounter the convention of using three dots to show that a sequence continues—1, 2, 3, 4, . . . , for example. It's not essential to teach this convention in the elementary grades, but if it occurs naturally in the context of an investigation, then it's an opportune time to inform students about it. This convention points out how we can look at mathematical symbolism in the way that we look at punctuation. The three dots are a mathematical way to represent the idea of "and so on" or "et cetera," and the convention isn't difficult for children to understand.

▲ *I noticed that sometimes in the lesson you ask students to talk with a neighbor, but sometimes you don't. How do you decide?*

Talking in pairs gives more students a chance to voice their ideas, and that supports their learning. Also, if only a few students raise a hand to respond to a question, that tells me that most are not comfortable sharing their ideas. Talking with just one other person is easier for students and gives them a safe way to clarify their ideas. I find that after talking in pairs, more students typically are willing to share with the whole class.

CHAPTER EIGHT
CANCELING ZEROS

Overview

It's only sometimes appropriate to "cancel" 0s in the numerators and denominators of fractions. For example, if you cancel the 0s in $\frac{10}{20}$, the result is an equivalent fraction: $\frac{1}{2}$. However, canceling the 0s to change $\frac{101}{201}$ to $\frac{11}{21}$ is not correct. In this lesson, after thinking about how canceling relates to division by 10 and considering fractions for which canceling 0s makes sense, the students think about what happens when you cancel the 0s in $\frac{101}{201}$ to change the fraction into $\frac{11}{21}$. This lesson gives students valuable experience in thinking about equivalent fractions, justifying their ideas, and discovering how a rule may or may not be appropriate in all situations.

Materials

▲ none

Time

▲ two class periods

Teaching Directions

1. Write on the board: $\frac{10}{20} = \frac{1}{2}$. Have students explain why this is true. Repeat with other fractions where canceling zeros results in an equivalent fraction—$\frac{20}{40}$ and $\frac{20}{30}$, for example.

2. Discuss with the class how canceling a zero produces the same result as dividing a number by ten. To help the students see this pattern, write on the board several examples of dividing numbers that end in zero by ten:

$20 \div 10 = 2$

$60 \div 10 = 6$

$100 \div 10 = 10$

$110 \div 10 = 11$

Point out that canceling the zeros in both the numerator and denominator of a fraction is the same as dividing both numbers by ten.

3. Write on the board a few more examples of fractions with numerators and denominators that end in zero—$\frac{30}{40}$, $\frac{50}{100}$, $\frac{60}{80}$, $\frac{100}{200}$. Have the students, in pairs or small groups, discuss why canceling the zeros in each case results in an equivalent fraction.

4. Before posing the next problem, let them know that the question you're about to present is a hard one. Reassure them that you don't expect them to be able to figure it out easily. Let them know that you're interested in hearing their ideas, even if they aren't correct, because wrong ideas can be helpful for figuring out and seeing something in a new way.

5. Write on the board: $\frac{101}{201}$. Ask: "If I cancel the zeros and change the fraction to $\frac{11}{21}$, are the two fractions equivalent?" Write on the board:

$$\frac{101}{201} = ? \frac{11}{21}$$

6. Give the students time to talk in pairs or small groups about the question. Then call them to attention and lead a class discussion and give all who have ideas the chance to express them. It's helpful to record students' ideas on the board as a reference of the ideas presented.

7. To push students' thinking, after they have shared their ideas, point to $\frac{101}{201}$ and ask students whether it is more or less than $\frac{1}{2}$. Have them talk in pairs or small groups, then discuss the problem with the whole class to help students understand that it is more than $\frac{1}{2}$. Repeat for $\frac{11}{21}$.

8. Continue the discussion about whether $\frac{101}{201}$ and $\frac{11}{21}$ are equivalent until you think that the students have heard enough to be able to write about their ideas. Then ask them to explain their thinking in writing. It's most likely some students will not understand or be able to explain why the two fractions are not equivalent. Using their papers as an assessment can give you insights into their understanding that can help you guide their thinking in future lessons.

Teaching Notes

I remember that much of my early learning about fractions involved learning and practicing procedures. Canceling 0s was one of those procedures that I learned to apply, by canceling the 0s, for example, in a fraction such as $\frac{10}{20}$ to change it to $\frac{1}{2}$. But it wasn't until much later that I figured out that it made sense because canceling accomplished the same result as dividing the numerator and denominator both by 10, thus preserving the proportional relationship between the two numbers.

This lesson deals with the notion of canceling 0s by presenting students with a situation in which canceling is incorrect—changing $\frac{101}{201}$ to $\frac{11}{21}$ by eliminating the 0s in the numerator and denominator. I tried this lesson after watching a segment on a videotape of a fifth-grade class from the Mathematical Inquiry Through Video program, a project funded by the National Science Foundation. I tried a version of the lesson with fifth graders, and then with other classes, and feel that it is a valuable experience to offer students, even though it presents a challenge that will be a struggle for many.

Students who have had more experience relating fractions and decimals can convert $\frac{101}{201}$ and $\frac{11}{21}$ to decimals in order to compare them more easily and see that they are not equivalent. The students described, however, did not have this facility. They were comfortable comparing fractions by seeing how far they were from 0, $\frac{1}{2}$, or 1. As you'll read in other lessons, they were used to figuring out that $\frac{5}{8}$ is more than $\frac{7}{12}$, for example, by comparing them both to $\frac{1}{2}$. They would reason that $\frac{5}{8}$ is $\frac{7}{12}$ more than $\frac{1}{2}$ while $\frac{7}{12}$ is only $\frac{1}{12}$ more than $\frac{1}{2}$, so $\frac{5}{8}$ has to be larger than $\frac{7}{12}$. It was much more difficult, however, for them to use this reasoning with $\frac{101}{201}$ and $\frac{11}{21}$. Along with dealing with fractions, the lesson also draws on students' number sense about whole numbers. In this class, Elizabeth knew that 101 is a prime number and, therefore, can't have a factor in common with 201. Elizabeth, however, was an extremely gifted student, and this idea hasn't come up in other classes.

It's important to encourage students to take risks in math class to explain their thinking. They should feel that you value their willingness to try out ideas and offer them to the class, that there are no penalties for expressing incorrect ideas. They should learn that incorrect ideas can be valuable for helping lead to understanding and seeing ideas in new ways.

The Lesson

▲▲

DAY 1

To begin class, I wrote on the board:

$$\frac{10}{20} = \frac{1}{2}$$

"Is this true?" I asked. Most of the students indicated that it was.

"Who can explain why?" I asked. More than half of the students raised their hands, and I called on Sahara.

"Ten is half of twenty, and one is half of two," she said. This satisfied me and seemed to satisfy the others as well.

Next I wrote on the board:

$$\frac{20}{40} = \frac{2}{4} = \frac{1}{2}$$

Kurt gave an explanation similar to Sahara's. "Twenty and twenty are forty, so twenty is half of forty, and so it's one-half.

And two-fourths is the same as one-half, just in smaller pieces."

I then wrote on the board:

$$\frac{20}{30} = \frac{2}{3}$$

This also seemed obvious to the students, but only about half a dozen students volunteered to explain. I called on Emma first.

She said, "One-third of thirty is ten, so two-thirds of thirty has to be twenty."

"I have a different way to explain," Raquel said. "You divide twenty by ten and you get two, and you divide thirty by ten and you get three."

Emma, Raquel, and the few others who had raised their hands were nodding in agreement, but most of the other students were noncommittal. I drew a circle, divided it into thirds, and shaded in two sections.

"That's two-thirds," Miguel called out.

"Yes," I confirmed. "Can I use this drawing to prove that two-thirds and twenty-thirtieths would be the same amount of pizza?"

Kalila said, "Just divide each of the thirds into ten small pieces." I followed her instructions.

"That shows it," Anisa said. "See, twenty of the pieces fit into the two-thirds."

I then said to the class, "When I was learning fractions in fifth grade, I remember learning about canceling zeros in fractions. I learned that if you crossed out the zero at the end of the numbers in the numerator and denominator of a fraction, the new fraction was equivalent to the first one. It was the same as dividing both numbers by ten." To help the students see this pattern, I wrote on the board several examples of dividing numbers that ended in zero by ten:

$20 \div 10 = 2$

$60 \div 10 = 6$

$100 \div 10 = 10$

$110 \div 10 = 11$

Even though the students hadn't heard about this rule or the terminology of canceling, what I said seemed to make sense to them. To be sure, I presented a few more examples. I wrote on the board:

$\frac{30}{40}$

$\frac{50}{100}$

$\frac{60}{80}$

$\frac{100}{200}$

"Talk at your tables about how to apply the rule that I learned and if it makes sense with these fractions," I directed the class. As discussion broke out among the groups, I circulated and listened. I noticed that Kalila, who had been clear about dividing each third into ten equal slices to show that twenty-thirtieths and two-thirds were equivalent, was explaining to her group how to use the same strategy to show that thirty-fortieths and three-fourths were equivalent.

It seemed obvious to all groups that fifty–one hundredths was equivalent to five-tenths. "They're both a half," Midori said matter-of-factly to the others at her table.

I overheard a group struggle with why sixty-eightieths and six-eighths were equivalent. "It has to work," Alexa said, "but I can't explain it."

Elizabeth responded, "Well, six-eighths is the same as three-fourths, right?" The others agreed and Elizabeth continued, "Well, sixty-eightieths has to be, too. Look, there are four twenties in eighty—twenty, forty, sixty, eighty. And there are three twenties in sixty—twenty, forty, sixty." This seemed clear to Alexa, but Miguel and Sahara weren't convinced. Alexa started to make a drawing to explain it to the group in another way.

I then heard Dario exclaim to the others in his group, when they were talking about why one hundred–two hundredths and ten-twentieths were equivalent, "Look, you can cross them out again, and it's one-half! That's cool." Dario had noticed that you could cancel zeros twice.

I called the class back to attention and we talked about what the students had learned.

Presenting the Problem

Before posing the problem that I wanted them to discuss, I talked with the students about the challenge I was about to offer. I let them know that the question I was about to present was a hard one. I said, "I don't expect you to be able to figure this out or understand it easily. But I'm interested in hearing the ideas that you'll come up with. Even wrong ideas can help lead us to figure out something or see something in a new way." I said this to encourage the students to take the risk of sharing their ideas, even if they weren't sure they were correct. Then I wrote on the board:

$$\frac{101}{201}$$

"If I cancel the zeros in these two fractions, I wind up with eleven over twenty-one," I said. "Are these two fractions equivalent?" Next to $\frac{101}{201}$ on the board, I wrote an equals sign, a question mark, and then $\frac{11}{21}$:

$$\frac{101}{201} = ? \frac{11}{21}$$

Hands shot up from students who wanted to respond. But before taking any of their responses, I asked them to talk among themselves at their tables. I've found that when only some of the students want to respond, small-group conversations can help loosen up others' thinking, give students a safe way to try out ideas, and provide more students the chance to express themselves than a whole-class discussion would. After a few moments, I interrupted the groups and brought the class to attention.

"Before I hear your ideas," I said, "I'm interested in how many of you think that the fractions are equivalent, how many think they aren't equivalent, and how many aren't sure. Put a thumb up if you think the two fractions are worth the same, a thumb down if you think they aren't worth the same, and a thumb sideways if you're not sure." About half of the students showed thumbs up; the rest were divided between showing thumbs down and thumbs sideways.

I then gave guidelines for a whole-class discussion. "I'll give everyone who

has an opinion the chance to talk," I said. "When you start, first state whether or not you think the fractions are equivalent, and then give your reasoning. Please listen to what others say to see if someone else has the same idea as you do, or if someone else's argument convinces you to change your position."

The students' arguments were varied.

Letitia began. She said, "I think they're both the same. You can just cross out the zeros."

Elliot agreed with Letitia. He said, "Zeros aren't really anything. They just hold a place, so you can get rid of them."

Miguel took the opposite point of view. He said, "No, you can't. If you take out a zero, the whole number changes."

Emma spoke to the general point of removing zeros from numbers. She said, "You can only take away zeros in decimals, after the decimal point."

Nick returned to the fraction question and said, "But if you take them away in both numbers, it's OK, like it worked before."

Abby disagreed, "You can't just do that. Then you make tens out of the hundreds."

Elizabeth, a truly gifted math student, said, "They can't be the same because you can't divide the numerator and denominator by the same number. I know that because one hundred one is prime."

Tillie had two ideas. "My first idea is that if you wrote one hundred over two hundred, you could take out the middle zeros and you'd have ten over twenty, and they're the same. My second idea is that a hundred one plus a hundred one equals two hundred two, and that's one away from two hundred one. And eleven plus eleven equals twenty-two, and that's one away from twenty-one. They're just both one away. So I think they're the same." I recorded on the board as Tillie spoke:

$$\frac{1\cancel{0}0}{2\cancel{0}0} = \frac{10}{20}$$

101 + 101 = 202, 202 is 1 away from 201

11 + 11 = 22, 22 is 1 away from 21

So $\frac{101}{201}$ is the same as $\frac{11}{21}$.

Kalila offered a different explanation for why they were the same. "If you write one hundred one over two hundred two, and you cross out the zeros, you get eleven over twenty-two, and they're both half." I recorded Kalila's idea on the board:

$\frac{101}{202} = \frac{11}{22}$

"Oh yeah, that's right!" Pedro said.

"But that's not our problem," Midori said.

I then entered the discussion, returning the focus to the problem I had posed. I pointed to where I had recorded $\frac{101}{201}$ on the board and asked, "Is this fraction more or less than half?" The students' opinions were divided, so I again had them talk in their groups. I felt this was a question they could resolve, and they did. At least, all reported they were convinced that $\frac{101}{201}$ was more than $\frac{1}{2}$. I had several explain why.

"If you add one hundred one and one hundred one, you get two hundred two, not two hundred one," Dario said. "So it can't be half." I wrote on the board:

101 + 101 = 202

101 + 101 ≠ 201

Raquel said, "We think it has to be more than half because half of two hundred one is a hundred and a half, and a hundred one is bigger."

$\frac{1}{2}$ of 201 = $100\frac{1}{2}$

101 is greater than $100\frac{1}{2}$

$\frac{100\frac{1}{2}}{201} = \frac{1}{2}$

$\frac{101}{201}$ is greater than $\frac{1}{2}$

"What about eleven over twenty-one?" I asked, pointing to $\frac{11}{21}$ on the board. "Is this more or less than half?" Again, I had them discuss in their groups and then I asked for their attention. Several students had ideas.

"One-half is the same as ten and a half over twenty-one, so it's bigger," Midori said.

Letitia said, "It has to be bigger than one-half because eleven over twenty-two is one-half, and they both have the same number of pieces, but if you cut something into twenty-one pieces, the pieces are bigger than if you cut something into twenty-two pieces." I recorded on the board:

$\frac{11}{22} = \frac{1}{2}$

$\frac{11}{21}$ is greater than $\frac{1}{2}$ because the pieces are bigger.

I turned the discussion back to comparing $\frac{101}{201}$ and $\frac{11}{21}$. Geoff said, "They're both more than one-half, and that's why I think they're the same."

Sahara said, "I agree that they're both bigger than one-half, so they could be the same, but it doesn't seem right."

Elizabeth had been fiddling with a calculator. "I proved it!" she said. "I divided and eleven–twenty-firsts is definitely more."

"What did you divide?" Raquel asked.

"I did one hundred one divided by two hundred one, and then I divided eleven by twenty-one," Elizabeth said. I asked her for the answers she got and recorded on the board:

101 ÷ 201 = 0.5024875

11 ÷ 21 = 0.5238095

"What does dividing have to do with it?" Miguel asked. I knew that many of the students didn't yet understand the relationship between fractions and division.

Pedro then said, "I thought it would be right, but now I think it isn't. What I did was start with eleven over twenty-one and then timesed both by two and got twenty-two over forty-two, so I know they're the same. Then I timesed them by three and got thirty-three over sixty-three. I kept on going to see if I would get one hundred one over two hundred one, but I didn't. After ninety-nine over one eighty-nine I got one ten over two ten, so I don't think they're the same." I had Pedro repeat his calculations and I recorded on the board:

$\frac{11}{21} \times \frac{2}{2} = \frac{22}{42}$

$\frac{11}{21} \times \frac{3}{3} = \frac{33}{63}$

$\frac{11}{21} \times \frac{4}{4} = \frac{44}{84}$

$\frac{11}{21} \times \frac{5}{5} = \frac{55}{105}$

$\frac{11}{21} \times \frac{6}{6} = \frac{66}{126}$

$\frac{11}{21} \times \frac{7}{7} = \frac{77}{147}$

$\frac{11}{21} \times \frac{8}{8} = \frac{88}{168}$

$\frac{11}{21} \times \frac{9}{9} = \frac{99}{189}$

$\frac{11}{21} \times \frac{10}{10} = \frac{110}{210}$

I pointed to the original problem on the board—$\frac{101}{201} = ? \frac{11}{21}$—and asked Pedro, "Are you sure that they're not the same, or are you still thinking about it?"

Pedro hedged his bets. "I think they're not the same," he said, still tentative.

Kurt said, "I think they're the same because I just think it's OK to cross out the zeros because like Elliot said, they're just placeholders."

Abby said, "You can't just take a zero out of the middle of a number and expect it to disappear."

Raquel said, "I think you can change eleven over twenty-one to one hundred ten over two hundred ten, like Pedro did, but not to one hundred one over two hundred one. I agree with Abby. You can't put zeros in the middle of numbers, so you can't take them away, either."

Geoff said, "It's wrong. If you divide eleven into one hundred one, it's not equal to twenty-one divided into two hundred one."

Sonia said, "They're not the same because Geoff is right. I used the calculator, but I did something different from Elizabeth. Can I come up and write what I got?" I agreed. Sonia came up and carefully copied from her paper:

101 ÷ 11 = 9.1818181

201 ÷ 21 = 9.5714285

A Writing Assignment

By this time, the discussion had gone on for almost half an hour. The board was filled with different students' ideas, and although hands were still raised, everyone who had wanted to speak had had at least one chance to do so. I made the decision to end the conversation. But, rather than try to bring closure to the discussion, I decided to have them write about their thinking. I've learned that writing can be a useful tool for students to sort out their thinking, and I wanted to give them as much time as possible to do so.

I said, "This is a difficult idea to think about, and you've had a chance to hear a lot of different viewpoints. I'd like to find out now where each of your thinking is." The students were used to writing to help me understand their thinking.

"You still may not be sure about the answer to the question," I continued, "but I'm interested in hearing about what you're thinking so far." I left all of the students' ideas on the board for their reference.

The students' writing revealed their confusion. Of the twenty-five students present that day, six had a firm grasp. For the others, their writing revealed either soft spots in their understanding or glaring misconceptions. I left the students' ideas on the board so that we could refer to them again the next day. (See Figures 8–1 through 8–6.)

101/201≠11/21 because a Fraction is a division problem. To turn a remainder into a fraction you make the remainder the numerator and the devisor the denominator. Or if you wanted a decimal you would add a decimal point and divide again. So therefore you would divide the numerator by the denominator.
101/201=0.5024875
11/21=0.5238095

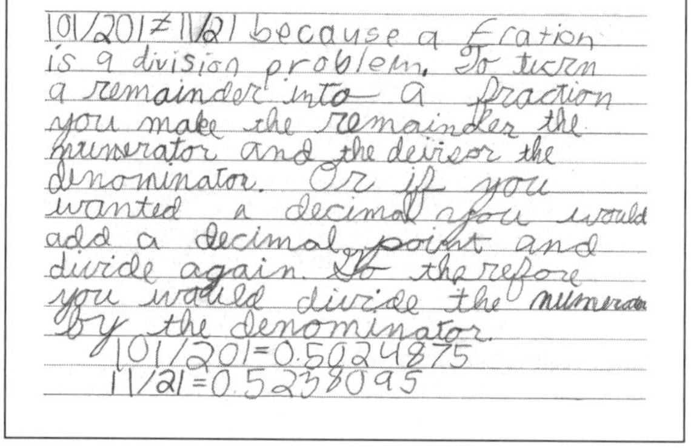

▲▲▲▲▲**Figure 8–1** *Elizabeth was a gifted math student. Her paper showed her understanding of the relationship between fractions and division and her comfort with decimals.*

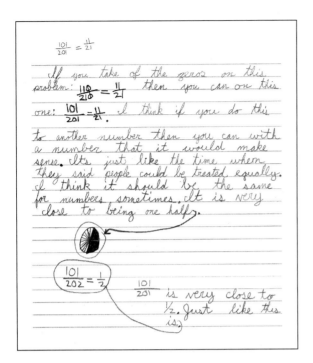

$\frac{101}{201} = \frac{11}{21}$

If you take of the zeros on this problem: $\frac{110}{210} = \frac{11}{21}$ then you can on this one: $\frac{101}{201} = \frac{11}{21}$. I think if you do this to another number then you can with a number that it would make sense. Its just like the time when they said people could be treated equally. I think it should be the same for numbers sometimes. It is very close to being one half.

$\frac{101}{202} = \frac{1}{2}$

$\frac{101}{201}$ is very close to $\frac{1}{2}$. Just like this is.

▲▲▲▲▲▲**Figure 8–2** *Letitia's conclusion was based on a notion of equality that isn't mathematical. However, she was correct that the two fractions are both very close to $\frac{1}{2}$.*

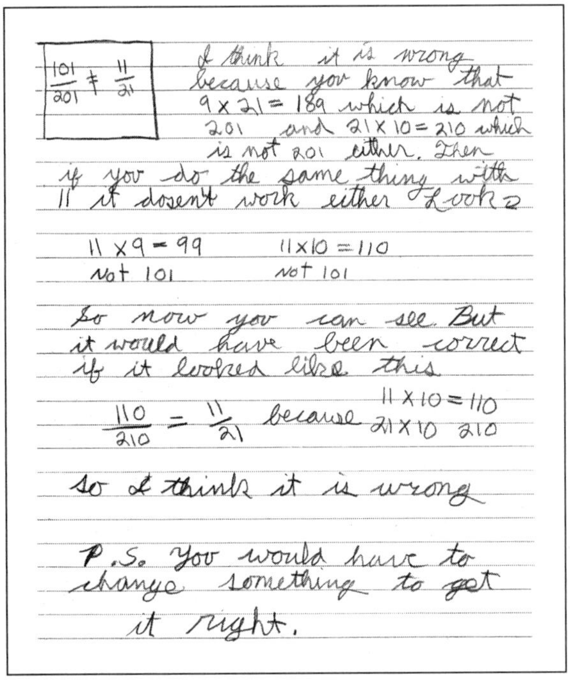

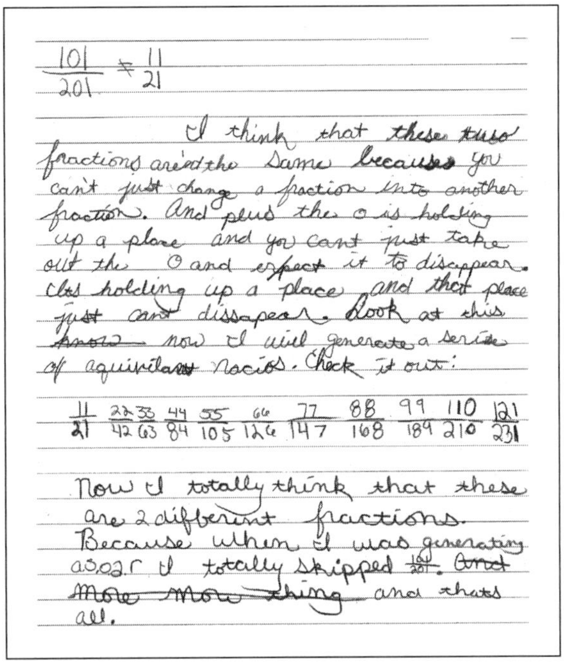

$\frac{101}{201} \neq \frac{11}{21}$

I think that these two fractions are'nt the same because you can't just change a fraction into another fraction. And plus the 0 is holding up a place and you cant just take out the 0 and expect it to disappear. cbs holding up a place and that place just cant dissapear. Look at this know — now I will generate a series of aquivilant racios. Check it out:

| $\frac{11}{21}$ | $\frac{22}{42}$ | $\frac{33}{63}$ | $\frac{44}{84}$ | $\frac{55}{105}$ | $\frac{66}{126}$ | $\frac{77}{147}$ | $\frac{88}{168}$ | $\frac{99}{189}$ | $\frac{110}{210}$ | $\frac{121}{231}$ |

Now I totally think that these are 2 different fractions. Because when I was generating a 202 I totally skipped $\frac{101}{201}$. And that more more thing and thats all.

▲▲▲▲▲▲**Figure 8–4** *Abby generated a series of equivalent fractions to explain why $\frac{101}{201}$ could not equal $\frac{11}{21}$.*

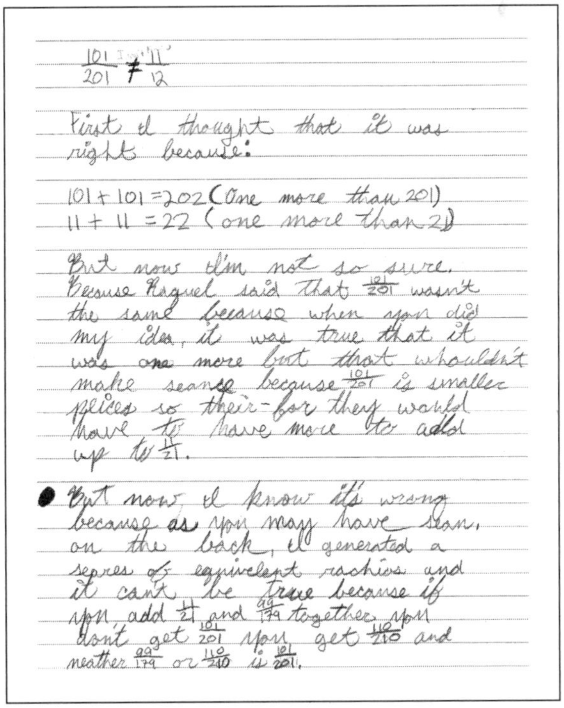

$\frac{101}{201} \neq \frac{11}{21}$

I think it is wrong because you know that $9 \times 21 = 189$ which is not 201 and $21 \times 10 = 210$ which is not 201 either. Then if you do the same thing with 11 it dosent work either Look

$11 \times 9 = 99$ — Not 101 $11 \times 10 = 110$ — not 101

So now you can see But it would have been correct if it looked like this

$\frac{110}{210} = \frac{11}{21}$ because $11 \times 10 = 110$ $21 \times 10 = 210$

so I think it is wrong

P.S. You would have to change something to get it right.

▲▲▲▲▲▲**Figure 8–3** *Sahara was convinced that the fractions were not equivalent and stated her argument clearly.*

$\frac{101}{201} \neq \frac{11}{12}$

First I thought that it was right because:

$101 + 101 = 202$ (One more than 201)
$11 + 11 = 22$ (one more than 2)

But now I'm not so sure. Because Raquel said that $\frac{101}{201}$ wasn't the same because when you did my idea, it was true that it was one more but that whouldn't make seanse because $\frac{101}{201}$ is smaller pieces so their — for they would have to have more to add up to $\frac{11}{21}$.

● But now, I know it's wrong because as you may have San, on the back, I generated a sepres of equivelent rachios and it cant be true because if you add $\frac{11}{21}$ and $\frac{99}{189}$ together you dont get $\frac{101}{201}$ you get $\frac{110}{210}$ and neather $\frac{99}{189}$ or $\frac{110}{210}$ is $\frac{101}{201}$.

▲▲▲▲▲▲**Figure 8–5** *Tillie revised her conclusion after hearing Raquel's argument.*

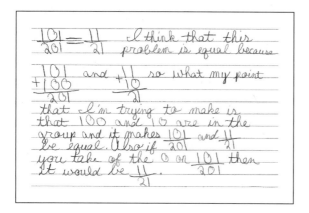

▲▲▲▲▲**Figure 8–6** *Magda's paper showed the fragility of her understanding.*

DAY 2

The next day, I returned to the conversation for part of the class. I complimented the students for sticking with the discussion about a difficult idea and for working hard on their papers to sort out their thinking. I wrote on the board:

$$\frac{101}{201} \neq \frac{11}{21}$$

"Not all of you came to this conclusion," I said, "but the two fractions are not equivalent. They both are very close to one-half, and they both are just a little bit more that one-half, but they're not worth exactly the same." The students were used to comparing fractions by seeing how far they were from 0, $\frac{1}{2}$, or 1, so I used their experience to try to explain the relationship between $\frac{101}{201}$ and $\frac{11}{21}$. I wrote on the board:

$$\frac{100\frac{1}{2}}{101} = \frac{1}{2}, \text{ so } \frac{101}{201} \text{ is } \frac{\frac{1}{2}}{201} \text{ more than } \frac{1}{2}$$

$$\frac{10\frac{1}{2}}{21} = \frac{1}{2}, \text{ so } \frac{11}{21} \text{ is } \frac{\frac{1}{2}}{21} \text{ more than } \frac{1}{2}$$

$$\frac{\frac{1}{2}}{201} \text{ is less than } \frac{\frac{1}{2}}{21}, \text{ so } \frac{101}{201} \text{ is closer to } \frac{1}{2}$$

I tried to give this explanation with a light touch, realizing that not everyone would understand it. After I explained, I assured them, "We'll be continuing to learn more about fractions and how to make sense of complicated ideas. The more you study, the easier it will be to understand ideas like these." I try to remind my students that not understanding is always an opportunity for learning something new.

EXTENSION

Ask students to come up with fractions for which canceling 0s in the middle "works," that is, the two fractions are equivalent. In this class, Kalila offered the idea that $\frac{101}{202} = \frac{11}{22}$, so in this case, removing the 0s in the middle resulted in an equivalent fraction. If, however, no student comes up with this idea, or a similar one, present a few pairs of fractions that work in this way, for example:

$$\frac{203}{406} \qquad \frac{1,001}{2,002} \qquad \frac{402}{804}$$

Then have them come up with other examples. Most likely, students will come up with fractions that are equivalent to one-half, since these are fractions that are easy for them to analyze.

Questions and Discussion

▲▲

▲ *Is seems that this problem was too hard for most of the students. Is it something that would be better to present in a later grade?*

I think that it's a problem that *also* should be presented in a later grade. These students were fifth graders and, yes, the problem was difficult, even for some of those who had a strong understanding of fractions. But thinking about the problem, even for those for whom it was out of reach, helped reinforce for students that following rules without understanding is a risky mathematical strategy. Also, I feel that this lesson can provide a helpful basis for a later discussion of the same idea, after students have had more time and experience with fractions.

▲ *Do you think it makes sense to teach the rule for canceling zeros if you're careful to explain how to apply the rule correctly?*

I don't recommend teaching the rule for canceling 0s as a procedure that you would then expect students to practice, master, and apply. Rather, I want them to know that canceling 0s is the same as dividing both the numerator and denominator by 10, and that dividing the numerator and denominator by the same number always results in an equivalent fraction. It's obvious to students that, for example, $\frac{10}{20} = \frac{1}{2}$, $\frac{30}{60} = \frac{3}{6}$, and $\frac{40}{80} = \frac{4}{8}$. With fractions such as these, students don't need a rule but instead rely on their number sense. It isn't as obvious to all students, however, that $\frac{20}{30} = \frac{2}{3}$ or that $\frac{60}{80} = \frac{6}{8}$. In instances like these, students should be encouraged to explain why the fractions are equivalent and not be satisfied because they applied a rule. Also, applying a rule incorrectly, as with $\frac{101}{201}$, occurs more often when students are not reasoning but are relying on following a procedure instead of seeking to make sense of a situation.

▲ *What did you do next with these students?*

I learned from the lesson what I needed to emphasize in later lessons. I realized that I had to make the relationship between fractions and division clear so that students understood that another interpretation of, for example, $\frac{3}{4}$ is $3 \div 4$. I also needed to spend more time relating fractions to decimals. I've come to see that developing understanding of fractions is complex for most students, and the more ways I can offer students to look at concepts about fractions, the more ways I strengthen their understanding.

▲ *It seems that the discussion continued for a very long time. Is such a long discussion typical when you teach this or other lessons?*

The length of the discussion depends on the interest of the students, their mathematical understanding, and my encouragement for expecting them to think hard and share their thinking. In the discussion I described here, the students were wonderfully engaged and willing to discuss. I think it helped that I let them know in advance that the question I was posing was a hard one that I didn't expect them to understand easily. I think this helped them not be intimidated and be more willing to take the risk of sharing ideas, even if they weren't sure they were correct. It takes time and encouragement to build an atmosphere of trust in a class so that students feel free to express their ideas and take intellectual risks.

CHAPTER NINE
INTRODUCING ADDITION AND SUBTRACTION

Overview

This lesson introduces addition and subtraction of fractions and mixed numbers. The lesson builds on students' understanding of equivalent fractions and gives them experiences combining fractions and mixed numbers and finding differences. Rather than teaching algorithms, this lesson relies on having students use their own reasoning strategies. Taught over a period of days, this lesson allows the class to think about a variety of problems and also asks students to practice on their own.

Materials

▲ none

Time

▲ one class period to introduce, plus time for additional experiences over several days

Teaching Directions

1. Draw two circles on the board and divide each into four equal parts. Ask students how much one part is worth and label the parts each $\frac{1}{4}$.

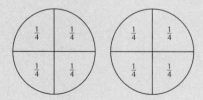

2. Then ask how many fourths there are in the two circles. Explain that you could count the fourths and model how to do so: "One-fourth, two-fourths, three-fourths, four-fourths, five-fourths, six-fourths, seven-fourths, eight-fourths." Record on the board:

$\frac{1}{4} + \frac{1}{4} + \frac{1}{4} + \frac{1}{4} + \frac{1}{4} + \frac{1}{4} + \frac{1}{4} + \frac{1}{4} = \frac{8}{4} = 2$

3. Draw two more circles on the board, divide each into eighths, and label the pieces. Ask how many eighths are in the two circles and model counting by eighths.

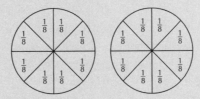

4. Write on the board: $\frac{1}{8} + \frac{1}{8} + \frac{1}{8} + \frac{1}{8}$. Ask students to talk with a neighbor about their ideas for an answer to this problem. Then ask students to share their thinking with the class. Explain that the answer could be four-eighths or one-half. Record:

$\frac{1}{8} + \frac{1}{8} + \frac{1}{8} + \frac{1}{8} = \frac{4}{8} = \frac{1}{2}$

5. Write a problem on the board, for example, $\frac{1}{4} + \frac{1}{2}$. Ask students to talk with a neighbor about how to solve it. Then have all students who would like present their ideas. For each method presented, record their thinking on the board.

6. Repeat Step 5 for other problems, presenting a mixture of addition and subtraction problems. Below are the problems presented in the lesson that follows:

$\frac{3}{4} - \frac{1}{4}$

$1 - \frac{1}{2}$

$2\frac{1}{2} - \frac{1}{4}$

$1\frac{1}{4} + \frac{1}{2} + \frac{1}{8}$

$\frac{1}{2} + \frac{3}{4}$

$1\frac{1}{4} - \frac{1}{2}$

7. Give an individual assignment of three problems to solve. Following are the problems I gave to this class:

$\frac{1}{2} + \frac{1}{3}$

$\frac{3}{8} + \frac{3}{4}$

$\frac{2}{3} - \frac{3}{8}$

8. Over the next several days, continue presenting more problems for the class to discuss and for students to do individually. See page 100 for suggestions for additional problems.

Introducing Addition and Subtraction   93

Teaching Notes

Learning to add and subtract fractions and mixed numbers requires that students understand the idea of equivalence and can represent fractions as equivalent fractions. The previous lessons in this book and in the Teaching Arithmetic book *Lessons for Introducing Fractions, Grades 4–5*, especially Chapters 2 and 15, about using fraction kits, focus on developing this understanding. (See the booklet, *The Fraction Kit Guide*.) This lesson is appropriate once students have a firm understanding of equivalence and are able to write fractions as equivalent fractions. Then they have the foundation necessary to combine fractions and mixed numbers and find differences.

Rather than teaching students particular recording systems or algorithms, this lesson presents them with problem situations that call for adding and subtracting and introduces them to a variety of strategies. The instructional procedure for each problem presented is the same. Students first talk with a neighbor, then a volunteer presents a solution to the class, and then the teacher records, modeling for the students how to record their thinking. The problems increase in difficulty, beginning with like denominators, then moving to fractions with halves, fourths, and other easy denominators, and finally challenging students with other denominators.

The Lesson

▲▲

I began the lesson by relating to students' early mathematics learning. I said, "When you were much younger, you learned to count using whole numbers—one, two, three, four, and so on. And you used counting when you were first learning to add and subtract. Now that we're studying fractions, counting can also come in handy, this time for addition and subtraction problems with fractions." I stopped and drew two circles on the board and divided each into fourths.

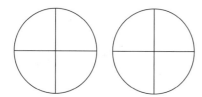

"Who can describe what I drew?" I asked.

Carla said, "There are two circles and you made each into four parts."

I pointed to one section of the first circle and said, "And how much is this part worth? Let's answer in a whisper voice."

"One-fourth," the students said.

"And this part?" I asked, pointing to another section in the same circle.

"One-fourth," the students said again. I wrote $\frac{1}{4}$ in each section of the two circles:

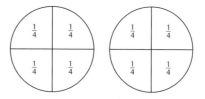

"How many fourths are there in the two circles altogether?" I asked. After a few moments, I asked them to answer again in a whisper voice.

"Eight," they said.

"Who can explain why there are eight-fourths in two whole circles?" I asked.

Brendan said, "There are four in each circle and there are two circles. Four plus four is eight."

Kayla added, "Or you could do two times four."

"Brendan and Kayla are right," I said. "I could also figure out how many fourths there are by adding up the fourths." I wrote on the board:

$$\frac{1}{4} + \frac{1}{4} + \frac{1}{4} + \frac{1}{4} + \frac{1}{4} + \frac{1}{4} + \frac{1}{4} + \frac{1}{4}$$

"To add fractions like these, if I didn't have a picture, I could count up the fourths." I pointed to each fourth in turn and counted, "One-fourth, two-fourths, three-fourths, four-fourths, five-fourths, six-fourths, seven-fourths, eight-fourths. So there are eight-fourths in two whole circles." I recorded:

$$\frac{1}{4} + \frac{1}{4} + \frac{1}{4} + \frac{1}{4} + \frac{1}{4} + \frac{1}{4} + \frac{1}{4} + \frac{1}{4} = \frac{8}{4} = 2$$

I then drew two more circles on the board, divided each into eighths, and labeled the pieces. I said, "Count up these eighths and figure out how many are in two wholes."

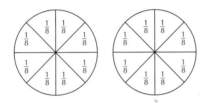

David answered. "It's sixteen-eighths. You have eight in one circle and eight in the other." I recorded:

$$\frac{16}{8} = 2$$

I then wrote on the board:

$$\frac{1}{8} + \frac{1}{8} + \frac{1}{8} + \frac{1}{8}$$

Hands shot up. "Talk to your neighbor about your idea for the answer to this problem," I said. After a moment, I interrupted them and called on Helene.

"It's four," she said. Helene's answer was a common error, and I responded by recording what she said and giving her a chance to correct the answer. I recorded:

$$\frac{1}{8} + \frac{1}{8} + \frac{1}{8} + \frac{1}{8} = 4$$

Students raised hands to object and Helene looked flustered. "That's not what I meant," she said. "I meant four-eighths." I corrected what I had written:

$$\frac{1}{8} + \frac{1}{8} + \frac{1}{8} + \frac{1}{8} = \frac{4}{8}$$

"I thought that was what you meant, Helene, and it's good that you noticed. Remember, when we're first learning something new, it's natural to make a mistake. Making a mistake like this can be useful for helping you remember what to write when you're working on problems like these."

"Hey, that's the same as one-half," Craig said.

"What's the same as one-half?" I asked. If Craig hadn't made this comment, I would have suggested that we could represent the answer as $\frac{1}{2}$.

"The answer," Craig said. "Four-eighths is the same as one-half." I added to what I had recorded:

$$\frac{1}{8} + \frac{1}{8} + \frac{1}{8} + \frac{1}{8} = \frac{4}{8} = \frac{1}{2}$$

"Does it make sense that you're adding eighths and you wind up with one-half?" I asked.

Clark said, "Four-eighths is the same as one-half. You just have more pieces."

Celia said, "If you times the top and bottom of one-half by four, you get four-eighths."

"What about this problem?" I asked, writing on the board a problem that called for adding fractions with unlike denominators:

$$\frac{1}{4} + \frac{1}{2}$$

I chose fractions that I thought the students could deal with easily. (If they weren't able to solve this problem handily, then that would have told me that I needed to give them more experiences with equivalent fractions.) Some hands shot up immediately. I waited to give others the chance to think. After more hands went up, I asked the students to talk with their neighbor about how to combine these fractions. The room got noisy, then began to quiet. I asked for their attention and called on Julio.

"All you have to do is change the one-half so it's fourths," Julio said matter-of-factly. "Then it's one-fourth plus two-fourths, and that's three-fourths." I wrote on the board:

$\frac{1}{4} + \frac{1}{2}$

$\frac{1}{4} + \frac{2}{4} = \frac{3}{4}$

"When Julio changed the one-half into two-fourths, then I could count up the number of fourths there are," I commented as I wrote.

"I just knew the answer," Pierre said. "I did it in my head."

"That's fine," I said. "But sometimes it's helps to do what Julio did—change the fractions so they have the same denominator and you can count them up. Did anyone think about the problem in a different way?" No one volunteered, so I then wrote a subtraction problem on the board:

$\frac{3}{4} - \frac{1}{4}$

After giving the students time to talk, I brought them to attention and called on Sachi. "I think it can either be two-fourths or one-half," she said. "I thought that if I had three of the fourths and took away one of them, I would have two of them left, and two-fourths is the same as one-half." I recorded:

$\frac{3}{4} - \frac{1}{4} = \frac{2}{4} \ or \ \frac{1}{2}$

PROBLEMS WITH WHOLE NUMBERS AND MIXED NUMBERS

"Here's another subtraction problem," I said and wrote on the board:

$1 - \frac{1}{2}$

This problem was easy for the students. Sabrina explained, "If you start with one whole cookie and give away

one-half, then you have one-half left." I presented another problem:

$2\frac{1}{2} - \frac{1}{4}$

Francis explained, "One-half minus one-fourth is one-fourth because one-fourth plus one-fourth is one-half."

"So what do you think the answer is?" I asked, not sure if Francis remembered the whole number.

"It's two and one-fourth," he said. I recorded:

$2\frac{1}{2} - \frac{1}{4} = 2\frac{1}{4}$

Damien raised his hand. "I don't get that. Shouldn't you take the one-fourth away from the two, too?" Saying "two, too" made him and others giggle.

I said, "Let's talk about this. It's really good that you let me know when you're not sure about something. Are you thinking that you need to take the one-fourth away from the one-half and also from the two?" Damien nodded. I drew two and one-half circles on the board and wrote $2\frac{1}{2}$ underneath my drawing:

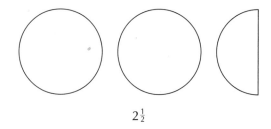

$2\frac{1}{2}$

I explained, "So the problem says that we have two and one-half circles, and we need to subtract one-fourth. Francis says that we're left with two and one-fourth circles." I altered my drawing by shading one-fourth:

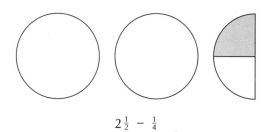

$2\frac{1}{2} - \frac{1}{4}$

"But why is my idea wrong?" Damien asked.

"I think you're solving two problems. You're getting the right answer if I had asked you to do this." I wrote on the board:

$2 - \frac{1}{4}$ and $\frac{1}{2} - \frac{1}{4}$

"When I get confused about a problem with fractions," I added, "I try to think about a similar problem with whole numbers." I wrote on the board:

$6 + 4 - 3$

"What's the answer?" I asked.

"Seven," Damien and several others answered.

"How did you get that answer?" I asked Damien.

"I did six plus four makes ten, minus three is seven," he said.

Brendan's hand was waving. "I did four minus three is one, plus six is seven," he said.

"You each did one addition and one subtraction," I said, pointing to the plus sign and then to the minus sign. "And that's right. We wouldn't get the same answer if we did six minus three and then also four minus three. That would be subtracting three twice." Damien nodded.

"So I could write the fraction problem like this," I said, writing:

$2 + \frac{1}{2} - \frac{1}{4}$

"You subtract one-fourth just one time," I said. Damien nodded, but I knew that he needed more time to think about this idea and reconcile his confusion.

I then returned to an addition problem. "Try this one. Talk with your neighbor." I wrote on the board:

$1\frac{1}{4} + \frac{1}{2} + \frac{1}{8}$

Conversations broke out and I let the students talk for a moment. Then I called them to attention. Most were willing to report and I called on Gloria.

"We left the one alone and made the fractions into eighths so we could count them up. One-half is easy, that's four-eighths. One-fourth is half that many, and that's two-eighths. So you have four plus two plus the one at the end, and it adds up to seven-eighths." Others nodded their agreement and I recorded:

$1\frac{1}{4} + \frac{1}{2} + \frac{1}{8}$

$1\frac{2}{8} + \frac{4}{8} + \frac{1}{8} = 1\frac{7}{8}$

"Talk with your neighbor about this problem," I said, and wrote on the board:

$\frac{1}{2} + \frac{3}{4}$

After a few moments, I interrupted their conversations and called on Maggie. She said, "It's two-fourths plus three-fourths, and that's five-fourths." I recorded:

$\frac{1}{2} + \frac{3}{4}$

$\frac{2}{4} + \frac{3}{4} = \frac{5}{4}$

"Don't you have to change it to one and one-fourth?" Hassan asked. I recorded:

$\frac{2}{4} + \frac{3}{4} = \frac{5}{4} = 1\frac{1}{4}$

"Like this?" I asked. Hassan nodded.

"They mean the same thing," Celia said.

"Yes, they're equivalent, and both of these answers are correct," I said.

A SUBTRACTION PROBLEM WITH REGROUPING

"How about this subtraction problem," I said. "We start with one and one-fourth and we have to take away one-half." I wrote on the board:

$1\frac{1}{4} - \frac{1}{2}$

A few students noticed the relationship between this problem and the previous one and knew immediately that the answer was three-fourths. Others, however, didn't notice. I chose this problem purposely because I could verify the answer in several ways, relying on the previous problem and working with these numbers. I had the students talk with their neighbors and then I began a discussion.

"I'm interested in all of the different ways you thought of to solve this problem," I said. "Who would like to go first?" I called on Sabrina.

"I changed them to fourths. I made the one and one-fourth into five-fourths and the one-half into two-fourths. Then it's easy. The answer we got is three-fourths." I recorded:

$$1\tfrac{1}{4} - \tfrac{1}{2}$$

$$\tfrac{5}{4} - \tfrac{2}{4}$$

$$\tfrac{3}{4}$$

"Who else solved the problem this way?" I asked. About eight or so hands went up.

Kayla went next. "I didn't really have to think about it because it's kind of like the problem we just did. We did one-half plus three-fourths and got one and one-fourth, and this problem starts with one and one-fourth and takes away one-half, so the answer has to be three-fourths." I recorded on the board:

$$\tfrac{1}{2} + \tfrac{3}{4} = 1\tfrac{1}{4}$$

$$1\tfrac{1}{4} - \tfrac{1}{2} = \tfrac{3}{4}$$

Others expressed their surprise, impressed with what Kayla had noticed.

David had another way to think about the problem. "I thought of one and one-fourth as two numbers, one plus one-fourth," he began. "Then I knew that I had to subtract the one-half only one time, so I did one whole minus one-half, and that's one-half. And one-half plus one-fourth is three-fourths." I recorded:

$$1\tfrac{1}{4} - \tfrac{1}{2}$$

$$1 + \tfrac{1}{4} - \tfrac{1}{2}$$

$$1 - \tfrac{1}{2} = \tfrac{1}{2}$$

$$\tfrac{1}{2} + \tfrac{1}{4} = \tfrac{3}{4}$$

"So we have three different ways to arrive at the same answer of three-fourths," I said. "Does anyone have another way?" No one volunteered. Even though this traditionally is a problem that calls for regrouping, the students solved it in other ways. Their methods worked fine. I then said, "I'll show you how I learned to do this kind of subtraction problem." I did this not to imply that my way was better or the right way, but to show the students another recording system. I wrote the problem vertically:

$$1\tfrac{1}{4}$$

$$-\tfrac{1}{2}$$

"First I changed the fractions so that they had the same denominators," I said. I wrote:

$$1\tfrac{1}{4} = 1\tfrac{1}{4}$$

$$-\tfrac{1}{2} = \tfrac{2}{4}$$

"Then I knew that I couldn't subtract two-fourths from one-fourth, but instead of doing what David did and subtract it from the one whole, I did sort of what Sabrina did. I took the whole, changed it to four-fourths, and added it to the one-fourth already there to get five-fourths. Then I could subtract." I recorded:

$$1\tfrac{1}{4} = \tfrac{4}{4} + \tfrac{1}{4} = \tfrac{5}{4}$$

$$1\tfrac{1}{4} = \tfrac{5}{4}$$

$$-\tfrac{1}{2} = \tfrac{2}{4}$$

$$\tfrac{3}{4}$$

"It's kind of the same, but you wrote them one under the other," Sabrina said.

"Yes," I agreed.

An Individual Assignment

I then wrote three problems on the board for students to solve by themselves, two addition problems and one subtraction problem:

$\frac{1}{2} + \frac{1}{3}$

$\frac{3}{8} + \frac{3}{4}$

$\frac{2}{3} - \frac{3}{8}$

"Can we work together?" Kara asked.

"Yes, that's fine," I said. "It's good for you to talk over how to solve these. But you each need to record on your own paper."

The first problem was easy for the students and most handily changed the fractions to $\frac{3}{6}$ and $\frac{2}{6}$. Two of the students, Craig and Gloria, figured out that the answer to $\frac{1}{2} + \frac{1}{3}$ was $2\frac{2}{3}$. Even though this was an unconventional answer, both were able to explain why it made sense. Juanita also indicated that she knew that the answer was also $\frac{5}{6}$. Hassan figured the answer as $\frac{20}{24}$, also correct.

For the second problem, $\frac{3}{8} + \frac{3}{4}$, most students converted the fractions to eighths and got the answer of $1\frac{1}{8}$. However, there were other correct answers. Julio, for example, converted the fractions to $\frac{12}{32}$ and $\frac{24}{32}$ and reported the answer as $1\frac{4}{32}$. Sabrina reported it as $\frac{9}{8}$. Sachi figured the answer as $\frac{18}{16}$. She first changed $\frac{3}{4}$ to $\frac{12}{16}$ and then wrote: *There are 12 sixteenths plus three eights and two sixteenths go into one eight but there are three eights which equals six sixteenths and 12 + 6 = 18.* Although Sachi incorrectly wrote eights for eighths, her reasoning was correct. Pierre had another unique solution for $\frac{3}{8} + \frac{3}{4}$. He wrote: *4 is half of 8 so $\frac{3}{8}$ cut in half is $1\frac{1}{2}\frac{}{4} + \frac{3}{4} = 4\frac{1}{2}\frac{}{4}$.* Pierre's language wasn't accurate, but he was correct that $\frac{3}{8}$ is equivalent to $1\frac{1}{2}\frac{}{4}$.

Three students, Clark, Eddie, and Kara, had difficulty with all three problems and needed a good deal of help. Using the fraction pieces from their fraction kits helped. See Figures 9–1 through 9–4 for four students' work on these problems.

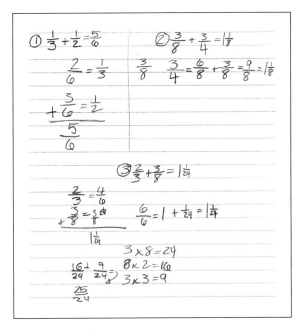

▲▲▲▲▲▲Figure 9–1 *Maria correctly solved all three problems, but incorrectly solved the third problem as an addition problem instead of as a subtraction problem.*

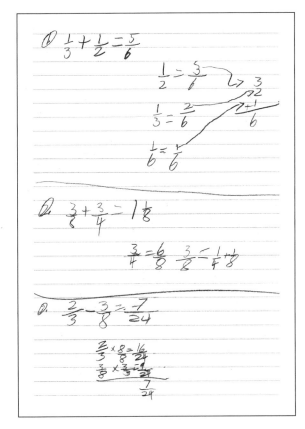

▲▲▲▲▲▲Figure 9–2 *Brendan reasoned correctly to get the right answers on all three problems.*

Introducing Addition and Subtraction 99

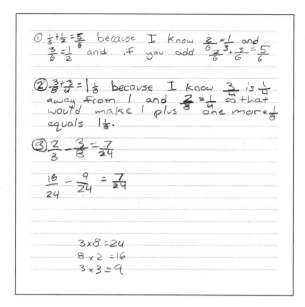

▲▲▲▲▲▲Figure 9–3 *Maggie solved the second problem by adding on to the $\frac{1}{4}$ to make 1, and then adding on the extra $\frac{1}{8}$.*

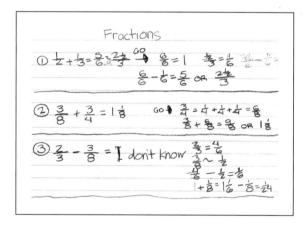

▲▲▲▲▲▲Figure 9–4 *While Gloria was able to solve the first problem in a unique way, getting an answer of $2\frac{\frac{1}{2}}{3}$, she was unable to figure out the third problem.*

CONTINUING WITH MORE PROBLEMS

Over the next several days, I continued in the same way, presenting the class with other problems, discussing them, and having students solve problems on their own. However, I didn't spend entire class periods doing this, as I had done before. Rather, I interspersed these discussions with the other things we were doing in math, spreading out the experiences to give the students the opportunity over time to build their understanding and develop their skills. Following are some of the problems I presented and discussed with the students.

$$\frac{1}{2} + \frac{2}{3}$$

$$\frac{1}{2} - \frac{1}{3}$$

$$1\frac{1}{2} + \frac{2}{3}$$

$$4 - \frac{2}{3}$$

$$\frac{1}{3} + 2\frac{1}{4}$$

$$1\frac{2}{3} + 1\frac{3}{4}$$

$$4\frac{3}{4} - \frac{1}{2}$$

$$\frac{1}{8} + \frac{1}{3}$$

$$\frac{3}{8} + \frac{2}{3}$$

$$2\frac{1}{2} - \frac{2}{3}$$

Questions and Discussion

▲▲

▲ *Why do you present addition and subtraction problems together? Doesn't this confuse students?*

The same understanding and skills are necessary for adding and subtracting, and I think that presenting the problems together helps students become more flexible in their thinking. Also, I want students to think about addition and subtraction in relationship to each other, and presenting combining and comparing problems together helps with this.

▲ *What if my students don't come up with strategies, or different ways to solve problems?*

This would be an indication that the problems were out of the students' reach. They either would need simpler problems, more instruction, or more experience with situations that would help them become more comfortable with representing equivalent fractions. Or you might try suggesting a strategy for a problem, then giving a similar problem and asking the students to try your idea.

▲ *I notice that you didn't require students to change improper fractions to mixed numbers. Are there times when they should convert them?*

I think that it's important for students to be able to represent an improper fraction as a mixed number and vice versa. When I was in elementary school, we couldn't ever leave answers as improper fractions and always had to change them to mixed numbers. (The very name—*improper* fractions—made them seem like fractions to be avoided!) However, I don't think this is necessary and I accept both. The only situations I can think of in which a mixed number would be a better way to express an answer are in solutions to problems where it would be more colloquial to say, for example, that "each person received one and a half cookies" rather than "each person received three-halves cookies."

▲ *My students seem to understand what to do when the denominators are easy numbers for them—halves, fourths, and eighths. But they don't seem to transfer their understanding to more difficult denominators. How do you help students when denominators present difficulties?*

My instructional strategies include giving students many opportunities to solve problems, talk with others, and listen to other students' solution strategies. I rely on concrete materials, most often the fraction kits I mentioned earlier. I check that they are comfortable with whole number relationships and spend more time on factors and multiples if needed. And I give individual students as much help as possible. While I believe that all of my students can learn, I know that they learn in different ways and at different rates. For some, concrete materials are essential; for others, pictures can help; still others rely on reasoning numerically. I try to match students with methods that are most useful to them. Also, when I make assignments, I find that it's good to list six problems, in order of difficulty, and ask students to solve any three of them. That way, I can provide challenges for students who are ready for more while giving needed practice with simpler problems for students who need that support.

CHAPTER TEN
PROBLEMS WITH ORANGES

Overview

In this lesson, students consider several variations of the same problem in which friends share oranges. The context and format of all of the problems are the same, but the fractions differ, making it possible to present problems of varying difficulty. For each problem, the students present their strategies for figuring out how many oranges the friends had and how much orange was left.

Materials

▲ *The Orange Problems* worksheet, 1 per student (see Blackline Masters)

Time

▲ one class period

Teaching Directions

1. Write on the board:

Three friends were eating oranges.
Alan ate $\frac{1}{2}$ of an orange.
Billy ate $\frac{1}{4}$ of an orange.
Carla ate $\frac{1}{2}$ of an orange.
How many oranges did they have?
How much was left?

2. Clarify the question about how many oranges they had. Explain that they could have had an entire basket of oranges, but that you're interested in the fewest number of oranges they could have had.

3. First ask the students to think by themselves, then ask them to talk about their ideas with a neighbor. Next, lead a class discussion for students to present their answers to both questions. Record their thinking on the board.

4. Erase the fraction in the problem for Carla and replace it with $\frac{5}{8}$ so that Alan now ate $\frac{1}{2}$ of an orange, Billy ate $\frac{1}{4}$ of an orange, and Carla ate $\frac{5}{8}$ of an orange. Repeat Step 3 for this problem.

5. Change the fractions for Billy and Carla for a new problem—Alan ate $\frac{1}{2}$ of an orange, Billy ate $\frac{1}{3}$ of an orange, and Carla ate $\frac{3}{4}$ of an orange—and follow Step 3.

6. Change the fraction for Carla for a new problem—Alan ate $\frac{1}{2}$ of an orange, Billy ate $\frac{1}{3}$ of an orange, and Carla ate $\frac{5}{8}$ of an orange—and follow Step 3.

7. Distribute *The Orange Problems* worksheet and have students solve the three problems. Circulate and offer assistance as needed.

Teaching Notes

Learning to add and subtract fractions and mixed numbers requires that students understand the idea of equivalence and can represent fractions as equivalent fractions. Once students have this understanding and skill, they are able to combine fractions and find differences. This lesson is appropriate once students have a firm understanding of equivalence and are able to write fractions as equivalent fractions. Rather than teaching students particular recording systems or algorithms, this lesson presents them with problem situations that call for adding and subtracting. The context for all of the problems is the same, but changing the fractions makes the problems easier or more difficult.

Although adding the fractions provides an exact answer of how many oranges the three friends ate, the answer to the first question—How many oranges did they have?—is always a whole number of oranges. This both gives a real-world context and also encourages students to estimate. Answering the second question—How much was left?—requires that students figure accurately.

The Lesson

▲▲▲

As the students watched, I wrote a problem on the board, choosing fractions that I knew would be easy for the students to think about:

> Three friends were eating oranges.
> Alan ate $\frac{1}{2}$ of an orange.
> Billy ate $\frac{1}{4}$ of an orange.
> Carla ate $\frac{1}{2}$ of an orange.

> How many oranges did they have?
> How much was left?

After giving the students time to read the problem, I asked, "How many oranges did they have?" Then I clarified. "They could have had an entire basket of oranges, but I'm interested in the fewest number of oranges they could have had."

I gave the students a few moments to think quietly and then said, "Talk with your neighbor about your ideas." After a few more moments, I interrupted the students and asked who was willing to share his or her idea. I called on Pierre to answer the first question.

"They had to have two oranges," he said, "because one-half plus one-half makes one whole orange, and that's what Alan and Carla ate, and Billy ate one-fourth more, so they had to have another orange, too." Others nodded their agreement. I wrote on the board:

$$\tfrac{1}{2} + \tfrac{1}{2} = 1$$

$$1 + \tfrac{1}{4} = 1\tfrac{1}{4}$$

I commented, "Pierre saw the two friendly fractions, the two one-halves, and combined them. Then he knew that there was one-fourth more." I then asked, "How much was left?"

Anita answered, "Three-fourths of an orange."

"How did you figure that out?" I asked.

Anita said, "Well, if they had two oranges and they ate one whole orange and one-fourth of another, then three-fourths of the second orange is left." I wrote on the board:

$$2 - 1\tfrac{1}{4} = \tfrac{3}{4}$$

A SECOND PROBLEM ABOUT ORANGES

I then changed the fraction that told how much Carla ate from $\tfrac{1}{2}$ to $\tfrac{5}{8}$:

Three friends were eating oranges.

Alan ate $\tfrac{1}{2}$ of an orange.

Billy ate $\tfrac{1}{4}$ of an orange.

Carla ate $\tfrac{5}{8}$ of an orange.

How many oranges did they have?

How much was left?

I gave the students time to think and then had them check their thinking with a neighbor. After a few moments, I asked for

their attention and called on Juanita. "Maybe two still," she said. "You still have the one-half, and if you subtract one-eighth from the five-eighths, you get four-eighths. One-half plus four-eighths is one, and that's one orange. And you still have one-eighth left over to add to one-fourth, and that's three-eighths of another orange. They ate one and three-eighths, and that means that they had two oranges." I recorded on the board:

$$\tfrac{5}{8} - \tfrac{1}{8} = \tfrac{4}{8}$$

$$\tfrac{1}{2} + \tfrac{4}{8} = 1$$

$$\tfrac{1}{8} + \tfrac{1}{4} = \tfrac{3}{8}$$

$$1\tfrac{3}{8}$$

I pointed to the second equation and asked, "Who can explain why one-half plus four-eighths is equal to one?" I called on Hunter.

"Four-eighths is the same as one-half," he said, "so they make one together." I wrote on the board:

$$\tfrac{4}{8} = \tfrac{1}{2}$$

I pointed to the third equation and asked, "Who can explain why one-eighth plus one-fourth equals three-eighths?" I called on Carla.

She said, "One-fourth is equal to two-eighths, so one-eighth and two-eighths make three-eighths." I wrote on the board:

$$\tfrac{1}{4} = \tfrac{2}{8}$$

Sabrina raised a hand to explain how she solved the problem. "Or you could say from the beginning that one-half is equal to four-eighths, and four-eighths plus four-eighths is eight-eighths, and that's the same as one whole." I recorded:

$$\tfrac{1}{2} = \tfrac{4}{8}$$

$$\tfrac{4}{8} + \tfrac{4}{8} = \tfrac{8}{8} = 1$$

"How much was left?" I asked. "Raise your hand when you know the answer."

Damien said, "It's five-eighths. Two minus one is one, and then minus three-eighths leaves five-eighths." I wrote on the board:

$$2 - 1\tfrac{3}{8} = \tfrac{5}{8}$$

A THIRD PROBLEM ABOUT ORANGES

This time I changed two of the fractions in the problem. Again, I asked the students to think first and then talk with a neighbor about how to answer the questions:

> Three friends were eating oranges.
>
> Alan ate $\tfrac{1}{2}$ of an orange.
>
> Billy ate $\tfrac{1}{3}$ of an orange.
>
> Carla ate $\tfrac{3}{4}$ of an orange.
>
> How many oranges did they have?
>
> How much was left?

After the students had time to talk, I interrupted them and called on Maria to tell how many oranges they had. She said, "I kind of did what Juanita did on the other problem. I took one-fourth from the three-fourths to get one-half, and I put it with the one-half, so that's one orange. Then I had the problem of figuring out one-third plus the extra one-fourth, and I know that's not enough to make more than another orange because those are small pieces. So they had two oranges." Even though Maria didn't figure out exactly how much they had eaten, she answered the question correctly. I recorded:

$$\tfrac{3}{4} - \tfrac{1}{4} = \tfrac{1}{2}$$
$$\tfrac{1}{2} + \tfrac{1}{2} = 1$$
$$\tfrac{1}{3} + \tfrac{1}{4} < 1$$

Brendan thought about the problem differently. He said, "I made them all into twelfths. One-half is six-twelfths, and one-third is four-twelfths, and three-fourths is nine-twelfths. Then you add them all up and it's nineteen-twelfths, and that's one and seven-twelfths." I wrote on the board:

$$\tfrac{1}{2} = \tfrac{6}{12}$$
$$\tfrac{1}{3} = \tfrac{4}{12}$$
$$\tfrac{3}{4} = \tfrac{9}{12}$$
$$\tfrac{19}{12} = 1\tfrac{7}{12}$$

"So how many oranges do you think they had?" I asked.

"Oh," Brendan said, "it's two, like Maria said."

Julio had another explanation. He said, "Kayla and I thought about a clock. We did what Maria did sort of and got one orange, but we added the extra one-third and one-fourth on a clock and got seven-twelfths." I drew a clock face on the board. Then Julio came up and showed how one-third went to four o'clock, and one-fourth more went to seven o'clock.

Kayla concluded, "So the whole orange plus the seven-twelfths is one and seven-twelfths."

I recorded:

$$\tfrac{1}{2} + \tfrac{1}{2} = 1$$
$$\tfrac{1}{3} + \tfrac{1}{4} = \tfrac{7}{12}$$
$$1 + \tfrac{7}{12} = 1\tfrac{7}{12}$$

ONE MORE PROBLEM ABOUT ORANGES

I now changed the last fraction in the sentence to pose the challenge of combining thirds and eighths together. I wrote:

> Three friends were eating oranges.
>
> Alan ate $\tfrac{1}{2}$ of an orange.

Billy ate $\frac{1}{3}$ of an orange.

Carla ate $\frac{5}{8}$ of an orange.

How many oranges did they have?

How much was left?

I thought that the students could determine that the children had two oranges. But I thought that figuring exactly how much the children ate, which would allow them to figure out how much was left, would be difficult for some of the students. I again asked them to talk with their neighbor about the problem. This time, more of the students reached for paper and pencil than had done so for the other problems. Some also reached for their fraction kits. (For information about fraction kits, see the Teaching Arithmetic book *Lessons for Introducing Fractions, Grades 4–5,* Chapters 2 and 15, or the booklet, *The Fraction Kit Guide.*)

The room was noisy as the students worked. After a few minutes, I asked for their attention and called on Celia. Celia was a capable math student who was able to explain her thinking clearly and concisely. I chose her hoping for an example of a correct solution, and Celia delivered just that.

Celia said, "First I thought about one-half plus one-third. I changed them both to sixths, so it's three-sixths plus two-sixths, and that's five-sixths." I interrupted Celia to record what she had done so far and give the others a chance to think about her idea. I wrote:

$$\frac{1}{2} + \frac{1}{3}$$

$$\frac{3}{6} + \frac{2}{6} = \frac{5}{6}$$

"Any questions for Celia so far?" I asked. There were none so I signaled Celia to continue.

Celia said, "Then I needed to add five-sixths and five-eighths, and I thought about what I could change them to so I could add them, and I thought twenty-fourths.

Five-sixths is twenty–twenty-fourths, and five-eighths is fifteen–twenty-fourths." Again I interrupted Celia to record:

$$\frac{5}{6} + \frac{5}{8}$$

$$\frac{20}{24} + \frac{15}{24}$$

"Any questions?" I asked.

Clark said, "I see why she wanted them both to be the same size pieces, but I don't get how she got those numbers on the top."

I said, "Who can explain what Celia did to change those fractions?"

David said, "To change six to twenty-four, you multiply by four, so you have to do the same to the numerator. And for the other one, eight times three is twenty-four, so five times three is fifteen." This explanation seemed to satisfy Clark.

"Is that how you thought about it?" I asked Celia. Celia nodded.

Kara had a question. "I get how you make them into twenty-fourths like David said, but I don't get how you decide to do twenty-fourths. How do you pick the right number?"

Celia explained, "You have to use a number that works for eight and six, that both can go into."

Kara brightened. "Oh, I see, eight times three is twenty-four and six times four is twenty-four, so you know it works."

Celia then continued. "So I added, and that's thirty-five–twenty-fourths, and that's one and eleven–twenty-fourths, so it's two oranges again. Should I tell how much is left?" I nodded and she added, "It's thirteen–twenty-fourths." I recorded:

$$\frac{20}{24} + \frac{15}{24} = \frac{35}{24}$$

$$\frac{35}{24} = 1\frac{11}{24}$$

$$2 - 1\frac{11}{24} = \frac{13}{24}$$

The class was quiet for a moment as the students contemplated what I had written. Then Francis said, "I don't get how you can have thirteen–twenty-fourths of an orange. I mean, I see how she got that fraction, but how can you have that much of an orange?"

"Can anyone explain?" I asked.

Sabrina raised a hand. "You can think about an orange that breaks into twenty-four little pieces," she said. "Then you would have only thirteen of them. That's just one piece more than half."

"Oh, I get it," Francis said.

Craig then said, "I think that Celia's right, but I got a different answer and I'm not sure what happened. I changed all of the fractions to twenty-fourths first." I listed the three fractions from the problem and then recorded as Craig reported how he changed them to twenty-fourths.

$$\frac{1}{2} = \frac{12}{24}$$

$$\frac{1}{3} = \frac{8}{24}$$

$$\frac{5}{8} = \frac{20}{24}$$

Kayla's hand flew up. "The last one isn't right," she said. "You have to multiply eight times three to get twenty-four, so you multiply five times three and you get fifteen, not twenty."

Craig slapped his forehead with his hand and said, "That's it. I multiplied by four, not three. Now I bet it will work." I corrected what was on the board and Craig helped me do the rest of the math:

$$\frac{1}{2} = \frac{12}{24}$$

$$\frac{1}{3} = \frac{8}{24}$$

$$\frac{5}{8} = \frac{15}{24}$$

$$\frac{35}{24} = 1\frac{11}{24}$$

Sam raised his hand. "I got the wrong answer, but I see what I did. I did three-sixths plus two-sixths, but I thought it was four-sixths and it's really five-sixths."

Helene said, "I thought the answer was one and one-fourth, but Celia's idea makes sense."

"How did you figure one and one-fourth?" I asked.

"I pictured in my head what it would look like with the fraction kit," Helene answered.

I responded, "Picturing is a good way to estimate an answer. Let's see what the fraction kit pieces show." I placed a half piece, a one-third piece, and five one-eighth pieces end-to-end. Then, above, I placed a whole strip and a quarter piece.

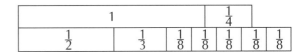

"Oooh, it's too short," Helene said. "You can fit in another one-fourth piece." I added another one-fourth piece.

1				$\frac{1}{4}$	$\frac{1}{4}$
$\frac{1}{2}$	$\frac{1}{3}$	$\frac{1}{8}$	$\frac{1}{8}$	$\frac{1}{8}$	$\frac{1}{8}$	$\frac{1}{8}$

"Isn't that right?" Helene asked.

The inaccuracy of the pieces, and the general nature of inaccuracy in measurement, made it appear correct. I said to Helene, "Remember that the pieces we cut aren't exact. Folding and cutting makes for some variation. The fraction kit pieces show you that the total of what they ate is just about one and two-fourths, which is the same as one and one-half, and this is a good estimate. Celia's figuring produced an answer of one and eleven–twenty-fourths. To be exactly one-half, Celia's answer would have to be one and *twelve*–twenty-fourths, which is only one–twenty-fourth away." I wrote on the board:

$$\frac{1}{2} = \frac{12}{24}$$

$1\frac{11}{24}$ *is* $\frac{1}{24}$ *smaller than* $1\frac{1}{2}$

I concluded, "One–twenty-fourth is an awfully teeny piece to show with the fraction kit pieces."

Pierre's hand flew up. He was excited and said, "I just realized something. If you add the one-half and the one-third, you get five-sixths, like Celia said. To make a whole, you need one more sixth. But all we have is eighths. When you put an eighth, there's a little extra space right there. Can I come up and show?" I nodded. Pierre came up and removed the two quarter pieces and four of the eighth pieces.

1		
$\frac{1}{2}$	$\frac{1}{3}$	$\frac{1}{8}$

He said, "See, there's a little space after the one-eighth piece to the end of the whole because you really need one-sixth, and one-eighth is a little smaller than one-sixth. That has to be the one extra twenty-fourth from the eleven–twenty-fourths to make twelve–twenty-fourths." Several others got excited, too, but I wasn't sure that all of the other students were following how Pierre had reasoned.

Anita then raised a hand. "I thought of a different way. If you start with four-eighths from the five-eighths, it's one-half, and you can add it with the one-half and you have one whole. Then all you have left is to add the one-third and the extra one-eighth." I recorded on the board:

$$\frac{4}{8} = \frac{1}{2}$$

$$\frac{4}{8} + \frac{1}{2} = 1 \text{ whole}$$

$$\frac{1}{3} + \frac{1}{8}$$

"How much is one-eighth plus one-third?" I asked.

"Make them twenty-fourths," Anita said. "It's three–twenty-fourths plus eight–twenty-fourths, and that's eleven–twenty-fourths, so it's one and eleven–twenty-fourths altogether." I recorded:

$$\frac{8}{24} + \frac{3}{24} = \frac{11}{24}$$

$$1 + \frac{11}{24} = 1\frac{11}{24}$$

AN INDIVIDUAL ASSIGNMENT

I then gave the students the assignment I had prepared with three more problems about oranges. As I distributed *The Orange Problems* worksheet, I said, "You can work together on these, but you each should do your own paper." Then I circulated, helping students who needed assistance.

The first problem, in which the friends ate three-eighths, one-fourth, and one-half of an orange, was accessible to most of the students, and those who had difficulty with the problem were able to get help from a neighbor. The students' explanations differed for how they figured that the friends had two oranges and seven-eighths of an orange was left. Andrea, for example, wrote: $\frac{1}{2} + \frac{1}{4} + \frac{3}{8} = more$ *than 1, so the next whole # is 2.* $2 - \frac{1}{2} = 1\frac{1}{2}$. $1\frac{1}{2} - \frac{1}{4} = 1\frac{1}{4}$ *or* $1\frac{2}{8}$. $1\frac{2}{8} - \frac{3}{8} = \frac{7}{8}$.

Maria wrote the correct answers and explained how she figured out exactly how much they ate: *I converted all the fractions into $\frac{1}{8}$'s. I then added all the $\frac{1}{8}$'s and got $\frac{9}{8}$ which equals $1\frac{1}{8}$.*

Pierre also wrote the correct answers and explained how he figured the total they ate. He wrote: *Because $\frac{1}{2} + \frac{1}{3} - \frac{3}{4}$. Cut $\frac{3}{8}$ into $\frac{2}{8}$ and $\frac{1}{8}$. $\frac{3}{4} + \frac{2}{8}$ equals 1. But you have $\frac{1}{8}$ extra.*

Helene called me over when she realized that her answer to how much of an orange was left in the first problem was different from the answers of the students at her table. She had worked hard to figure out that one-eighth of an orange was left, drawing a circle, dividing it into eighths, and marking each share. However, she incorrectly showed Freda's share as three-eighths instead of one-half, and she counted the same one-eighth piece as part of David's share and as the leftover piece. Helene had written: *$\frac{1}{2} + \frac{1}{4}$ is $\frac{3}{4}$ because there are $\frac{2}{4}$ in $\frac{1}{2}$. So $\frac{3}{4} + \frac{2}{8} = 1$ whole plus $\frac{1}{8}$ left over, or remainder.*

I began by talking with Helene about how she had shaded in the shares on the circle. "Which is Elissa's share?" I asked.

"Here," Helene said, correctly pointing to a quarter of the circle. "It's two-eighths, and that's the same as one-fourth."

"And David's piece?" I asked.

Helene pointed to the three-eighths piece she had outlined. "See, it's one-eighth, two-eighths, three-eighths."

I then asked, "What about Freda's share? She ate one-half of an orange."

Helene pointed to the section she had shaded for Freda. She said, "She ate one-half and that's four-eighths." Then she counted and realized that she had only marked off a section with three-eighths. "Uh oh," she said. "That's not right. Hey, there's no room for one-half." Helene recounted what she had done for Elissa's and David's pieces, and then said, "I messed up."

"What do you think you did wrong?" I asked.

"Freda's piece is one-half, but there's no room for it," Helene said, puzzled.

"What about if they had another orange?" I suggested.

Helene brightened. "Oh, that's a good idea," she said and then pointed to the empty space at the bottom of her paper. "Can I do it again down here?" I nodded, and Helene now drew two circles and divided them both into eighths. On the first circle, she marked Elissa's piece again. Then she marked Freda's piece, saying, "I better get this in or I'll run out of room again." Then, on the second circle, Helene marked off a three-eighths section for David. She sat quietly, looking over what she had done.

"What are you thinking?" I asked.

"There are a lot of pieces left over," Helene said.

"How much is left over?" I asked.

Helene then put a check mark in each of the unclaimed eighths, counted them, and said, "Oh, that's how they got seven-eighths," referring to the answer that the others at her table had written. (See Figure 10–1.)

I left Helene to check on the others. I noticed that Celia had also drawn circles for the first problem, but she had split Elissa's share between them, showing one-eighth on one circle and one-eighth on the other. I asked Helene and Celia to compare their drawings of two circles. I think that encouraging this kind of communication between students can be helpful to their learning.

Maggie was stuck on the third problem. She had figured out that two–twenty-fourths of an orange was left, and the others at her table had figured out that one–twenty-fourth was left. Sachi was trying to help her see where she had made a mistake, but they couldn't find the error. Maggie had tried to change each share into twenty-fourths. She had written:

I changed $\frac{1}{2}$ into $\frac{6}{12}$ into $\frac{12}{24}$, I changed $\frac{1}{3}$ into $\frac{3\frac{1}{2}}{12}$ into $\frac{7}{24}$. I changed $\frac{1}{8}$ into $\frac{1\frac{1}{2}}{12}$ into $\frac{3}{24}$ so I add those together and got $\frac{22}{24}$. $\frac{22}{24} = 1$ and $\frac{22}{24}$ is only $\frac{2}{24}$ away so there is $\frac{2}{24}$ left.

I was fascinated by how she had converted one-third and one-eighth into twelfths. For one-eighth, Maggie thought for a moment and then told me, "Twelve is like one eight and half more of it, so I did half more of one to get one and a half–twelfths, and then I doubled them and got three–twenty-fourths."

"And how did you think about one-third?" I asked.

Maggie said, "OK, I figured it the same way. Oh, wait, I counted wrong."

"What did you count wrong?" I asked.

"Making twelve from threes," Maggie said. She then sat thinking, using her fingers to figure. "It's four, not three and a half," she said.

"That's it!" Sachi said. "If it's four-twelfths, then it's eight–twenty-fourths, and that's what I got." I left the girls to work together to fix Maggie's paper.

"You tricked us with the last one," Craig said as I walked by.

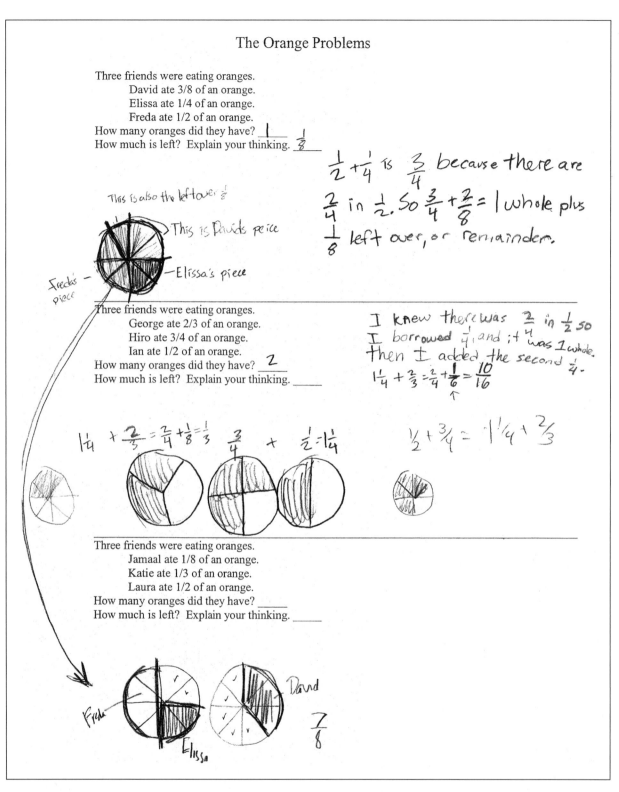

The Orange Problems

Three friends were eating oranges.
    David ate 3/8 of an orange.
    Elissa ate 1/4 of an orange.
    Freda ate 1/2 of an orange.
How many oranges did they have? 1
How much is left? Explain your thinking. 1/8

$\frac{1}{2} + \frac{1}{4}$ is $\frac{3}{4}$ because there are $\frac{2}{4}$ in $\frac{1}{2}$. So $\frac{3}{4} + \frac{2}{8} = 1$ whole plus $\frac{1}{8}$ left over, or remainder.

This is also the leftover 1/8

This is David's piece

Freda's piece

Elissa's piece

Three friends were eating oranges.
    George ate 2/3 of an orange.
    Hiro ate 3/4 of an orange.
    Ian ate 1/2 of an orange.
How many oranges did they have? 2
How much is left? Explain your thinking. _____

I knew there was $\frac{2}{4}$ in $\frac{1}{2}$ so I borrowed $\frac{1}{4}$ and it was 1 whole. Then I added the second $\frac{1}{4}$.
$1\frac{1}{4} + \frac{2}{3} = \frac{2}{4} + \frac{1}{6} = \frac{10}{16}$

$1\frac{1}{4} + \frac{2}{3} = \frac{2}{4} + \frac{1}{8} = \frac{1}{3}$ $\frac{3}{4} + \frac{1}{2} = 1\frac{1}{4}$

$\frac{1}{2} + \frac{3}{4} = 1\frac{1}{4} + \frac{2}{3}$

Three friends were eating oranges.
    Jamaal ate 1/8 of an orange.
    Katie ate 1/3 of an orange.
    Laura ate 1/2 of an orange.
How many oranges did they have? _____
How much is left? Explain your thinking. _____

Freda   Elissa   David $\frac{7}{8}$

▲▲▲▲▲▲Figure 10–1 *Helene's paper revealed her partial understanding of fractions. While she could reason with halves, fourths, and eighths, she was not able to solve problems when thirds were also involved. She needed more help.*

"How did I trick you?" I asked.

"They only had one orange, and for all of the others, they had two," he said.

The period was over and I asked the students to stop working. I collected their papers. When I looked over what Helene had done after I had left her, I saw that she had had difficulty with the second problem, too. To avoid running out of space shading shares in one orange, this time she drew three oranges, one for each friend, correctly marking off how much each ate. She had written *2* for the number of oranges they needed, which was correct, and she was able to combine two of the shares—$\frac{3}{4} + \frac{1}{2}$—to get $1\frac{1}{4}$. However, she wasn't able to add $1\frac{1}{4}$ and $\frac{2}{3}$, confusing eighths and sixths, and

she didn't have time to try the third problem.

Helene was one of the students who needed a good deal of extra help. Even though she made an error with the first problem, her explanations revealed that she was able to reason with halves, fourths, and eighths. But her understanding was fragile, and when thirds became involved, she was unable to move forward. At this time, Helene needed experiences that would help her understand relationships among halves, thirds, and fourths. Then I could build on that understanding to help her deal with fractions with other denominators.

See Figures 10–2 through 10–5 for other students' work on this assignment.

Questions and Discussion

▲▲

▲ *Is it necessary to record each student's way of thinking on the board?*

I think that recording on the board serves several important purposes. It provides a record of students' thinking that we can return to for further discussion. It models for students how to represent their ideas with correct mathematical notation. For students who do not learn easily just by hearing ideas, having them written on the board provides additional access to others' thinking. And when I record students' thinking on the board, I am indicating that I value their ideas. For these reasons, I make it a general practice to record on the board during lessons.

▲ *When Maria answered the third problem but didn't figure out the amount the children had eaten, why didn't you push her to explain the math?*

I felt that Maria's response was mathematically correct and showed good reasoning. If I had framed the question to ask for how much they had eaten altogether, then Maria's response would be incomplete. However, her answer was valid and I didn't push for more. Accepting her answer helped the children see that figuring out an exact number isn't always essential for solving a problem. Also, I knew that Maria could do the addition and produce the correct answer.

▲ *When you recorded the students' ideas, I noticed that sometimes you recorded horizontally and sometimes you recorded vertically. How do you decide which way to write fraction problems?*

I try to mix up the ways I record. One of my goals for students is for them to become flexible both in their thinking and in the ways they record their thinking. For that reason, just

Problems with Oranges 111

The Orange Problems

Three friends were eating oranges.
  David ate 3/8 of an orange.
  Elissa ate 1/4 of an orange.
  Freda ate 1/2 of an orange.
How many oranges did they have? _2_
How much is left? Explain your thinking. _1/8_

1/4 out of 3/8 plus 1/4 plus 1/2 =
but there is 1/8 left over
so 1 + 1/8 = 1 1/8.

Three friends were eating oranges.
  George ate 2/3 of an orange.
  Hiro ate 3/4 of an orange.
  Ian ate 1/2 of an orange.
How many oranges did they have? _2_
How much is left? Explain your thinking. _1/12_

1/2 Ian   Hiro 3/4
1 Whole 1/12

2/3 = 8 o'clock
1/2 = 6 o'clock
3/4 = 9 o'clock
23 o'clock = 1 11/12

Three friends were eating oranges.
  Jamaal ate 1/8 of an orange.
  Katie ate 1/3 of an orange.
  Laura ate 1/2 of an orange.
How many oranges did they have? _2_
How much is left? Explain your thinking. _4 1/48_

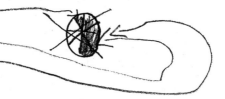

1/8 = 1:30
1/3 = 8:00
1/2 = 6:00
15:30 = 1 7/48

▲▲▲▲▲▲Figure 10–2 *Julio liked to think about fractions in relation to a clock face and successfully used a 24-hour clock for the second problem; however, in the third problem, he mixed a 12- and 24-hour clock and arrived at an incorrect solution.*

The Orange Problems

Three friends were eating oranges.
    David ate 3/8 of an orange.
    Elissa ate 1/4 of an orange.
    Freda ate 1/2 of an orange.
How many oranges did they have? __2__
How much is left? Explain your thinking. $\frac{7}{8}$

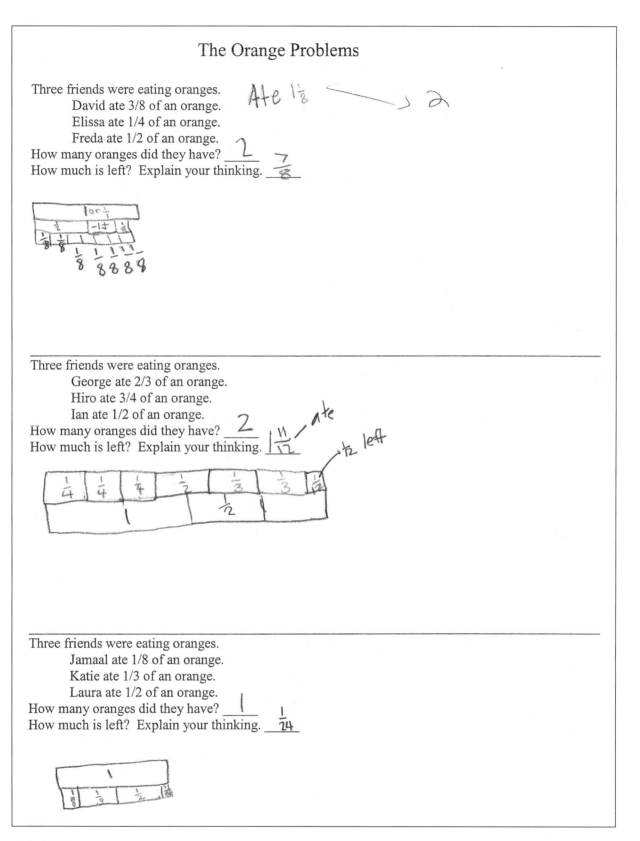

Three friends were eating oranges.
    George ate 2/3 of an orange.
    Hiro ate 3/4 of an orange.
    Ian ate 1/2 of an orange.
How many oranges did they have? __2__
How much is left? Explain your thinking. $1\frac{11}{12}$

Three friends were eating oranges.
    Jamaal ate 1/8 of an orange.
    Katie ate 1/3 of an orange.
    Laura ate 1/2 of an orange.
How many oranges did they have? __1__
How much is left? Explain your thinking. $\frac{1}{24}$

▲▲▲▲▲▲Figure 10–3 *Kara relied on drawing fraction kit pieces to solve each of the problems.*

The Orange Problems

Three friends were eating oranges.
    David ate 3/8 of an orange.
    Elissa ate 1/4 of an orange.
    Freda ate 1/2 of an orange.
How many oranges did they have? __2__ $\frac{7}{8}$
How much is left? Explain your thinking.

Because $\frac{1}{2} + \frac{1}{4} = \frac{3}{4}$. Cut $\frac{3}{8}$ into $\frac{2}{8}$ and $\frac{1}{8}$. $\frac{3}{4} + \frac{2}{8}$ equals 1. But you have $\frac{1}{8}$ extra.

Three friends were eating oranges.
    George ate 2/3 of an orange.
    Hiro ate 3/4 of an orange.
    Ian ate 1/2 of an orange.
How many oranges did they have? __2__
How much is left? Explain your thinking. $\frac{1}{12}$

Because $\frac{1}{2} + \frac{3}{4} = 1\frac{1}{4}$, $\frac{2}{3} + \frac{1}{4}$ is just smaller than 1, it's a $\frac{1}{2}$. Because $\frac{1}{4}$ is $\frac{1}{12}$ smaller than $\frac{1}{3}$, so if you add $\frac{1}{4}$ and $\frac{2}{3}$ you would get $\frac{11}{12}$. Add 1 and $\frac{11}{12}$, and you get $1\frac{11}{12}$!

Three friends were eating oranges.
    Jamaal ate 1/8 of an orange.
    Katie ate 1/3 of an orange.
    Laura ate 1/2 of an orange.
How many oranges did they have? __1__ $\frac{1}{24}$
How much is left? Explain your thinking. $\frac{1}{24}$

$\frac{1}{8} \times \frac{3}{3} = \frac{3}{24}$

$\frac{1}{3} \times \frac{8}{8} = \frac{8}{24}$

$\frac{1}{2} \times \frac{12}{12}$ $\frac{12}{24}$

$+\,\frac{}{}$

$\frac{23}{24}$

▲▲▲▲▲▲Figure 10–4 *Pierre illustrated his thinking for the first problem, relied on words for the explanation for the second problem, and solved the third problem numerically.*

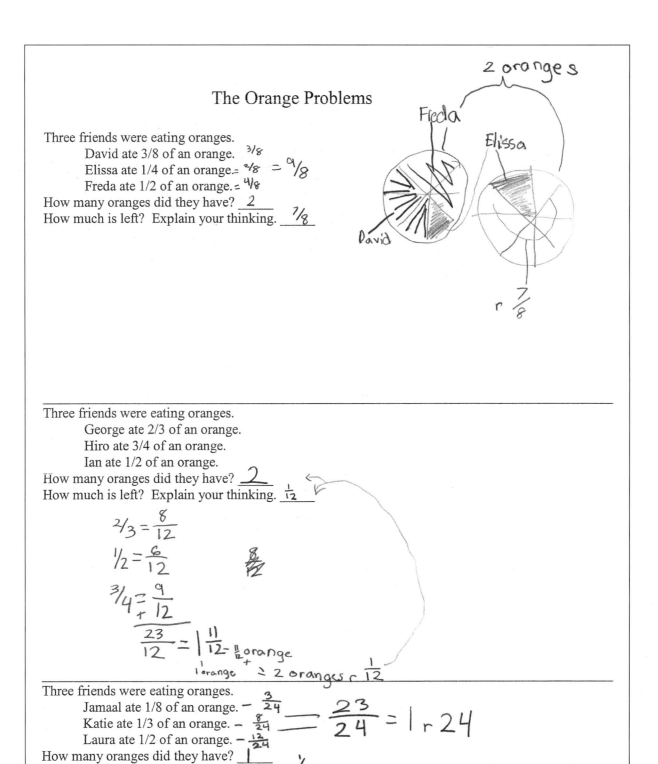

The Orange Problems

Three friends were eating oranges.
David ate 3/8 of an orange.   3/8
Elissa ate 1/4 of an orange. = 2/8 = 9/8
Freda ate 1/2 of an orange. = 4/8
How many oranges did they have? 2
How much is left? Explain your thinking. 7/8

2 oranges
Freda
Elissa
David
r 7/8

Three friends were eating oranges.
George ate 2/3 of an orange.
Hiro ate 3/4 of an orange.
Ian ate 1/2 of an orange.
How many oranges did they have? 2
How much is left? Explain your thinking. 1/12

$2/3 = \frac{8}{12}$

$1/2 = \frac{6}{12}$ 8/12

$3/4 = \frac{9}{+12}$

$\frac{23}{12} = 1\frac{11}{12} = \frac{11}{12}$ orange

1 orange = 2 oranges r 1/12

Three friends were eating oranges.
Jamaal ate 1/8 of an orange. — 3/24
Katie ate 1/3 of an orange. — 8/24 $\frac{23}{24} = 1 r 24$
Laura ate 1/2 of an orange. — 12/24
How many oranges did they have? 1
How much is left? Explain your thinking. 1/24

▲▲▲▲▲Figure 10–5 *Celia used the same strategy for all three problems, changing all of the fractions to fractions with common denominators.*

as I encourage the students to present different ways of thinking, I also try to present alternative ways to record. This models for students that what they record is a way of keeping track of how they reason, not a way to follow some set procedure.

▲ *When Celia explained her solution, you interrupted her several times to record and discuss what she had done. Did you do this because you thought that the others might have trouble following her reasoning?*

Exactly. I've learned from experience that thinking about thirds and eighths poses a problem for some students. While they can visualize many fractions, helped by the work we've done with fraction kits, which give the students models for halves, thirds, fourths, sixths, eighths, twelfths, and sixteenths, some have difficulty expanding their thinking. Their understanding of equivalent fractions is still fragile. However, they need opportunities to stretch their thinking in ways that they can follow, and taking extra time with Celia's explanation allowed me to present such an opportunity.

CHAPTER ELEVEN
MAKE A ONE

Overview

This activity gives students a problem-solving experience that also provides practice with combining fractions. Students first solve a problem with multiple solutions—finding five fractions that add to one. They then revisit the problem, this time with the limitation of using cards they draw from a deck with ten each of 1s, 2s, 4s, and 8s to form the fractions. For a second version of the activity, students use a deck with ten cards each of 1s, 3s, 6s, and 12s; for a third version, they use the two decks combined.

Materials

▲ decks of forty cards, with ten each of 1s, 2s, 4s, and 8s, 1 deck per six students (**Note:** It's helpful to use a different-colored index card to make each deck so that it's easy to keep them sorted. Also, 3-by-5-inch index cards cut in half make manageable-sized cards for students to handle and spread out on their desks.)

▲ decks of forty cards, with ten each of 1s, 3s, 6s, and 12s, 1 deck per six students (**Note:** Make these the same size and colors as the original decks.)

▲ *Make a One* worksheet, at least 3 per pair of students (see Blackline Masters)

▲ optional: *Make a One* rules, 1 per group (see Blackline Masters)

Time

▲ at least two periods

Teaching Directions

1. Write on the board *Make a One* and draw one round of boxes from the worksheet.

Make a One

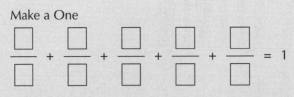

$$\frac{\square}{\square} + \frac{\square}{\square} + \frac{\square}{\square} + \frac{\square}{\square} + \frac{\square}{\square} = 1$$

2. Pose the problem to the students of thinking of five fractions that add to one. Have them first think on their own and then discuss their ideas with a partner.

3. Ask for a volunteer to present a solution. Record it on the board and ask the volunteer to explain why the fractions add to one. Then draw another set of boxes and repeat with another volunteer. Continue until you have recorded five solutions.

4. Introduce the scoring system for the activity. Hold up a worksheet and point out that there are spaces for five solutions, just as you recorded on the board, and that next to each set of boxes there is a line for the score for that round. Explain: "You score one point for each number you write in the numerator or denominator. Each of the five solutions on the board used ten numbers, so each round scores ten points. The total for these five rounds is fifty points."

5. Introduce the first deck of cards, explaining to the students that it contains forty cards, ten each of 1s, 2s, 4s, and 8s. Explain the directions, either writing them on the board as you do so or distributing them to the students.

Make a One Rules

You need:
> deck of forty cards, ten each of 1s, 2s, 4s, and 8s (for Version 1)
> deck of forty cards, ten each of 1s, 3s, 6s, and 12s (for Version 2)
> *Make a One* worksheet
> a partner and another pair to play with

Rules for Version 1
1. One person mixes the Version 1 deck of cards and leaves them facedown.
2. Each pair takes ten cards.
3. Try to use as many of your cards as you can to make fractions that add to one. Write the fractions on your worksheet and fill in your score. You score one point for each box you fill in when making your fractions.
4. When everyone has completed the round, return to Step 1 and continue.
5. Play five rounds and figure your total score. The team with the highest score wins.

Rules for Version 2
Play the same way as you do for Version 1, but use the Version 2 deck of cards.

Rules for Version 3
Play the same way as you do for Versions 1 and 2, but shuffle both decks of cards together.

---

6. Tell students that with this limited set of numbers, it's difficult to use the ten cards they draw to make five fractions that add to one. They may be able to make only four, three, two, or one fraction, but their goal is to use as many of their cards as they can on each round to get as high a score as possible. You may want to model an example by drawing ten cards and having them think of how to use as many of the numbers as possible to make fractions that add to one.

7. As students play in pairs, circulate and offer help as needed. Make additional worksheets available so that students who finish more quickly can repeat the activity.

8. List the even numbers from *10* to *50* on the board. (These are the possible total scores.) After all students have completed one worksheet, have them report their scores and mark each with a tally next to the appropriate number. Discuss the data.

9. Introduce the second deck of cards and have students repeat the activity.

10. Introduce a third version of the activity by having the students shuffle the two decks together.

11. Optional: Draw ten cards, give the numbers to the students, and ask them, for homework, to use the numbers from the cards to make the maximum score possible.

Teaching Notes

This lesson was inspired by the article "An Activity Involving Fraction Squares," from the December 2000 issue of *Teaching Children Mathematics*. The author, Enrique Ortiz, teaches mathematics education courses at the University of Central Florida in Orlando. I had clipped the article when my journal arrived and put it in my fractions folder, but I didn't try it with students until May 2002. After the success I experienced, I wrote to Enrique, shared the students' reactions, and discussed with him the changes I had made.

Three versions of the activity are included in the lesson, using one deck of cards, then a different deck, and finally the two decks combined. The first deck produces only halves, fourths, and eighths and is a good way to introduce the game; the second deck produces thirds, sixths, and twelfths; the combined deck includes all of these possibilities.

Using 3-by-5-inch index cards cut in half, as suggested in the "Materials" section, produces cards that are easy to handle and also small enough for students to spread out on their desks as they think about the possible fractions to make. Once students are satisfied that they've done the best they can with their particular cards, they record on their worksheet.

One extension to the lesson suggests that students figure out the different solutions for two, three, four, and five fractions. Using the first deck, and ignoring the order of the fractions, there are seven different five-fraction solutions:

$$\frac{1}{2} + \frac{1}{8} + \frac{1}{8} + \frac{1}{8} + \frac{1}{8} = 1$$

$$\frac{2}{4} + \frac{1}{8} + \frac{1}{8} + \frac{1}{8} + \frac{1}{8} = 1$$

$$\frac{4}{8} + \frac{1}{8} + \frac{1}{8} + \frac{1}{8} + \frac{1}{8} = 1$$

$$\frac{2}{8} + \frac{2}{8} + \frac{2}{8} + \frac{1}{8} + \frac{1}{8} = 1$$

$$\frac{1}{4} + \frac{2}{8} + \frac{2}{8} + \frac{1}{8} + \frac{1}{8} = 1$$

$$\frac{1}{4} + \frac{1}{4} + \frac{1}{4} + \frac{1}{8} + \frac{1}{8} = 1$$

$$\frac{2}{8} + \frac{1}{4} + \frac{1}{4} + \frac{1}{8} + \frac{1}{8} = 1$$

However, students more typically form only four, three, or two fractions using the particular cards they draw. There are six four-fraction solutions, nine three-fraction solutions, and six two-fraction solutions.

The Lesson

▲▲▲

DAY 1

To begin the lesson, I wrote on the board *Make a One* and drew one round from the worksheet the students would use for the activity.

Make a One

I asked, "Can anyone think of numbers to put in the boxes so that the five fractions add to one? Think quietly about this for a moment by yourselves. If you'd like, you can use paper and pencil to test your ideas." The class was quiet as students worked to find five fractions that added to one.

After a few moments, a few students had found solutions and raised their hands. Before having anyone report, however, I asked for everyone's attention and said, "Some of you have thought of a solution and some of you are still thinking. Please take a few moments now to share your ideas with your partner."

A moment after partners began to confer, Nick raised his hand. He had interpreted the problem differently from his partner, Alice. Nick thought that the fractions all had to be the same while Alice thought that wasn't necessary, and they wanted clarification. I assured them that the fractions didn't have to be the same and thanked them for bringing this possible interpretation to my attention. Their question was a reminder to me of how difficult it is to give clear and precise directions.

A moment later I interrupted the discussions and asked who had an idea about how I could fill in the boxes. I called on Manjit first.

"Put all ones in the numerators and all fives in the denominators," he said. "Then it's one-fifth plus one-fifth plus one-fifth plus one-fifth plus one-fifth, and that's five-fifths, so it's one." I filled in the boxes as Manjit directed.

$$\frac{1}{5} + \frac{1}{5} + \frac{1}{5} + \frac{1}{5} + \frac{1}{5} = 1$$

"Did anyone else come up with that solution?" I asked. About half a dozen students raised their hands.

I added, "Manjit's solution uses the same fraction five times, but it isn't necessary to use the same fraction. It's fine for this activity to have different fractions in the boxes. Who else has a solution?" I drew another set of boxes underneath the first example.

Alice reported next. "Nick found the same solution that Manjit did, and that made me think of another one that is kind of the same, but it's different. It starts the same with one-fifth, then you go two-tenths, four-twentieths, eight-fortieths, and sixteen-eightieths." I recorded as Alice reported.

$$\frac{1}{5} + \frac{2}{10} + \frac{4}{20} + \frac{8}{40} + \frac{16}{80} = 1$$

"Can you explain your solution?" I asked.

Alice explained, "See, they're all worth the same as one-fifth, so that's why it's like Manjit's. But they look different."

I drew another set of boxes and Alec reported next. He said, "I did one-half for the first fraction and then one-fourth for all of the others." I filled in the boxes as Alec directed.

$$\frac{1}{2} + \frac{1}{4} + \frac{1}{4} + \frac{1}{4} + \frac{1}{4} = 1$$

"Can you explain why you think these fractions add to one?" I asked Alec.

Alec replied, "Because first you have one-half so the rest of the fractions have

to add to the other one-half so . . . hey . . . wait a minute . . . that doesn't work . . . oh, I know, they should be eighths, not fourths."

"Tell me what to write," I said.

Alec said, "Leave the one-half and then change the fours to eights. Four-eighths make another half, so that works." I made the change.

$$\frac{1}{2} + \frac{1}{8} + \frac{1}{8} + \frac{1}{8} + \frac{1}{8} = 1$$

I drew another sets of boxes and Marisa gave her solution. She said, "I did one-fourth three times and then one-eighth two times." I recorded her idea.

$$\frac{1}{4} + \frac{1}{4} + \frac{1}{4} + \frac{1}{8} + \frac{1}{8} = 1$$

Marisa continued, "It works because if you use all one-fourths, you can only use four of them to make one, so I split the last fourth into one-eighth plus one-eighth."

Gabe went next. I drew another set of boxes and recorded as he reported.

$$\frac{1}{5} + \frac{3}{10} + \frac{1}{10} + \frac{1}{5} + \frac{1}{5} = 1$$

Gabe then explained, "Three-tenths and one-tenth is four-tenths, and that's the same as two-fifths. So with the first one-fifth, you have three-fifths, so you need two more fifths."

There were now five solutions on the board, the same number students would do to complete a worksheet. Even though more students were ready to give solutions, I took this opportunity to

Make a One   121

introduce the scoring system they would use. I held up a worksheet and pointed out, "Notice that next to each set of boxes there is a line for you to write your score for that round. You score one point for each number you write in the numerator or denominator. Each of the five solutions on the board used ten numbers, so each round scores ten points. Then what's the total for these five rounds?"

"Fifty," several students answered together.

Kamila was waving her hand, eager to contribute. She said, "I'm really close to getting another solution, but I'm stuck, and I want to know if it's possible." Kamila often posed challenges for herself and was tenacious about solving problems. I was ready to move on, but I decided to hear her question.

"Tell us what you're thinking," I said.

"Can you draw more boxes?" she asked. I drew another set and recorded the fractions as she reported them.

$$\frac{1}{15} + \frac{2}{10} + \frac{3}{10} + \frac{1}{10} + \frac{\Box}{\Box} = 1$$

Kamila said, "I know that the tenths add up to six-tenths, and I need four-tenths more. One-fifteenth is way less than four-tenths. It's not even one-tenth. But I can't figure out the last fraction. It's driving me nuts." A buzz broke out in the room as students began to talk about Kamila's problem. After a few moments, I interrupted the class. No one had found a solution.

June commented, "I know that one-fifteenth plus something has to equal to four-tenths, but I can't figure it out."

Since I wanted to get students working on the activity I had prepared, I wrote the problem on a piece of chart paper and said, "Let's leave Kamila's

problem for a while and come back to it. Now I'd like to explain how you'll work with your partner on this activity." This seemed to satisfy Kamila as well as the others. I knew that some students would enjoy working on this problem while others wouldn't be interested. (Kamila came back to class the next day with the correct answer of one-third for the missing fraction. I gave Kamila the opportunity to report her solution to the class and how she had found it.)

Introducing the Activity

I held up one of the decks of cards I had prepared and explained to the students that it contained forty cards, ten each of 1s, 2s, 4s, and 8s. "One deck is enough for six of you to use," I explained, "and these are the only numbers you can use to write in the boxes on the worksheet." I held up a worksheet and continued explaining, writing the directions on the board as I did so.

1. *One person mixes the cards and leaves them facedown.*
2. *Each pair takes ten cards.*
3. *Try to use as many of your cards as you can to make fractions that add to one. Write the fractions on your worksheet and fill in your score.*
4. *When everyone has completed the round, return to Step 1 and continue.*
5. *Play five rounds and figure your total score.*

I added, "With this limited set of numbers, it's more difficult to use the ten cards you draw to make five fractions that add to one. You may be able to make only four fractions, or three fractions, or maybe only one or two fractions. Your goal is to use as many of your cards as you can on each round so you can get as high a score as possible. You score one point for each number you write. Ten is the most you would get." I then returned to the example that Alec had first given, before he replaced the 8s with 4s.

$$\frac{1}{2} + \frac{1}{4} + \frac{1}{4} + \frac{1}{4} + \frac{1}{4} = 1$$

I erased the last two fractions:

$$\frac{1}{2} + \frac{1}{4} + \frac{1}{4} + \frac{\square}{\square} + \frac{\square}{\square} = 1$$

I explained, "Alec's equation is now correct because one-fourth plus one-fourth is one-half, and one-half plus one-half makes one. Suppose these were the only fractions that Alec could use with his cards. Raise your hand if you know how many points he would score for this round." About two-thirds of the students raised their hands. I called on Indira.

"I think he'd get six points because he wrote six numbers," she said.

"That's right," I confirmed and then wrote on the board:

$$\tfrac{1}{8} + \tfrac{1}{8} + \tfrac{1}{4} + \tfrac{1}{2} = 1$$

"Talk with your partner about whether or not this is a true equation and, if so, what the score would be," I said. In a moment, hands were up. Althea explained why it was correct and that it earned 8 points.

"What's the least you can score on a round?" I asked.

"Two," Eliana answered.

"No, you could get zero," Francesca countered.

"I guess that's so," Eliana conceded, "but I bet you could always do something with the cards."

I then organized the class to work on the activity. I had made five decks and organized the twenty-six students into three groups of six and two groups of four. I gave one last direction; "If you finish a sheet

before I call you back to attention, come up and get another sheet and try again."

Observing the Students

There was the typical flurry of questions when students have to do something new, some from groups and others from pairs of students. When questions were procedural, I referred the students to the directions I had written on the board, asking them to read them and making sure that they interpreted them correctly.

Other questions related to the mathematics. For example, Taber asked, "Is it possible to use more of our numbers?" This was a common question from students eager to maximize their scores with the cards they had. The numbers that Taber and Indira had drawn for their second round were 1, 1, 1, 1, 2, 2, 2, 4, 4, 4 and they had recorded $\tfrac{2}{4} + \tfrac{1}{4} + \tfrac{1}{4} = 1$. When students ask me a question like this, I scan their numbers. If I notice that they could use more of their cards for a higher score, I tell them so without revealing how they can do it. If I can't see what else they might do, I say, as I did to Taber and Indira at this time, "It may be possible to score more, but I can't see how you could do any better than what you've done." Then, to check that they understood the scoring system, I asked, "So what's your score for this round?"

"Six," they answered in unison. They continued and wound up with a total score of 36. (See Figure 11–1.)

The comment at the bottom of Taber and Indira's paper was an indication of their competitive spirit, which was typical for Taber. One of the groups in the class, however, didn't focus on competing for the highest score, but instead worked together, trading cards among pairs to help each other get the highest score possible. They worked together as a team.

Twice during the class, a pair of students scored 10 on a round, and each time they whooped with excitement. On their third round, Amalia and Tomo recorded

$\frac{1}{8} + \frac{1}{8} + \frac{2}{8} + \frac{1}{4} + \frac{1}{4} = 1$ and, also on their third round, Angelo and Sandra recorded $\frac{2}{8} + \frac{1}{4} + \frac{1}{4} + \frac{1}{8} + \frac{1}{8} = 1$ (see Figure 11–2).

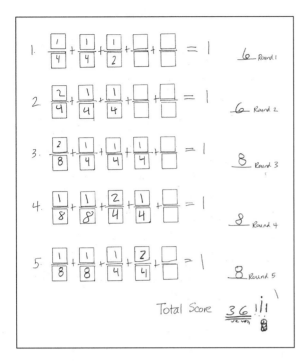

▲▲▲▲▲▲**Figure 11–1** *Taber and Indira scored 6 for their first two rounds and then 8 for the last three. Their total of 36 was the highest in their group but not in the class.*

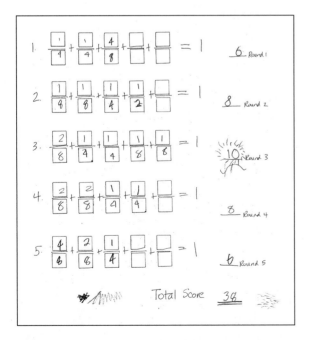

▲▲▲▲▲▲**Figure 11–2** *Angelo and Sandra had a total score of 38, the most any group in the class scored.*

By the end of the class, all of the students had completed one worksheet and some were working on a second. I collected all of their papers and told them that we would continue the next day.

DAY 2

Before returning their papers, I asked the students for their reactions so far to the activity. I gave all the students who wanted a chance to report.

Sandra said, "It was kind of easy. I think it was more luck than anything else. We got really lucky."

Marisa said, "I think it was easy, but it was fun, too. We scored eight every time."

Aviva said, "I think it's both luck and skill. It depends. Each round is different and you make the best out of the cards you get."

Gabe said, "It's a good activity. It seems like we always got the same thing, but then we saw how we could put in a different number."

Lila said, "I didn't like getting too many twos. That made it hard for Francesca and me."

Paolo, also competitive like Taber, said, "I liked that we got the most points at our table. That made it fun."

Analyzing the Scores

I then said to the class, "Before I give your papers back to you, I want to explain how we'll analyze the scores you got. What's the highest possible total score you could get from all five rounds?" Hands shot up and I called on Paolo.

"Fifty, but that would be really hard," he said.

"You'd have to be really, really lucky," Amalia added.

"And I think that the lowest possible score would be ten," I said. "You could always score two points on a round by using the same number in the numerator and denominator of the first fraction." To illustrate this idea, I wrote on the board:

$$\frac{1}{1}, \frac{2}{2}, \frac{4}{4}, \frac{8}{8}$$

"I also think that all of your total scores should be even," I said. "Who can explain why I think that?"

Only a few hands went up, so I said, "Talk with your partner about why I think the total scores all have to be even."

After the students had a chance to talk about my idea, more than half of the students had their hands raised. Max explained, "You need two numbers for a fraction, so you can only get an even number on a round. There's no way to add all even numbers and get an odd total."

On the board, I listed the even numbers from *10* to *50*, the minimum and maximum scores for a complete worksheet. I said to the class, "I'll return your papers now. Before you continue working, I'd like you to report your total score and I'll make a tally mark next to the number. Then we'll have what's called a 'frequency distribution' of our class scores." I distributed the papers and had the students report their scores.

10
12
14
16
18
20
22
24
26
28 |
30
32
34 ||
36 ||||| |
38 |||
40 |
42
44
46
48
50

I took the opportunity to inject some statistical ideas into the lesson. I explained that since the scores went from 28 to 40, we could subtract these numbers to figure that the range of the scores was 12. I explained that 36 was the mode because it had more tally marks than any other score. And, the middle score of the thirteen scores was also 36, so 36 was the median as well as the mode. I didn't find the mean but could have done so by adding the thirteen scores and dividing by thirteen. (Doing this produces 35.846.)

Introducing Variations on the Activity

Before the students returned to work, I explained two variations on the activity. "The directions for playing are the same," I said, "but you use different decks of cards." I showed them the second set of decks I had prepared, in the same colors as the first set. These decks also had forty cards each, but they contained ten each of 1s, 3s, 6s, and 12s. The students were excited about trying the activity with the new decks.

I explained, "After your group finishes your second worksheet with the first deck, take a third worksheet and switch decks. Then, when you've finished a worksheet with the second deck, shuffle the two decks together and draw from all eighty cards." The students were even more curious about this third version.

Observing the Students

A few of the students used the fraction kits we had cut earlier in the year to help them. (See *Teaching Arithmetic: Lessons for Introducing Fractions, Grades 4–5*, Chapters 2 and 15, or the booklet, *The Fraction Kit Guide*.) Bjorn and Juan, for example, used their kits to verify that $\frac{1}{3} + \frac{1}{6} + \frac{6}{12} = 1$. Marisa, however, who was sitting next to them, said, "It has to be true. A third plus a sixth makes a half, and six-twelfths is a half, so together they make one." Still, Bjorn and Juan, and also a few others, continued to use their fraction kits as they worked.

When Paolo and Eliana figured out how to use all of their cards for the fourth round of the second version of the activity, they were thrilled. "I think we were too lazy with the first rounds," Eliana said. They had scored only 4 points in Rounds 1 and 3, and 6 points in Round 2. (See Figures 11–3 and 11–4.)

Before the end of class, we analyzed the scores from the second version of the activity and I recorded the results next to the results from the first version.

```
10
12
14
16
18
20
22
24
26          |
28 |        |
30 |||
32
34 ||       |
36 ++++ |
38 |||      ||
40 |        ||
42
44          |
46
48
50
```

The scores for this version went from 26 to 44, resulting in a range of 18, which was larger than for the first activity. The mode for this version was 30; the median was again 36. I gave this information with a light touch. Our sample size wasn't large enough to draw valid conclusions about the activity, but I felt that exposing students to these ideas could be beneficial. I didn't analyze the results for the third version of the activity. The students didn't seem interested and it didn't seem necessary to belabor the analysis. Figure 11–5 shows one pair's results for the third version.

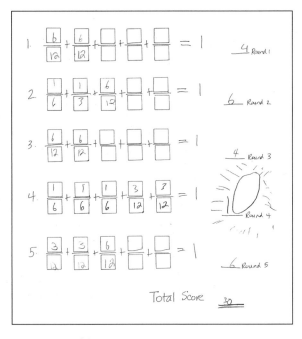

▲▲▲▲▲▲Figure 11–3 *Paolo and Eliana were excited to score 10 in their fourth round for the second version of the activity, but they were disappointed in their total score.*

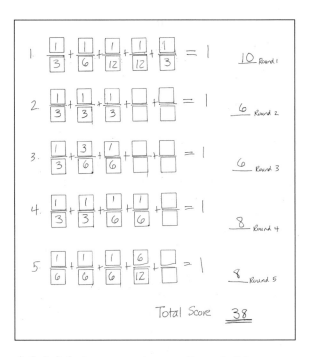

▲▲▲▲▲▲Figure 11–4 *Manjit and Althea were pleased with their total score of 38 for the second version but frustrated that they could score 10 only once.*

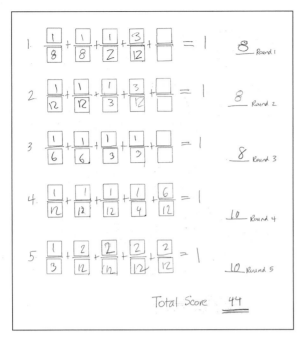

▲▲▲▲▲▲**Figure 11–5** *Nick and Alice had the highest score for the third version.*

1. Change the activity to include subtraction as well. For example:

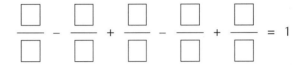

2. Change the goal of adding to one to adding to two, three, or another number.

3. Ask students to find all the possible five-fraction solutions using the first deck of cards. (See the "Teaching Notes" section for the possibilities.) Also ask them to find all the possible two-, three-, and four-fraction solutions.

Questions and Discussion

▲▲

▲ *How do you deal with errors on students' papers?*

It's important to look over students' papers and check that the fractions they recorded for each round add to one. When I find an error, I talk with the students who made it. Depending on what I know about the students' understanding, I either tell them that the round has an error and ask them to find it on their own or sit with them and talk through the problem. Occasionally I use an error for a whole-class discussion, writing the incorrect number sentence on the board and having the students discuss how they might correct it. Doing this presents the class with a problem that has multiple solutions, thus involving them in a problem-solving experience while giving practice with combining fractions.

▲ *Do you recommend having students repeat the activity at home for homework?*

I think that this activity is ideal for homework, as long as you're willing to invest the time and materials for each of them to make the cards they need. To me, it's worth the effort and expense because it's a way not only for students to have a worthwhile mathematical experience at home but also to help parents understand how a problem-solving experience can also provide practice with the basic skill of adding fractions. I didn't have the class I described in this lesson make the cards. Instead, for homework, I gave them an imaginary set of cards and asked them to figure out the maximum score they could get. If you take this route, you might choose cards that include those that can produce ten points; see the list in the "Teaching Notes" section for suggestions.

CHAPTER TWELVE
FRACTION CAPTURE

Overview

Fraction Capture is a two-person game that gives students practice with representing and combining fractions. The game requires a game sheet of eleven circles, a pair of dice, and pencils in two different colors. Players take turns rolling the dice and using the numbers to make a fraction that is less than or equal to one. They sketch and shade a pie-shaped piece to represent that fractional part, either on a blank circle or on a circle with a part already shaded. When a player shades in more than one-half of any circle, then the player has captured that circle. The winner is the player who captures more circles.

Materials

▲ *Fraction Capture* worksheet, 1 per game (see Blackline Masters)
▲ dice, 2 per pair of students
▲ optional: *Fraction Capture* rules, 1 per pair of students (see Blackline Masters)

Time

▲ two class periods, plus additional time for playing

Teaching Directions

1. Teach or review with the class how to divide circles into halves, thirds, fourths, fifths, sixths, and eighths. To do this, draw six circles on the board, each about 6 inches in diameter. Ask a student to come up and divide one of the circles into halves, shade in half, and outside the circle label the shaded part $\frac{1}{2}$. Continue by asking other students to divide each of the other circles into thirds, fourths, fifths, sixths, and eighths. See the "Teaching Notes" section for suggestions about helping students divide circles.

2. To make room on the board to teach the game, erase the circles that the students divided and, as a class reference, draw six circles at the top of the board and divide them as the students had done.

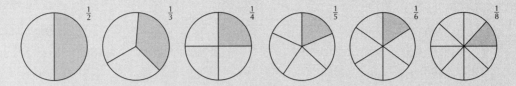

3. Draw eleven circles on the board, each about 6 inches in diameter.

4. Ask two volunteers to come to the board to demonstrate how to play. Explain the rules for playing *Fraction Capture,* pointing out the difference between Version 1 and Version 2. Tell the two students that they'll play Version 1 and use 8 for any 5 they roll on the dice. However, do not explain the rule about splitting fractions. Do so after a few rounds and when the opportunity comes up from one of their rolls.

Fraction Capture Rules

You need:
  Fraction Capture worksheet
  two dice
  pencils or thin markers in two different colors
  a partner

Rules for Version 1
1. Each player uses a different color pencil or marker.
2. Take turns rolling the dice. On your turn, use the numbers that come up to make a fraction that is less than or equal to one. If a 5 comes up on one or both of the dice, replace it with an 8. For example, if you roll a 3 and a 5, the fraction you use is $\frac{3}{8}$.
3. Draw and shade in a pie-shaped piece equal to your fraction in one of the circles. You may do this in a blank circle or add to a circle that already has a shaded piece. Record your fraction outside the circle. For example:

4. If you wish, you may shade parts of more than one circle on your turn. For example, if your number is $\frac{2}{3}$, you may either color $\frac{2}{3}$ of one circle or $\frac{1}{3}$ of one circle and $\frac{1}{3}$ of another circle. You can only split a fraction by keeping the same denominator; that is, you can't split $\frac{2}{3}$ into $\frac{1}{6}$ and $\frac{3}{6}$, even though $\frac{4}{6}$ is equivalent to $\frac{2}{3}$.
5. When you've shaded in more than half of any circle, write your initial beside it to show that you have captured it.
6. The winner is the player who captures more circles.

Rules for Version 2
Play the same way as you do for Version 1 except that when you roll a 5, do not substitute an 8 for it. For example, if you roll a 3 and a 5, the fraction you use is $\frac{3}{5}$.

---

5. As the volunteers play, supervise their moves and answer questions from the class. Also, to make the play easier for others to follow, each time a player rolls the dice, record on the board the fraction they'll be using. And introduce the splitting rule when there is an opportunity to do so as an alternative for one of the player's turns.

6. When you feel comfortable that the other students understand the rules, distribute dice and game sheets so that they can play Version 1 in pairs. (Let the volunteer players finish their game at the board.) Tell the students to play Version 2 for their second game.

7. As students play, circulate and assist as needed. At the end of class, collect the students' papers to return to them the next day.

8. On Day 2, begin with another demonstration game, this time with two students playing Version 2. (Skip this step if you think that your students don't need this extra support.)

9. Return students' unfinished game sheets from the day before and have them continue playing in pairs. When students finish a game, they can start a new one. Circulate and assist as needed.

10. About fifteen minutes before the end of the class, interrupt the students and lead a class discussion about what they noticed. Pose questions such as:

> What did you think about the game?
> What confused you about playing?
> What strategies did you use?
> What did you learn about rolling doubles?
> How did you use splitting fractions?
> How would you add one-half onto a circle with one-fifth already shaded? (Or present some other situation that you noticed as you circulated.)

Teaching Notes

When thinking about fractions, it's often helpful for students to make sketches, and *Fraction Capture* provides the opportunity to teach and reinforce for students how to divide circles into fractional parts. While sketches are not sufficient by themselves for proofs, the more accurate students' sketches are, the more useful they can be to help them reason and explain their reasoning. Generally, it's easy for students to divide circles into halves, fourths, and eighths. However, thirds, fifths, and sixths can pose problems. For thirds, I suggest to students that they think of an upside-down uppercase letter Y, or a peace sign. For fifths, I suggest they think of a person standing with legs apart and arms up; it helps to draw a stick figure on the board:

For sixths, I advise them to start with thirds and then divide each of the thirds in half.

Also, it helps some students to think about dividing a clock face. For thirds, for example, on a clock face you need lines drawn from the center to the 12, the 4, and the 8. If you feel this model will help students, present it to them as an alternative way to divide circles into fractional parts.

The game also gives the students practice with adding fractions. However, the context of the game keeps the focus on visualizing how to combine fractional parts of circles, not on adding the symbolic fractions. This experience helps students build mental models for adding fractions and emphasizes reasoning and making sense rather than learning procedures.

Two more tips: If you think that your students will need more support for thinking about the fractions and playing the game, have pairs of students play against other pairs of students. That way, students are less likely to get stuck or make errors that then go unnoticed.

Also, when teaching the game, I've found it more effective not to introduce the rule about being allowed to split fractions into two or more circles right away. This rule has no meaning for students, or confuses them, until they see it in practice. I choose to have the two volunteer students play a few rounds before I introduce the splitting option. The lesson described here illustrates how I did this with this particular class.

The Lesson

▲▲

DAY 1

To begin the lesson, I said, "Today I'm going to teach you how to play a fraction game called *Fraction Capture*. But before I teach you how to play, I want to make sure that you're comfortable dividing circles into fractional parts." I drew six circles on the board, each about 6 inches in diameter.

I pointed to one of the circles and asked, "Who would like to come up and divide this circle into halves?" Most of the students raised their hands and I called on

Sahara. She came to the board and quickly drew a vertical line to split the circle in half.

"Can you shade in one-half of the circle and then, outside the circle, next to section you shaded, write one-half?" I asked. Sahara nodded and did as I asked. She then returned to her seat.

I pointed to another circle and asked, "Who would like to divide this circle into fourths?" I purposely skipped thirds, choosing to ask them to divide a circle into fourths because I knew they would all be able to do so. Dividing a circle into thirds is more difficult for some students, and I wanted two successes on the board before a possible error. Again, many hands were raised. I called on Jimmy.

Jimmy came to the board and quickly drew a vertical line, then a horizontal line, correctly splitting the circle into fourths. He then shaded one of the sections.

"Could you also label your section outside of the circle?" I asked. Jimmy nodded, wrote $\frac{1}{4}$ next to the shaded section, and returned to his seat.

"Who would like to shade one-third of the next circle?" I asked, pointing to another circle. Not as many students raised their hands this time. I called on Jonah. He came up to the board and split the circle into three sections with three vertical lines.

Some students giggled and others looked puzzled. Jonah looked back at his picture, now confused. I scowled at the gigglers.

"What are you thinking?" I asked Jonah.

"The middle part looks too big," he responded.

"Yes, it does to me, too," I said. "But if I asked you to divide a square into thirds, then your idea would look right."

Jonah thought for a moment, then drew a square and divided it with two vertical lines into thirds. He commented, "This is right." Then he pointed to the circle he had divided and added, "This isn't right. It's not exact."

Carolyn commented, "The pieces aren't the same size."

Anisa added, "The middle looks definitely too big."

"Can you think of a way to divide a circle into thirds so that it would be more exact?" I asked Jonah. He thought again for a moment and then he divided another of the circles I had drawn into thirds by drawing an upside-down uppercase Y.

Several students commented. "That works." "It looks right." "That's better."

"How did you decide how to draw the lines?" I asked Jonah.

Jonah answered, "I remembered you could do it with a peace sign, like a Y inside a circle."

"Can you shade one-third and label it?" I asked. Jonah did this easily. I erased the circle that Jonah had divided incorrectly and drew at blank one in its place.

I then said to the class, "Sometimes I use a clock to help me divide circles into equal parts." To the side, I drew another circle. I drew lines to mark the hours on a clock and wrote the numbers. I also drew a line from the center of the circle to the 12.

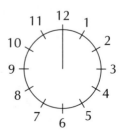

"Where else would I have to draw hands to show thirds?" I asked. "Talk with your neighbor about this." There was a buzz of conversation as students talked.

When I called them back to attention, Elliot reported, "Four and eight." The others agreed. I drew the lines on the clock I had drawn.

"How did you figure this out?" I asked.

Elliot said, "Well, you want them to be even, so if you skip four from the twelve, you get to four. Then you skip four more and you get to eight. And then it takes four more to get back to the twelve. It works." As Elliot explained, I moved my finger to show the skips he was referring to.

I then pointed to another blank circle and asked, "Who can divide this circle into sixths?" I chose to do sixths after thirds to help the students see the relationship between sixths and thirds. Some students looked puzzled, others thoughtful, and about eight students raised their hands. I called on Pedro. He came up to the board, divided the circle into thirds, and then divided each third in half to make sixths. He then shaded one section and labeled it $\frac{1}{6}$.

I pointed to the clock that showed thirds and asked, "Where do I have to draw lines to divide this clock face into sixths?" It was easy for the students to identify the correct hours—2, 6, and 10. I drew the lines.

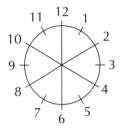

Jake explained, "That was easy. You just go to the number in the middle of the others."

"Who can divide the next circle into eighths?" I asked, saving fifths for last. I called on Libby.

When Libby came up to the board, she asked, "Can I draw on the fourths circle?"

"Do you think starting with fourths will help you draw eighths?" I asked. Libby nodded.

"How about starting by drawing fourths on the blank circle?" I asked.

"Oh, OK," Libby said. She divided the circle into fourths and then divided each fourth in half to make eighths. She shaded and labeled one of the sections.

"And who can divide the last circle into fifths?" I asked. A few students volunteered. I waited and a few more hands went up. I called on Letitia. She came up to the board, made marks on the circle to show a clock face, and drew lines to divide it. But she was dismayed when she realized that she had divided the clock into sixths instead of into fifths.

"Do you want to try again?" I asked. Letitia said no and sat back down. I erased the clock and redrew a blank circle.

Alexa came up next. "I think I can do it on a blank circle," she said. She slowly and carefully divided the circle into fifths, shaded one section, and labeled it.

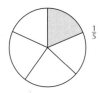

I said to the class, "When I'm trying to divide a circle into fifths, it helps me to think about drawing a stick figure with no head, and with arms and legs outstretched." I sketched a stick figure and then moved my legs apart and held my arms out to show the students what I was trying to draw. This seemed to make sense to them.

I then said, "But I think that Letitia had a good idea." I drew another clock face. "Let's think about how we could divide a clock face into fifths. How many minutes are there in an hour?"

"Sixty," about half of the students responded.

"How many minutes are in one-fifth of an hour?" I asked. "Talk to your neighbor about this." Some students seemed to figure this out right away while others struggled. When I called them back to attention, I called on Kendra.

"Five goes into sixty twelve times," she said, "so it's every twelve minutes."

Braheem added, "It works because if you count by twelves, you land on sixty, and it takes five times."

"Can you count by twelves?" I asked him.

Braheem nodded and said, "Twelve, twenty-four, thirty-six, . . . forty-eight, sixty, like that." I asked Braheem to say the numbers again as I drew hands to each on the clock face I had drawn.

Introducing the Game

Next I said, "Now that I see you can divide circles into halves, thirds, fourths, fifths, sixths, and eighths, I'll explain how to play the game. I'll erase the circles you divided to make room, but first I'll draw them again up here at the top of the board so that you can check them if you need to as you play." I erased the six circles, drew them again, and divided, shaded, and labeled each.

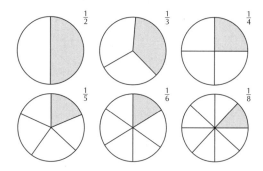

Doing this not only produced a reference for the class but also gave students the chance to see again how to divide circles into halves, thirds, fourths, fifths, sixths, and eighths. As I drew the circles, I talked aloud about how I divided and labeled them. I then drew eleven circles on the board, again each about 6 inches in diameter, and asked the students how many there were. They counted quickly. "These circles are for a two-person game called *Fraction Capture*. Both players try to capture circles, and whoever captures more circles wins. What's the fewest number of circles you have to capture in order to win?" Hands flew up. "Turn and talk to your neighbor about my question," I said. Animated conversation broke out. When I brought the class back to attention, I said, "Let's all answer together in a whisper voice."

"Six," they chorused.

I asked for two volunteers to come to the board and learn how to play the game while everyone else watched. Practically everyone volunteered and I chose Emma and Kurt. I explained the rules. "On your turn, you roll the two dice and use the numbers that come up to make a fraction that's less than or equal to one. That means if the numbers you roll are different, you need to use the smaller number for the numerator. There are two versions of this game. In Version One, when you roll a five, you call it eight instead. In Version Two, the five stays a five. We're going to start with Version One because I think it's easier to draw eighths than fifths."

"It's like closing up the top and bottom," Elliot said. I didn't understand what he was saying, so Elliot came up, wrote a *5* on the board, and converted it into a crude 8.

I continued with the rules. "OK, first you roll the dice to find out what your fraction is. Then, on any one of the circles, you shade in and label a pie-shaped piece in the amount that matches your fraction. If you shade in more than one-half of a circle, you capture it and write your initial next to it. You don't have to start a new circle each time you roll; you can shade in part of any circle that already has some of it shaded, no matter who started it. But your fraction has to fit in the space left. I think you'll understand the game better once you see it played." I didn't introduce the rule about splitting fractions. I find that it's better to get a game started and introduce that option in the context of play.

Kurt went first and reported that he rolled a 3 and a 6. I wrote $\frac{3}{6}$ and $\frac{6}{3}$ on the board. "Which fraction does Kurt have to make with his numbers?" I asked.

Manuel answered, "It has to be three-sixths because you said the fraction has to be smaller than one, and six-thirds is the same as two." As Manuel was answering, Kurt divided a circle into sixths, shaded in three of them, and wrote $\frac{3}{6}$.

"Do I have to write my initial next to the three-sixths?" Kurt asked.

"Did you capture that circle?" I asked.

"No," Kurt answered.

"Then you don't write your initial," I said. Then I explained, "You only write your initial when you've captured a circle."

Jake had a question. "If Emma rolls one-half, could she go on Kurt's circle?"

I answered, "Yes, she could. You can mark on any circle, as long as your fraction fits. If Emma rolls one-half, she can add it on to Kurt's three-sixths and capture the circle."

There were no other questions so I signaled Emma to roll. "I got a four and a six," she said, "so that's four-sixths." I wrote $\frac{4}{6}$ on the board so all of the students could see the fraction that Emma was working with. Emma was confused. "It's too much to add to Kurt's circle," she said.

I said, "That's true, but it's OK to start a new circle."

"Oh yeah," Emma said. She shaded in four-sixths of a new circle and labeled it. "Did I capture it?"

"Did you shade in more than half?" I asked.

"Oh yeah! I captured it!" Emma said.

"Now you can write an E underneath the circle so we know that you captured it," I said. Emma wrote an *E*.

Kurt rolled a 1 and a 4. I wrote $\frac{1}{4}$ on the board. He stood looking at the first circle, on which he had shaded $\frac{3}{6}$. "What are you thinking?" I asked.

Kurt said, "I thought I would shade in some more of my circle and capture it, but I don't know how to make fourths when there already are sixths."

"How much of your circle is still unshaded?" I asked.

"Three-sixths, and that's the same as one-half," Kurt answered.

"So is there room to shade in one-fourth more?" I asked.

"Yes, but the lines are in the way," Kurt said.

"Can you ignore the lines and just pretend they're not there?" I asked. "How would you show one-fourth? Just draw what you think in the blank part of the circle, over the lines that are already there." My explanation helped Kurt. He did as I suggested and marked the circle with a *K*.

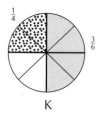

K

"How much of the circle is now shaded in?" I asked the class.

Paul answered, "Three-fourths, because three-sixths is one-half, and that's the same as two-fourths, so one more fourth is three-fourths." I recorded Paul's thinking on the board:

$$\frac{3}{6} = \frac{1}{2} = \frac{2}{4}$$
$$\frac{2}{4} = \frac{1}{4} = \frac{3}{4}$$

Emma next rolled a 4 and a 6 again. I wrote $\frac{4}{6}$ on the board and took this opportunity to introduce the rule about splitting fractions. "I'd like to tell you one more rule of the game," I said. "You're allowed to split your fraction and put part on one circle and part on another. Or you can split it among more than two circles. Let me explain." I pointed to the $\frac{4}{6}$ on the board and continued. "Emma could play all four-sixths on a new circle and capture it, as she did on her first move. That may be the best play here. But she could also split up the sixths and, for example, play two-sixths on one circle and two-sixths on another circle."

"But then she wouldn't capture either one," Dario said.

"In this case, that's true," I said. "But sometimes splitting can help you capture two circles, depending on what was already shaded in on them. But you have to keep the denominator of your fraction the same. For example, you can't split three-fourths by putting two-fourths on one circle and then splitting the remaining fourths into one-eighth and one-eighth—you have to use only fourths and shade them in on any circles you want."

Emma said, "I'm going to capture a new circle." She divided a new circle into sixths, shaded in four of them, labeled the section, and wrote an *E* underneath.

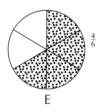

E

Kurt next rolled a 3 and a 6. He commented, "That's weird. I got that before." I wrote $\frac{3}{6}$ on the board and Kurt shaded in three-sixths of a new circle.

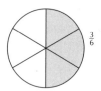

Emma rolled a 3 and a 5, and since they were playing Version 1, she now had the fraction three-eighths to play. I wrote $\frac{3}{8}$ on the board.

Elizabeth got excited. She said, "Emma, just add one of the eighths on Kurt's circle. Then you can use the other two-eighths to start a new circle." Emma followed Elizabeth's advice.

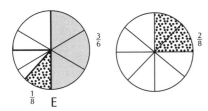

Kurt next rolled a 3 and a 4. I wrote $\frac{3}{4}$ on the board, and Kurt captured a circle.

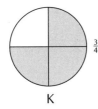

Emma rolled a 3 and a 5. I wrote $\frac{3}{8}$ on the board, reminding the students that the 5 was an 8 in this version of the game. Emma added three-eighths onto the circle with two-eighths shaded and wrote an *E* next to it to show that she had captured it.

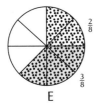

I then said, "OK, I think you've got the hang of the game, even though Emma and Kurt didn't finish. While they finish at the board, the rest of you can get started playing at your seats. Play Version One. After you complete your first game, for your second game, try Version Two." I distributed a copy of the rules to each pair of students for their reference.

As I circulated, I stopped to help students who asked. Sometimes I interrupted students to ask for clarification or an explanation or to remind them to label the sections they had shaded. There wasn't much time left in the class. Most of the students finished a game and started another, but some didn't. At the end of class I collected their papers. "Tomorrow you can start where you left off," I told them.

DAY 2

I decided to start the class with another demonstration game, this time of Version 2 so that we could talk about how to handle fifths. I drew eleven circles on the board and invited Braheem and Sadie to play.

Braheem went first. He rolled a 3 and a 6, divided one of the circles into sixths and shaded in three of them. "Do I capture it?" he asked.

"No, you don't," Sadie replied matter-of-factly. "You have to shade in more than half to capture it." Sadie was about to roll, but I stopped her and reminded Braheem to label what he had shaded. He wrote $\frac{3}{6}$.

Sadie rolled a 1 and a 4, divided a second circle into fourths, shaded one section, and labeled it. Sadie could have added the fourth onto the first circle and captured it, but she didn't. No one in the class commented about her choice, so I decided not to say anything.

Braheem rolled a 3 and a 4, divided the third circle into fourths and shaded in three fourths. "I capture it!" he exclaimed, writing a B at the top of the circle. I reminded him again to label the fractional part he had shaded.

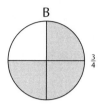

B

$\frac{3}{4}$

Sadie rolled a 1 and a 3 and groaned. She began to divide a blank circle when Tomas blurted out, "You can add on to one of the other circles!"

"Oh yeah," Sadie said and erased the marks she had begun to make. "Oh, no, I can't," she then said, "there aren't any thirds." Even though this situation had come up the day before, Sadie was still confused.

"What are you thinking?" I asked her.

"The first circle is in sixths and the second one is in fourths," Sadie said. "But I have to do thirds."

"You can add one-third on to to any circle as long as there's room," I said.

"Oh yeah," she said. "One-third is like two-sixths. I can capture the first circle." She shaded in two-sixths, wrote $\frac{1}{3}$, and wrote an S to claim the circle.

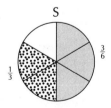

S

$\frac{3}{6}$

$\frac{1}{3}$

"How much of that circle is shaded altogether?" I asked, writing on the board $\frac{3}{6} + \frac{1}{3}$. "Talk to your neighbor about this and see if together you agree about how much of the circle is shaded." When I ask a question like this, there are always several students who immediately know the answer. By having students talk in pairs, I give time

for those who think more slowly to engage with the problem. After a moment, I called the students to attention and asked the class to say the answer softly together. Most knew that the answer was five-sixths.

"It's a tie so far," Kendra said. "They've got one circle each."

Braheem rolled again. "I got two fours," he reported. "That's four-fourths. I get another one." He started to divide a circle into fourths and then stopped. He said, "Wait! I can split them! I only need three-fourths to capture, so I have one extra fourth." He looked at the other circles and continued, "Uh oh, I don't want to put it on the other circle with one-fourth, 'cause then she'll capture it next time for sure." Braheem finally decided to use all four of the fourths on one circle. He continued dividing the circle he first marked into fourths, shaded it entirely, wrote $\frac{4}{4}$, and wrote a B above the circle.

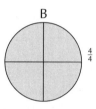

B

$\frac{4}{4}$

Sadie rolled 2 and 5 next and started a new circle. Braheem then rolled 5 and 6 and captured another new circle. Sadie rolled 1 and 2 and added on to the circle, on which she had shaded in one-fourth, to capture it.

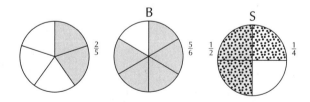

B   S

$\frac{2}{5}$ $\frac{5}{6}$ $\frac{1}{2}$ $\frac{1}{4}$

Braheem rolled 2 and 4. "This is the same as one-half," he said. "I think I can add it to the circle with two-fifths shaded, but I'm not sure how."

"What are you thinking?" I asked.

"I don't know," he said.

"Do you want help from someone else in class?" I asked.

Braheem paused and then said, "Oh, I see it. I have half, so that's two and a half–fifths." He divided one of the three remaining fifths in half and shaded in two and a half–fifths. He wrote $\frac{1}{2}$ and a *B*.

"But you rolled a two and a four," I said.

"Oh yeah," he said, "but it's the same." He erased the $\frac{1}{2}$ and wrote $\frac{2}{4}$.

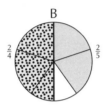

"How much is that sliver left over?" I asked the class. Only a few of the students were willing to answer. I again asked them to talk in pairs. After a few moments, I asked them for their attention and called on Jimmy.

"It's half of the fifth," he said. I wrote a fraction with $\frac{1}{2}$ in the numerator and *5* in the denominator:

$$\frac{\frac{1}{2}}{5}$$

"Oh, that's a tenth," Tamika said. "If you divide every fifth in half, you get ten pieces." Some of the others recognized why this made sense; others weren't so sure.

Braheem now had captured four circles and Sadie had captured three. As I did the day before with Kurt and Emma, I let Braheem and Sadie finish their game at the board while I returned the other students' papers so that they could also play.

Observing the Students

Booth and Midori were starting a game of Version 2. I watched Booth roll a 1 and a 5, divide a circle in fifths, shade a section, and label it $\frac{1}{5}$. "I think of what I draw when I play hangman," he said to explain how he divided a circle into fifths.

"I kind of start like I'm making thirds, but I add two more lines," Midori added.

Midori rolled and got two 3s. "I get a circle," she said, dividing a circle into thirds, coloring in all three of them, and recording $\frac{3}{3}$.

Booth took the dice, made a gesture of wishing for good luck, and rolled them. He got a 1 and a 2. He sat looking at the circles on the sheet.

"If I start a new circle, do I get it?" he asked.

"No," Midori answered, "you have to shade in more than one-half."

"Then I'll add on to the one-fifth," Booth said. He paused, not sure how to mark one-half on the circle that was already divided into fifths. But then he used the same idea that Braheem had. He extended one side of the fifth already shaded so it became a diameter, dividing the circle in half.

"That shows it," Booth said. He shaded in half, wrote $\frac{1}{2}$, and then wrote *B* to indicate that he had captured the circle.

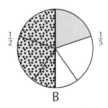

"How much of the circle is shaded in now?" I asked.

"It looks like two-thirds," Midori said. To show what she meant, she drew a circle on another sheet of paper, divided it into thirds, and shaded in two of them.

I said, "I think that two-thirds is very close to what's shaded in on Booth's circle, but you haven't convinced me. I think that drawings are often not exact and I need to hear another explanation."

Dario, sitting at the same table, had been eavesdropping and said, "I think it's three-fifths."

"Why do you think that?" I asked.

"Because three-fifths is more than half, and that's the number of fifths that's more than half," he answered.

"Do you agree that one-fifth plus two-fifths is three-fifths?" I asked, writing on a sheet of paper:

$$\frac{1}{5} + \frac{2}{5} = \frac{3}{5}$$

"Yeah," Dario said.

"But we added one-half to the one-fifth," I said, recording underneath what I had already written:

$$\frac{1}{5} + \frac{2}{5} = \frac{3}{5}$$

$$\frac{1}{5} + \frac{1}{2} =$$

"How does two-fifths compare with one-half?" I asked him, pointing first to the $\frac{2}{5}$ I had written and then to the $\frac{1}{2}$.

Dario answered, "It's the same. No, it's less. I'm not sure because five is odd."

"It has to be less," Dario's partner, Sahara, said.

"Oh yeah," Dario said, "it's a little less than a half."

"That's what I think, too," I said. "So if one-half is more than two-fifths, and two-fifths plus one-fifth is equal to three-fifths, then one-half plus one-fifth should be a little more than three-fifths. It's close, but not exact." I wasn't sure that Dario had followed my reasoning, but he nodded and admitted his error.

Booth suddenly got very excited. "It's seven-tenths," he said. "Look, there's a fifth and half of a fifth left. Half of a fifth is a tenth, and one-fifth is two-tenths, so it's three-tenths left over. So there are seven-tenths." He drew arrows to the unshaded pieces and wrote the fractions to explain his thinking.

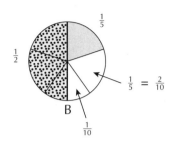

"Oooh, cool," Midori said.

"I don't get it," Dario said.

Booth divided each of the segments on the circle in half (more or less). "These are tenths," he said. Then Booth counted the tenths that had been shaded. "And seven of them are colored in. So it's seven-tenths."

I left them to observe another table. "Can you show me how to draw fifths? I'm not good at it," I heard Magda ask Pedro. She had rolled a 2 and a 5.

"Sure," Pedro said. He divided a circle into fifths while Magda watched.

As Magda shaded in two of the fifths, Pedro got ready to roll the dice. "I hope I don't get snake eyes," he said.

"Ms. Burns," Niko called to me. "Can you help us?" He had rolled a 2 and a 3 and was puzzled about how to show two-thirds in a circle that already was half shaded.

"It's too much to fit on that circle," I said. "Two-thirds is more than half, and half is already shaded in. If you shade in two-thirds of a new circle, you'll capture it."

"Hey, that's right!" he said.

Miguel, who had overheard Pedro's earlier comment, called out, "Hey, Pedro, you're wrong about snake eyes. It's great to get."

Pedro responded, "Yeah, I figured that out."

"Any doubles are good," Katie chimed in.

Emma giggled. "I rolled doubles twice," she said. "They're great."

"It's rotten to get one-half," Elizabeth said.

"Why do you think that?" I asked her.

"Because then the next person gets to capture no matter what they get," she said.

"Oh yeah," Alexa said. "I hadn't thought of that."

Magda, often tentative, wanted my help. She had rolled a 2 and a 4. "If I add two-fourths to this circle," she said, pointing to a circle on which one-sixth was already shaded, "will it go over a half?"

"What do you think, Pedro?" I asked. It became clear to me that Pedro hadn't been paying attention to what Magda was doing or thinking. I called his attention back to the game. Magda repeated her question.

"That works," he said. "Two-fourths is the same as one-half, so you can add it on and you have to have more than one-half colored."

"Do I color in three of them?" Magda asked.

"Why would you color in three of them?" I asked.

"They're sixths, and three of them are half?" she said in a questioning tone. I looked at Pedro.

"That works," he said again. "Three-sixths is the same as one-half and that's the same as two-fourths." Pedro was a patient boy, willing to be helpful to Magda.

Letitia came to me with a question. "Can I add on to a circle that's already been captured, but it still has some space left?" she wanted to know.

I answered, "It's OK to do that as long as there's room for your fraction. But why would you want to?"

"Well, it's a defensive move," Letitia explained. "I don't want to start a new circle for Anisa to capture on her turn."

"Is that fair?" her partner, Anisa, asked.

"Yes," I said, "as long as Letitia's fraction fits, she can put it on any circle."

The class continued with the usual disruptions of a few students leaving for music lessons and then returning. This coming and going seems to bother me more than it bothers the children. They just regroup, get new partners, and keep on playing.

Figures 12–1 through 12–3 show three pairs' games.

A Class Discussion

I interrupted the class about fifteen minutes before the end of the period for a class discussion about the game. "What do you think of this game?" I asked.

"I like the game," Kurt offered. "I like how when it's a five-five tie, the next roll could be sudden death."

"I like how you could fill in someone's circle if they didn't get more than half. But that was also hard if you didn't have the same denominator," Midori said.

"Using colored pencils worked great," Alexa said.

Tara added, "When one person captures six circles, the game is really over. There's no way the other person can win."

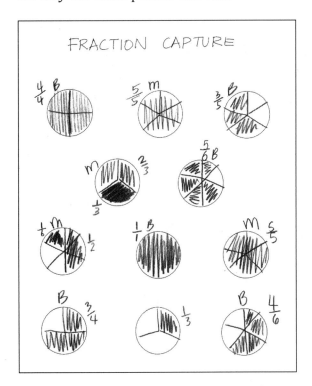

▲▲▲▲▲Figure 12–1 *After Manuel captured six circles, he and Bea ended the game, leaving one circle still uncaptured.*

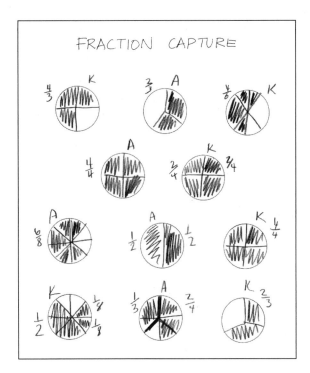

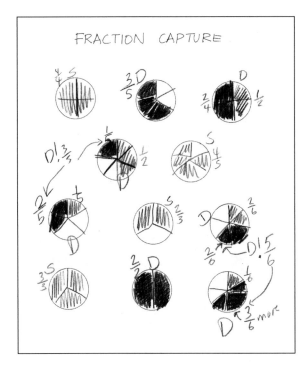

▲▲▲▲▲▲Figure 12–2 *Kurt captured six circles to win and Allison captured five.*

▲▲▲▲▲▲Figure 12–3 *Dario used a system of arrows to show when he split fractions on different circles. He captured seven of the eleven circles.*

No one had anything to add, so I asked, "Did anything confuse you about playing?"

Magda raised a hand. "I think the game got confusing when you had to add a fraction to a circle that already had a fraction and you needed to draw different lines," she said.

Jonah raised his hand. "I got confused like that when I had to put down one-third on a circle with one-fourth already on it."

"Did anyone else get confused as Magda and Jonah did?" I asked.

"It was hard for me, too," Paul said.

"It was hard, but I could figure it out," Sahara said. "The game helped me draw fractions better."

I then raised another question. "What strategies did you use?" I asked.

"I talked to the dice," Booth said. "It seemed to work."

"I split the fractions," Dario said.

"I tried to fill up circles before my partner did," Carolyn said.

"I think I need to play more to get a strategy," Niko said.

"I don't want to tell my strategy. Then I might not win," Elizabeth said.

"What do you know about rolling doubles?" I then asked.

"They're a guaranteed capture," Jake said.

"I rolled doubles three times in one game," Emma said.

"Are two sixes better than two twos or any other double?" I asked.

"No," they chorused.

"They're all worth one, so you can shade in a whole circle," Jimmy added. This was progress, as a few months ago it wasn't clear to some students that six-sixths, five-fifths, four-fourths, and so on were all equivalent. Using these fractions in the context of the game seemed to help.

"I'd like to discuss some of the situations I noticed when watching you play yesterday," I said. I brought up

Booth's problem with adding one-half on to a circle with one-fifth already shaded. Booth showed his solution, and then I raised the question for the class of how much was shaded in all. I also asked for ideas about how much of a circle was filled after one-sixth and two-fourths were shaded.

I then brought up the issue of splitting fractions, using what I had noticed Elizabeth do. I drew a circle on the board, shaded in half, and wrote $\frac{1}{2}$. I said, "This is the situation that Elizabeth was in when she rolled five-sixths."

"Can I tell what I did?" Elizabeth asked. "Sure," I replied.

"I split the five-sixths into one-sixth and four-sixths," she said, "and then I put the one-sixth on the one-half and the four-sixths on another circle. I captured two of them." She grinned.

"Cool!" Miguel commented.

It was now the end of the period, so I collected the students' papers and told them, "I'll add *Fraction Capture* to our list for choice time." This way, students would have the chance to continue playing the game over time.

Questions and Discussion

▲▲

▲ *It seems that you gave a lot of directions at once when introducing the game. Don't you find students get confused?*

Yes, a barrage of verbal directions can confuse some students. That's why I had two students come up to model how to play the game and saved the rule about splitting until they had some experience. I find that student demonstrations like this are useful when introducing new games or activities. Still, I've come to expect a certain amount of confusion from students no matter how clear directions are. Once students understand a game or activity, however, learning becomes more accessible.

▲ *What do you do for students that continue to have trouble dividing circles?*

A benefit of having the students play a game is that they are engaged, which allows me to give special attention to students who need more time. Sometimes I tell the class that I'll be working with a few students at the back table. I ask them to try to solve any problems they run into by checking with their neighbors or by writing their question on the board for me to answer in a little while. That way, I can have some uninterrupted time with students who need extra help.

CHAPTER THIRTEEN
SCORE THE DIFFERENCE

Overview

Score the Difference is a game that is similar to the *Comparing Game* (see Chapter 5) but also gives students practice with adding and subtracting fractions. Students play in pairs. For each round, they roll a die to determine the numerator and denominator of a fraction, trying to make the smallest fraction possible. Whoever has the smaller fraction wins the round and scores the difference between the two fractions, requiring the players to subtract. After four rounds, they total their scores from the rounds to see who has the greater total. Two versions allow for making the game easier or more difficult for students.

Materials

▲ dice, 1 per pair of students
▲ optional: *Score the Difference* worksheet, at least 1 per pair of students (see Blackline Masters)
▲ optional: *Score the Difference* rules (see Blackline Masters)

Time

▲ one class period to introduce the game, plus additional time for playing and discussion

Teaching Directions

1. On the board, draw a game board for two players.

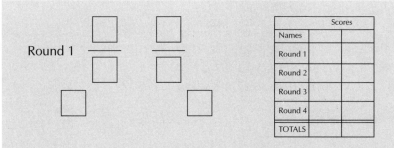

Round 1

	Scores	
Names		
Round 1		
Round 2		
Round 3		
Round 4		
TOTALS		

2. Tell the students that they will play the game in pairs. Explain the rules.

Score the Difference Rules

You need:
  a partner
  a die

Rules

1. You need a game board for four rounds like this:

2. Players take turns rolling the die and writing the number in one of their spaces on the game board. Once a number is written, it cannot be changed. The boxes to the side are reject boxes that give you one chance to write a number that you don't want to use in your fraction.

3. After writing a number, pass the die to the other player.

4. Play until both players have recorded a fraction. (Your reject box may be empty if you used your first two numbers to make a fraction.)

5. Whoever has the smaller fraction wins the round and scores the difference between the two fractions.

6. After four rounds, total your scores. Whoever has the larger total is the winner.

3. Ask for a volunteer to come up to the board and play a game with you.

4. Organize the students to play in pairs. Distribute a die and, if you wish, a copy of the rules to each pair. Also, you may want to distribute worksheets for the game boards instead of having students draw their own.

5. Circulate and offer help as needed.

Teaching Notes

This game is appropriate once students are comfortable comparing and combining fractions, and it's an engaging way to provide them practice. Also, the elements of strategy and luck contribute to make the game interesting for students.

When I teach the game, I first have the students play by using 8 whenever they roll a 5 on the die. This avoids having them deal with fifths, which is confusing for some students, who benefit from more experience working with friendlier denominators. When the students are successful with the game, then ask them to play using the 5 instead.

The game is useful as a choice activity for students who finish assignments early. It's also suitable for homework. When students have the chance to teach the game to someone at home, they help communicate about the kinds of activities they are doing during math class.

The Lesson

▲▲

I drew a game board for two players on the board:

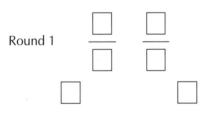

I said to the class, "This game is called *Score the Difference*. After I teach you how to play, you'll play in pairs. A game has four rounds, and you'll need one game board like the one I've drawn here. You take turns rolling one die, writing the number that comes up each time in one of your boxes. The boxes to the sides are reject boxes that give you one chance to write a number that you don't want to use in your fraction. You want to make the

smallest fraction possible because whoever has the smaller fraction wins the round."

Annie had a question. "Can you change a number after you write it?"

"No," I answered.

"Isn't it just luck?" Juanita asked.

"You're right that luck is involved," I said. "But you also have to think about where the best place is to play a number so you have the best chance of making the smaller fraction."

No one else had a question yet, so I continued. "There are two versions of the game. In the first version, when you roll a five, you pretend it's an eight. In the second version, a five will be a five. I'm going to show a game for Version One. Would someone like to come up and play with me?" Many of the students were eager to do so. I chose Craig and he came to the front of the room.

Hassan had a question. "Can you make an improper fraction?"

"That would be fine," I said.

Kayla said, "But if you want the smallest fraction possible, you don't want an improper fraction."

"Oh yeah," Hassan said.

PLAYING A SAMPLE GAME

"Who should go first?" I asked.

"Does it matter?" Craig asked.

Julio's hand shot up. "I think it's better to go second. Then you can see what the other person does first."

"You go first," Craig said to me. I rolled the die, a 2 came up, and I used it for the numerator.

Round 1
$$\frac{2}{\Box\ \Box} \qquad \frac{\Box}{\Box\ \Box}$$

Craig rolled a 4 and wrote it in his reject box. Then I rolled another 2 and wrote it in my reject box.

Round 1
$$\frac{2}{2\ \Box} \qquad \frac{\Box}{\Box\ \boxed{4}}$$

Next Craig rolled a 2 and wrote it in his numerator box.

Round 1
$$\frac{2}{2\ \Box} \qquad \frac{2}{\Box\ \boxed{4}}$$

"It's a tie so far," Pierre commented. I rolled the die and a 5 came up.

"Remember that a five is an eight in this version of the game," I said. Craig groaned. Then he rolled the die and groaned again when he saw that a 2 came up. Our round was complete.

Round 1
$$\frac{2}{2\ \boxed{8}} \qquad \frac{2}{2\ \boxed{4}}$$

"You win," Craig said.

"Well, I just win this round," I said. "That means that you score zero for this round. To figure out my score, I have to subtract our fractions to find the difference." I wrote on the board:

$$\frac{2}{2} - \frac{2}{8}$$

Then, talking out loud as I figured, I said, "Two over two is the same as one, and two-eighths is the same as one-fourth, so the problem is one minus one-fourth, and I know that that's three-fourths."

$$\frac{2}{2} - \frac{2}{8}$$
$$1 - \frac{1}{4} = \frac{3}{4}$$

"Do you agree?" I asked Craig. He nodded. I added, "When your partner figures his or her score, be sure that you agree. It could make a difference in the final outcome." I recorded our scores on the scoreboard.

	Scores	
Names	Ms. Burns	Craig
Round 1	$\frac{3}{4}$	0
Round 2		
Round 3		
Round 4		
TOTALS		

"Ready for Round Two?" I asked. Craig nodded.

"Do you want to go first or second?" I asked.

"You go first," Craig said.

I rolled a 2 and wrote it in the numerator box as I had done last time. This turned out to be unfortunate for me because I rolled a 1 for each of my next two turns. Craig rolled a 6 for his first roll and was pleased to write it in the denominator box. Then he rolled a 4 and wrote it in the reject box. Finally he rolled a

5, which forced him to write an 8 in the numerator. He groaned, but cheered up when he realized that because $\frac{8}{6}$ was smaller than two wholes, he had won the round.

Round 2

$$\frac{\boxed{2}}{\boxed{1}\;\boxed{1}} \qquad \frac{\boxed{8}}{\boxed{6}\;\boxed{4}}$$

"So what do I score?" Craig asked me.

I answered, "You have to figure the difference by subtracting our fractions, and I have to agree with your answer. Then you can record our scores."

Craig thought for a moment and then said, "I can do this. You have two, and I have one and two-sixths, and that's the same as one and two-thirds." On the board, he first wrote $2 - 1\frac{2}{3}$ but then realized his error and changed the $\frac{2}{3}$ to $\frac{1}{3}$. Then he figured the answer. "I mean two-thirds is the answer," he said and recorded our scores.

Scores		
Names	Ms. Burns	Craig
Round 1	$\frac{3}{4}$	0
Round 2	0	$\frac{2}{3}$
Round 3		
Round 4		
TOTALS		

For the third round, I again went first and wound up with $\frac{3}{8}$. Craig won with $\frac{2}{8}$.

Round 3

$$\frac{\boxed{3}}{\boxed{2}\;\boxed{8}} \qquad \frac{\boxed{2}}{\boxed{8}\;\boxed{}}$$

Craig had used his first two rolls for the numerator and denominator of his fraction so he didn't need to roll a third time since the number in the reject box would be moot. Craig subtracted $\frac{3}{8} - \frac{2}{8}$ to

figure his score of $\frac{1}{8}$ and then recorded both of our scores.

Scores		
Names	Ms. Burns	Craig
Round 1	$\frac{3}{4}$	0
Round 2	0	$\frac{2}{3}$
Round 3	0	$\frac{1}{8}$
Round 4		
TOTALS		

Round 4 had an exciting finish. I played my first roll of 5 as an 8 in the denominator. Craig rejected his first roll of 4. My second roll was a 2, and I played it in the numerator. Craig's second roll was a 5 and he wrote an 8 in the denominator.

Round 4

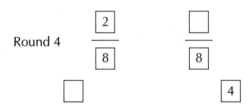

There was no need for me to roll again since my fraction was complete. Craig rubbed the die between his hands for luck, then let it go. The class was quiet, waiting to hear what came up. "Oh, no, you win!" Craig exclaimed when he saw that he had rolled a 4 to make his fraction $\frac{4}{8}$. He recorded the number.

Round 4

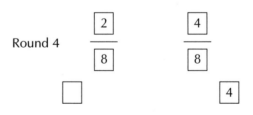

I said, "I think I score one-fourth this round. Do you agree?" I wrote on the board:

$$\tfrac{4}{8} - \tfrac{2}{8} = \tfrac{2}{8} = \tfrac{1}{4}$$

"Yes, I agree," Craig said. I recorded our scores.

Scores		
Names	Ms. Burns	Craig
Round 1	$\frac{3}{4}$	0
Round 2	0	$\frac{2}{3}$
Round 3	0	$\frac{1}{8}$
Round 4	$\frac{1}{4}$	0
TOTALS		

"Now we have to figure our total scores," I said. "Mine is easy. Three-fourths plus one-fourth is one, so my total is one. What about your total?"

Craig looked at his scores of $\frac{2}{3}$ and $\frac{1}{8}$ for a moment and then said, "I have to change them into twenty-fourths." He wrote on the board:

$\frac{2}{3} + \frac{1}{8}$

$\frac{16}{24} + \frac{3}{24} = \frac{19}{24}$

"You win," Craig conceded.

I agreed, "Yes, my score is five–twenty-fourths larger than yours." I recorded our totals on the board to complete our scoring and model for the students what they would have to do when they played.

Scores		
Names	Ms. Burns	Craig
Round 1	$\frac{3}{4}$	0
Round 2	0	$\frac{2}{3}$
Round 3	0	$\frac{1}{8}$
Round 4	$\frac{1}{4}$	0
TOTALS	1	$\frac{19}{24}$

"Are there any questions about the rules?" I asked. There weren't any and the students were eager to play. Before distributing the dice, I said, "After you play Version One, you can decide if you'd like to try Version Two. Who can explain what to do in Version Two?" I called on Maggie.

"The five stays a five," she said.

"Do you think this will change the game very much?" I asked.

Juanita said, "Then six will be the best number for the denominator."

I gave one final direction. "First each of you should set up a game board for a four-round game as I did on the board. Then you'll be ready to play two games."

OBSERVING THE STUDENTS

As I circulated, I observed the students construct their game boards. I reminded several students about making a chart for keeping track of their scores. I noticed that the boxes that Eddie drew were so small that there wasn't enough space to write numbers in them. When I pointed this out to him, he agreed and started over. Sabrina, on the other hand, was drawing boxes so large that it wouldn't be possible

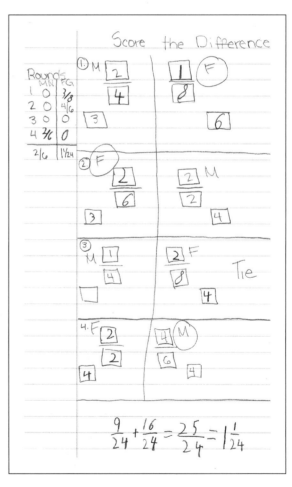

▲▲▲▲▲**Figure 13–1** *Francis won two rounds, Maria won one round, and they tied once. Francis showed at the bottom of their paper how he figured his total score of $1\frac{1}{24}$.*

to fit all four rounds on the page. She was about to start over when I suggested that she use what she had started and complete the game board on a second sheet.

After a few minutes, all of the students were involved in playing the game, and the sound in the room was one of enjoyment and activity. Francis cheered when he rolled a 5 for his last roll of Round 1 and was able to write an 8 in the denominator of his fraction (see Figure 13–1 on page 149). Celia and Brendan laughed after getting the same fractions in the first two rounds.

Annie and Josh had a bit of disagreement in Round 3. Annie rolled a 6 and mistakenly began to write it in the numerator. When she started to erase it, Josh objected. They called me over to referee.

Josh said, "You can't change a number once you've written it."

"But I hadn't even finished writing it," Annie protested.

"Do you think that Annie meant to write a six in the numerator?" I asked Josh.

"No," he said.

I responded, "Well, I would think of that the way I think when I play chess, that if I haven't lifted my fingers off the piece to complete a move, then I can change my mind. Annie didn't quite finish writing, so I think I'd agree that she could make the change."

"I guess I would be more harsh," Josh said, but he agreed that Annie could make the change. This didn't help Annie much, however, and Josh won all four rounds. (See Figure 13–2.)

Helene won all four rounds against Hassan. Hassan didn't seem to mind. "It's a good game," he commented. Pierre won

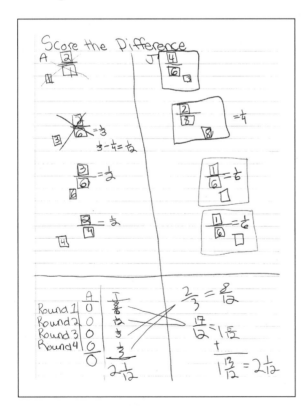

▲▲▲▲▲Figure 13–2 *Josh won all four rounds and showed how he combined his four scores of $\frac{8}{6}$, $\frac{1}{12}$, $\frac{1}{3}$, and $\frac{1}{3}$ to score $\frac{21}{12}$.*

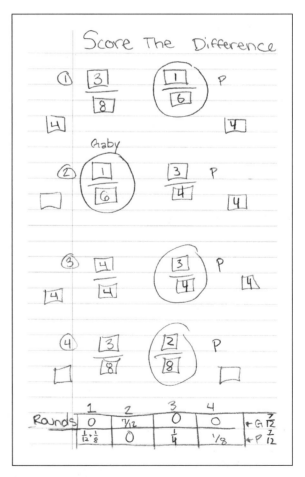

▲▲▲▲▲Figure 13–3 *Pierre won three of the four rounds, but he and Gloria wound up with the same scores at the end of the game.*

three of the four rounds, but he and Gloria both had scores of $\frac{7}{12}$ at the end of the game (see Figure 13–3). Sabrina also won three rounds against Carla, with a final score of $\frac{11}{24}$ to Carla's $\frac{1}{24}$.

EXTENSION

On following days, have the students play Version 2 of the game, keeping the 5 on the die instead of changing it to an 8.

Questions and Discussion

▲▲▲

▲ *Why do you have the students make their own game boards? Isn't it quicker if you have them duplicated ahead of time?*

Yes, it is quicker to provide the students with game boards already duplicated, and I provided a Blackline Master for that purpose if you would like to use it. However, I think it's valuable experience for students to have the chance to set up their papers for themselves. They then see the purpose of how a paper is organized and become, in a way, the producers as well as the consumers of the curriculum.

▲ *What can I do to support students who are less proficient?*

First of all, the game is a wonderful motivator for students. Because they like to play the game, they want to know how to figure their scores, and their interest is an asset to their learning. I encourage students who aren't sure how to find the difference to rely on their fraction kits. The kit provides them with a concrete model for fractions that builds their understanding and skill. (For information about fraction kits, see *Teaching Arithmetic: Lessons for Introducing Fractions Grades 4–5*, Chapters 2 and 15 and the booklet, *The Fraction Kit Guide*.)

▲ *Is it possible to play the same game but have the larger fraction win each round?*

Yes, this is possible and gives students more practice with dealing with improper fractions and whole numbers. When the larger fraction wins, students who roll a 1 place it in the denominator and wind up with a whole number. I chose having the smaller fraction win because it seems to give more practice with fractions. However, it's good to vary the game to keep students' interest, and your students may come up with other variations as well.

CHAPTER FOURTEEN
THE SMALLER ANSWER WINS

Overview

The Smaller Answer Wins is a two-person game that combines luck and strategic thinking to give students practice comparing and adding fractions. To play, students take turns rolling a die and writing the numbers that come up in the numerators and denominators of two fractions. They add their fractions and compare their totals. Whoever has the smaller answer wins the round. Several other versions of the game allow for variations that challenge the students in new ways.

Materials

▲ dice, 1 per pair of students
▲ optional: *The Smaller Answer Wins* worksheet, at least 1 per pair of students (see Blackline Masters)
▲ optional: *The Smaller Answer Wins* rules (see Blackline Masters)

Time

▲ one class period to introduce the game, plus additional time for playing and discussion

Teaching Directions

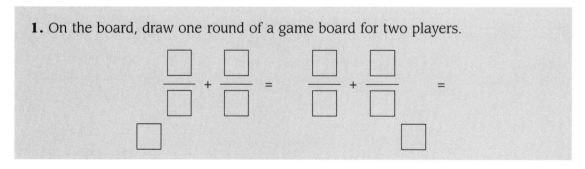

1. On the board, draw one round of a game board for two players.

2. Ask for a volunteer to play with you. Play a round, explaining the rules as you do so. You may want to post the rules so that there is a reference for the students when they play in pairs.

The Smaller Answer Wins Rules

You need:
   a partner
   a die

Rules
1. You need a game board for three rounds like this:

$$\frac{\square}{\square} + \frac{\square}{\square} = \quad \frac{\square}{\square} + \frac{\square}{\square} =$$

$$\square \qquad\qquad\qquad \square$$

2. Players take turns rolling the die and writing the number in one of their spaces on the game board. Once a number is written, it cannot be changed. The boxes to the side are reject boxes that give you one chance to write a number that you don't want to use in your problem.

3. After writing a number, pass the die to the other player.

4. Play until both players have recorded two fractions. (Your reject box may be empty if you used your first four numbers for the fractions.)

5. Add your two fractions. Check each other's sums. The winner of the round is the player with the smaller sum.

6. Play three rounds. Whoever wins more rounds wins the game.

3. Draw on the board an example of a game board for an entire game.

Round 1
$$\frac{\square}{\square} + \frac{\square}{\square} = \qquad \frac{\square}{\square} + \frac{\square}{\square} =$$
$$\square \qquad\qquad\qquad\qquad \square$$

Round 2
$$\frac{\square}{\square} + \frac{\square}{\square} = \qquad \frac{\square}{\square} + \frac{\square}{\square} =$$
$$\square \qquad\qquad\qquad\qquad \square$$

Round 3
$$\frac{\square}{\square} + \frac{\square}{\square} = \qquad \frac{\square}{\square} + \frac{\square}{\square} =$$
$$\square \qquad\qquad\qquad\qquad \square$$

4. Organize the students to play in pairs. Distribute a die to each pair and, if you wish, a copy of the rules to each pair. Also, you may want to distribute worksheets for the game boards instead of having students draw their own.

5. Circulate and offer help as needed. Also, look for students who are having difficulty comparing or combining fractions and for situations that might be useful for a whole-class discussion.

6. Interrupt the students so that there is time for a whole-class discussion. Ask students for their reaction to the game, and then discuss fractions that were particularly problematic or unusual for students to compare.

Teaching Notes

This game is purposely similar in format to the *Comparing Game* and *Score the Difference* (see Chapters 5 and 13). While these games aren't a prerequisite for playing this game, if students have experienced them, the students' familiarity with the format makes it easy to introduce *The Smaller Answer Wins*. The game is appropriate once students are comfortable comparing and combining fractions, and it's an engaging way to provide them practice. Also, the elements of strategy and luck contribute to make the game interesting for students.

Even if your students are familiar with playing the other games, I suggest modeling a game of *The Smaller Answer Wins* to review the rules. I also suggest having the students first play by using 8 whenever they roll a 5 on the die. This will present them with problems that involve eighths, which typically are easier for students to deal with than fifths are. For practice with fifths as well, students can then use the 5 instead.

The Lesson

▲▲

I wrote on the board *The Smaller Answer Wins* and drew a game board for one round of the game for each of two players:

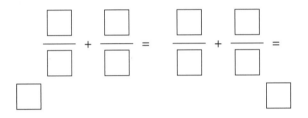

To introduce the game to the class, I said, "I'm going to teach you how to play a game. First I'd like a volunteer to play with me and help everyone learn the rules. Then you'll play in pairs." Hands shot up of volunteers willing to play. I called on Juanita and she joined me at the chalkboard.

I explained, "We'll take turns rolling the die. Each time we roll, we have to write our number in one of our five boxes. Once you write a number in a box, it has to stay there; you can't erase it and write it in another box. The idea is to place the numbers so that you'll have the smaller answer when we each add our fractions. And for this first version, if you roll a five, you'll use an eight instead." Juanita nodded to indicate that she understood.

"Would you like to go first or would you like me to go first?" I asked her.

"You go first," she responded.

I rolled the die. "It's a one," I said and then thought aloud about where I'd place it. "I think that if I want a small answer, I'll

write the one in the numerator of the first fraction."

I then said, "When it's your turn, hold on to the die until you're sure you've written the number where you want it. Then pass the die to your partner to take a turn. The other player shouldn't roll the die until the first player has written his or her number." I handed the die to Juanita and she rolled it.

"Tell the class what number came up," I said.

Juanita responded, "It's a six. I'll make it a denominator."

Next I rolled a 6, and I wrote it under the 1 to complete my first fraction. I passed the die to Juanita and she rolled a 6 again. She used it as her second denominator.

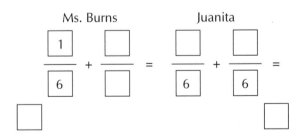

Juanita giggled. "This is lucky," she said.

"Not if Ms. Burns rolls a five and gets to write an eight in the denominator," Craig commented.

"Oh yeah, but it's pretty lucky so far," Juanita said.

I rolled next and a 3 came up. "I don't like this number very much," I said.

"Play it in the reject box," Pierre said.

"I think I'll do just that," I responded and did so.

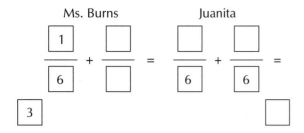

Ms. Burns   Juanita

$$\frac{1}{6} + \frac{\square}{\square} = \frac{\square}{6} + \frac{\square}{6} =$$

$$\boxed{3} \qquad\qquad\qquad \boxed{}$$

Juanita then also rolled a 3. She thought for a moment and then said, "I'm not sure where to write it." Some hands shot up of students who were interested in giving their suggestions.

"Would you like to hear some ideas from others?" I asked. Juanita nodded. She turned to the class and called on several of her classmates.

"I think that you should write it on top," Kara said. "That makes three-sixths, and that's one-half, and it's pretty small."

"Do you remember what we call the number in a fraction that's on the top?" I asked Kara to remind her to use the proper terminology.

"The numerator," she responded.

Francis disagreed. "I think you should reject it and hope for smaller numbers next time."

Kayla then said, "I agree with Kara. There are three numbers bigger than three and only two numbers smaller than three. I wouldn't take a chance. It's not great, but I think it's better in the numerator than in the reject box."

Juanita next called on David. He said, "If I rolled a three . . . . well, I'd reject anything more than a three, but I'd play the three in the fraction."

Other hands were still raised, but I said, "It's hard to be sure about a strategy when you're first learning a game. I appreciate that you're willing to help Juanita. As we play, keep thinking about what makes sense. Juanita, are you ready to write your number?"

Juanita responded, "I'll write it for the numerator of my first fraction."

Ms. Burns   Juanita

$$\frac{1}{6} + \frac{\square}{\square} = \frac{3}{6} + \frac{\square}{6} =$$

$$\boxed{3} \qquad\qquad\qquad\qquad \boxed{}$$

Juanita gave me the die and I rolled a 2. I said, "I'm going to take David's advice and write the two in the numerator of my second fraction." I handed the die to Juanita. She rolled a 5, groaned, and quickly wrote *8* in the reject box.

Ms. Burns   Juanita

$$\frac{1}{6} + \frac{2}{\square} = \frac{3}{6} + \frac{\square}{6} =$$

$$\boxed{3} \qquad\qquad\qquad\qquad \boxed{8}$$

"You better not roll a five again!" Damien said.

"A four or a six wouldn't be so good, either," Sachi added.

Juanita gave me the die and I rolled a 2 for my last roll. "I have no choice," I said as I wrote it in the denominator of my second fraction.

Ms. Burns   Juanita

$$\frac{1}{6} + \frac{2}{2} = \frac{3}{6} + \frac{\square}{6} =$$

$$\boxed{3} \qquad\qquad\qquad\qquad \boxed{8}$$

"That was too bad," Julio sympathized.

"Before Juanita rolls, let's think about whether I have any chance of winning the round," I said. "Two over two is one whole, so my sum is one and one-sixth." I recorded:

$$\tfrac{1}{6} + \tfrac{2}{2} = \tfrac{1}{6} + 1 = 1\tfrac{1}{6}$$

"Talk with your neighbor about what might happen with Juanita's last roll," I said. The room got noisy, and I talked with Juanita.

"What do you think?" I asked her.

Juanita looked at the board and then said, "If I roll one, two, or three, I'll be OK because my answer won't be more than one. And if I roll a four, then it's three-sixths plus four-sixths, and we'll tie. I'm doomed if I roll a five or a six."

"I agree with your reasoning," I said. "Let's call the class back to attention and see what happens."

I interrupted the students' conversations. Hands were raised and I called on Brendan. He said, "She wants a one or a two or a three to win, or a four to tie."

The class quieted as Juanita picked up the die to roll it. She rolled the die. "It's a four," she said and wrote it in her blank box.

Ms. Burns | Juanita

$$\frac{1}{6} + \frac{2}{2} = \frac{3}{6} + \frac{4}{6} = $$

3 | 8

$$\tfrac{1}{6} + \tfrac{2}{2} = \tfrac{1}{6} + 1 = 1\tfrac{1}{6}$$

"It's a tie!" several students said.

"Who can explain why?" I asked. I called on Clark.

He explained, "If you take one-sixth off the four-sixths, then you have three-sixths plus three-sixths, and that's six-sixths, and that's one whole. Then you add on the extra one-sixth." I recorded:

$$\tfrac{4}{6} - \tfrac{3}{6} = \tfrac{1}{6}$$

$$\tfrac{3}{6} + \tfrac{3}{6} = \tfrac{6}{6} = 1$$

$$1 + \tfrac{1}{6} = 1\tfrac{1}{6}$$

I gave the class one more direction. "For a complete game, you play three rounds and see who wins more of them," I said. "But Juanita and I won't continue our game. Instead, you'll all get a chance to play now." I thanked Juanita for playing and she returned to her seat.

"What questions do you have?" I asked the class. There were no questions, so I drew a complete game board on the board:

Round 1 $$\frac{\square}{\square} + \frac{\square}{\square} = \frac{\square}{\square} + \frac{\square}{\square} = $$ $$\square \qquad\qquad\qquad \square$$

Round 2 $$\frac{\square}{\square} + \frac{\square}{\square} = \frac{\square}{\square} + \frac{\square}{\square} = $$ $$\square \qquad\qquad\qquad \square$$

Round 3 $$\frac{\square}{\square} + \frac{\square}{\square} = \frac{\square}{\square} + \frac{\square}{\square} = $$ $$\square \qquad\qquad\qquad \square$$

I said, "If you each set up a game board like this, then you'll be ready for two games." I organized the students into pairs and distributed the dice.

OBSERVING THE CLASS

Playing the game went smoothly for the students. Because they had previously played the *Comparing Game* and *Score the Difference*, they were familiar with the format and the rules.

After their first round, Juanita and Julio called me over. "Is it OK if we figure our score for each round, not just who won?" Juanita asked.

"How would you do that?" I asked.

Julio answered, "Like we did for *Score the Difference*. We would subtract."

"Yes, that would be fine," I responded. (See Figure 14–1.)

Eddie and Sachi were giggling after their first round. "I had really, really bad luck," Eddie said. "I rolled a five for my last roll so I had to write an eight over a three." I took a look at what they had recorded (see Figure 14–2).

Eddie explained further. "My next-to-last roll was a two, and I didn't want to write it over the three because that would be two-thirds. But I made a mistake."

"It was good for me, though," Sachi said cheerfully.

I was interested in how they had added $\frac{8}{3} + \frac{1}{2}$ to figure Eddie's sum of $3\frac{1}{6}$. Eddie explained. "I changed eight-thirds to two and two-thirds, and I knew that I needed one-third more to get another whole. So I took the one-third from the one-half and that left me with one-sixth. So it's three and three-sixths. Sachi helped me do it."

"I'm pleased that Sachi was able to help, but I'm also pleased that you were able to explain it so clearly," I said. Eddie beamed. He was a hardworking student, but he lacked confidence, and this experience was somewhat of a triumph for him.

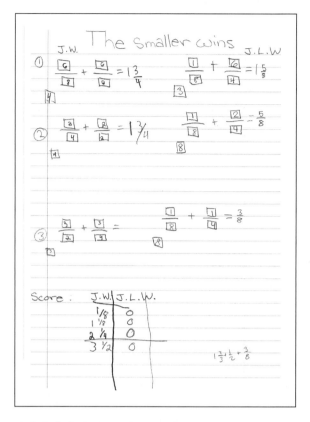

▲▲▲▲▲▲**Figure 14–1** *Julio and Juanita decided to figure the difference of their scores for each round. Juanita won all three rounds for a total score of $3\frac{1}{2}$.*

Clark came to me with a question. "If the fraction numbers are all filled in and the reject boxes are still empty, do we have to keep rolling the dice to fill in the reject boxes?" I came over to where Clark and Damien were playing and looked at

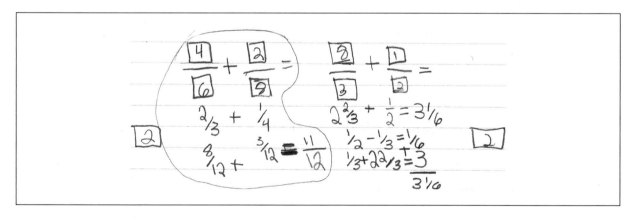

▲▲▲▲▲▲**Figure 14–2** *Eddie's last roll forced him to write an 8 in the numerator, causing him to lose the round.*

their paper. Damien had completed his five rolls and Clark had rolled the die only four times, but he had used the numbers in the fractions, leaving his reject box still open.

"What do you think?" I asked.

"It doesn't matter what he rolls, so I don't think he should have to," Damien said. Clark nodded his agreement, and I confirmed that the last roll wasn't necessary.

"Just figure your sums and see who has the smaller answer," I said, leaving to continue circulating around the room. In a few moments, however, Clark came to get me again.

"Now we're really stuck," he said. "We can't figure out who wins." I returned to their table and saw that the boys had figured their sums correctly.

Clark   Damien

$$\frac{2}{6} + \frac{2}{8} = \frac{1}{3} + \frac{1}{4}$$

$$\frac{16}{48} + \frac{12}{48} = \frac{28}{48} \qquad \frac{4}{12} + \frac{3}{12} = \frac{7}{12}$$

Damien said, "We know that forty-eighths are smaller pieces than twelfths, but we're not sure which fraction is smaller."

"Is your fraction more or less than one-half?" I asked Clark.

He thought for a moment and then said, "More. Half of forty-eight is twenty-four."

"Mine's more, too," Damien said, "so that doesn't help."

I asked Damien, "Can you change your fraction from twelfths to forty-eighths? Imagine taking a one-twelfth piece and cutting it in half."

"I'd have two–twenty-fourths," Damien said.

I nodded and asked, "And if you cut each of the twenty-fourths in half?"

Damien thought out loud, "If I cut a twelfth in half, I get twenty-fourths. Oh

yeah, I can cut them again into forty-eighths. So if I cut them twice, then I have to cut seven of them twice, and that gives me fourteen . . . twenty-eight pieces. Hey, I think we tie!"

"I don't get it," Clark said.

"Look," Damien said and began to explain to Clark. I left the boys huddled together over their paper.

Brendan won the first two rounds of his game with Celia. "Should we play the last round?" he asked me. "We already know that I won."

I responded, "Yes, please play the last round, too. Remember that the idea is to give you practice with fractions, and the more practice the better. Besides, playing again gives Celia another chance to win a round." They nodded and went back to their game. (See Figure 14–3.)

I noticed that Kayla had miscalculated her sum for her second round. Knowing that Kayla was a strong math student, I merely told her about the error and left her to find it. "I still won the round," she said, after making the correction. (See Figure 14–4.)

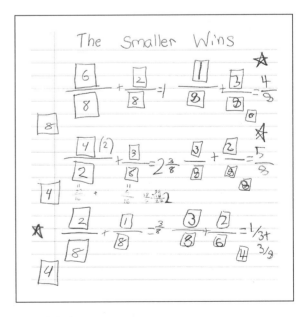

▲▲▲▲▲▲Figure 14–3 *For their third round, Brendan told me that he didn't need to bother adding the fractions to see that Celia won. He said, "She has three-eighths, and I have three-eighths plus one-third, so the wins."*

The Smaller Answer Wins 159

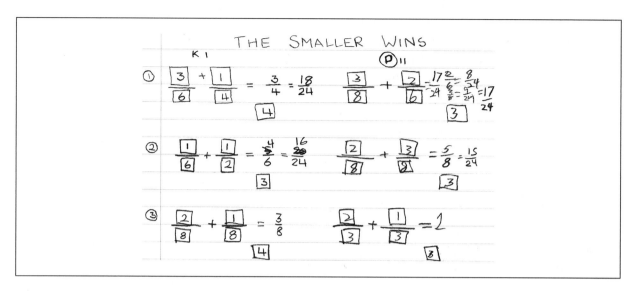

▲▲▲▲▲▲Figure 14–4 *After Kayla corrected her addition error in the second round, her sum was still larger than David's.*

I continued to circulate. When I do so, I try to notice situations that might be good for a whole-class discussion. Anita and Craig's last round presented an interesting situation. I gave the students a warning that they would have to stop playing in one minute and, as the students played, I recorded Anita and Craig's round on the board, leaving off Craig's last two rolls. As I was writing on the board, Brendan came to me to report, "Celia won Round Three."

A CLASS DISCUSSION

When I interrupted the students, about ten minutes remained in class. First I asked for their reactions. The students all enjoyed the game, and I told them they would have the chance to play it again on other days.

Then I said to them, "Craig and Anita had an interesting situation. This is where they were when I talked with them." I pointed to what I had drawn on the board.

Craig   Anita

$$\frac{}{6} + \frac{}{8} = \frac{3}{8} + \frac{2}{6} =$$

$$8 \qquad \qquad \boxed{}$$

I explained, "Anita had gone first. When they took turns, Anita didn't use her reject box, but Craig did. So now it was time for Craig's fourth roll."

Craig interjected, "Anita didn't need to roll anymore, and I had two rolls to go. I rolled a three next."

"Tell the class your dilemma," I said.

"My what?" Craig asked.

"Tell the class what you were puzzled about," I paraphrased.

"Oh yeah," Craig said. "I knew that if I put the three over the eight, then I'd have to roll a one to beat Anita or a two to tie. So I thought that maybe I should put the three over the six instead. So what I did is—"

I interrupted Craig and said, "Let's see what others think. Where would you play the three? Talk with your neighbors."

Conversation broke out and I called them back to attention after a few moments and called on Francis.

"It depends on what he rolls next, so you can't tell," Francis said.

Celia said, "I think he should do what Anita did. If he puts the three over the six, then you start with one-half, and both of Anita's fractions are less than one-half."

"That's just what Craig did. And then he rolled a two, so they tied. But I was wondering about what would have happened if Craig had played the three over the six and then the two over the eight. Then here's what they would have had. Who would have won?" I wrote on the board:

Craig   Anita

$\frac{3}{6} + \frac{2}{8}$ $\frac{3}{8} + \frac{2}{6}$

Conversation broke out again and most reached for pencil and paper. When I called them back to attention, I asked, "What would Craig's total have been?"

Sabrina answered, "Three-fourths. Three-sixths is one-half, and two-eighths is one-fourth, and one-half plus one-fourth is three-fourths." I recorded:

Craig   Anita

$\frac{3}{6} + \frac{2}{8}$ $\frac{3}{8} + \frac{2}{6}$

$\frac{1}{2} + \frac{1}{4}$

$\frac{3}{4}$

Maria said, "Anita got seventeen–twenty-fourths, didn't you, Anita?" Anita nodded.

"How did you figure?" I asked.

"I changed two-sixths to one-third, and then I changed them both into

twenty-fourths," Maria said. As she gave me the specifics, I recorded:

Craig   Anita

$\frac{3}{6} + \frac{2}{8}$ $\frac{3}{8} + \frac{2}{6}$

$\frac{1}{2} + \frac{1}{4}$ $\frac{3}{8} + \frac{1}{3}$

$\frac{3}{4}$ $\frac{9}{24} + \frac{8}{24}$

                $\frac{17}{24}$

Saul said, "That's what we did. Three-fourths is the same as eighteen–twenty-fourths, so Anita would have won by a teensy bit." I recorded:

$\frac{3}{4} = \frac{18}{24}$

"Those are the same two fractions we got for our first round," David said.

This discussion ended the class.

EXTENSIONS

1. For another version, ask students to play a 5 when they roll one, rather than changing it to an 8.

2. For a more difficult version of the game, instead of scoring 1 point for having the smaller answer in each round, the winner of the round scores the difference between the two answers.

3. To vary the game, change it to *The Larger Wins*. Then have students play play either the first or the second version.

Questions and Discussion

▲▲▲

▲ *How much time do you provide for students to play the game?*

In this lesson, I had the students play for most of the class period. Then I used the game in several ways on subsequent days. Sometimes it was an option for students who finished another assignment quickly when time was still left for math. Sometimes I had an entire period for choices, and this game was one of them. Also, sometimes I assigned it for homework and asked students to teach someone at home how to play.

▲ *When Clark and Damien were confused, why did you ask Damien to change seven-twelfths into forty-eighths instead of asking Clark to simplify twenty-eight–forty-eighths? Wouldn't this have been a good opportunity to show them how to convert fractions?*

These are two good questions that point out the kind of decision making we regularly have to make as teachers. To answer the first question, from my experience with Damien and Clark, I knew that they were more comfortable when they could visualize fractions. They relied regularly on their fraction kit pieces but didn't do so at this time because the kits don't have pieces that are forty-eighths. However, I thought they could imagine cutting twelfths in half and then half in again. Damien did so, and I left him and Clark to discuss the situation. I don't think that showing them a numerical procedure would have been helpful at this time. From knowing the boys, I knew that they needed more experiences reasoning with the fractions in ways that made sense to them rather than learning a procedure that they might not understand. Once they had a better foundation of understanding, introducing numerical procedures would be appropriate.

▲ *Do you believe that it's important for students to convert fractions to simplest form?*

I believe that it's important for students to be able to convert fractions to simplest form and also to know when a fraction is in simplest form. But I do not believe that all answers have to be expressed in simplest form in order to be considered correct. And sometimes the context of a problem implies that it makes sense for a fraction not to be in simplest form. For example, if five friends were sharing three pizzas, and each pizza was cut into eight pieces, it probably, would make more sense to refer to the slices as eighths, so that two slices would be two-eighths, not necessarily one-fourth.

ASSESSMENTS

This section suggests twelve assessments that are useful for tracking students' progress as they study fractions. *What Do You Know About Fractions?* asks students to reflect on their learning and can be used before, during, or after instruction. *The Broth Problem*, *A Class Party*, *Sharing Apples*, and *The Pizza Problem* measure students' ability to apply their understanding of fractions to problem-solving situations. *The Comparing Game Problem*, *In-Between Fractions*, *Fraction Capture*, and *Which Fractions Will Capture?* are follow-up assessments to Chapters 5, 6, and 12. *True or False*, *Comparing Five-Eighths and Two-Thirds*, and *Does $\frac{2}{1} - \frac{10}{6} = \frac{1}{3}$?* assess students' facility with comparing and combining fractions.

Teaching Notes

In the lessons presented in this book, students work together, collaborate on solving problems, play games, talk with one another about their ideas, and listen to the ideas of others. All of this interaction fosters students' learning and helps them develop understanding and skills about fractions. However, it's also important for students to have opportunities to think on their own, practice what they've learned, and face the challenge of applying their learning to new situations. Students' individual work is key for assessing their learning progress and informing your classroom instruction.

The assessments in this section differ from the assignments I was given when studying about fractions. My experience as an elementary student mainly involved doing computations and solving word problems, with the measure of my success being the number of correct answers. While correct answers are important to the assessments in this section, equal emphasis is put on how students think. In all of the assessments, students are asked to write about their ideas and describe how they reason.

As with the lessons, I've tried all of the assessments with several classes, and I've chosen student work to serve as examples of how students have responded. Some papers show acceptable or exemplary work; other papers reveal students' confusion or partial understanding. All of their papers are useful for me both for planning further instruction for the entire class and also for providing help as needed for individual students. At times, I use specific responses from students for whole-class discussions.

You'll notice that this section doesn't follow the format of the lessons presented. No teaching directions, vignettes, or question-and-answer reflections are included. Instead, for each assessment, I've included the prompt that I gave to the students, some comments about my experience with the assignment, and samples of student work.

What Do You Know About Fractions?

PROMPT

Diagram and explain all you know about fractions so far.

Giving this assessment is effective for getting a sense of your students' understanding before, during, or after you provide instruction on fractions. Be sure to let the students know that your purpose is to learn as much as possible about what they know so that you can better decide how to provide them the help that they need. Encourage the students to give you as much information as they can. If you give the assessment before you begin instruction, it's a good idea to give it again after the students have studied about fractions. Then both you and they can compare the results. The responses in Figures 1 through 4 are from fifth graders who had experienced most of the activities from the Teaching Arithmetic book *Lessons for Introducing Fractions, Grades 4–5* and some of the activities from this book.

Diagram and explain all you know about fractions so far.

1. The bottom number in a fraction tells you how many pieces the whole was divided into. The top number tells you how many of those pieces you have.

$\frac{1}{4}$ of this square is shaded in. The 4 tells you that the whole was divided into 4 pieces. The 1 tells you how much you have.

2. The bigger the number on the bottom, the smaller the fraction is. For instance, if I have $\frac{1}{2}$ of something, the number on the bottom is 2. If I divided that in half, I have $\frac{1}{4}$. The number on the bottom is 4. 4 is more than 2, and $\frac{1}{2}$ is more than $\frac{1}{4}$.

3. You can change fractions so that the written fraction looks different, but it's really the same. For instance, if I have $\frac{1}{2}$ of something, it's the same as $\frac{2}{4}$. $\frac{1}{2}$ is the same as $\frac{2}{4}$, $\frac{4}{8}$, $\frac{12}{24}$, and lots of other fractions, just as long as the top number is $\frac{1}{2}$ of the bottom number.

▲▲▲▲▲▲Figure 1 *Katarina wrote about the meaning of fractions and about fractions that are equivalent to $\frac{1}{2}$.*

Diagram and explain all you know about fractions so far.

1. I know that the bigger denomenater the smaller the fraction piece.
denomenator→$\frac{1}{2}$ $\frac{1}{4}$←denomenater

2. I know that if you take a fraction like $\frac{1}{12}$ then add it together with another $\frac{1}{12}$ then you will always get the number that is half of the number you added. $\frac{1}{12} + \frac{1}{12} = \frac{1}{6}$

3. I know that fractions can be usefull when you're sharing things like food.
We divided the extra cookie into fourths for the 4 of u

4. I know that fractions never end because you can always make another fraction out of what you have already
The fractions keep going

5. I know that even though some fractions sound different they're really the same like $\frac{4}{5}$ is the same as $\frac{2}{10}$ and $\frac{2}{4}$ is the same as $\frac{4}{8}$
See $\frac{1}{5}$ and $\frac{2}{10}$ are the same
See $\frac{2}{4}$ and $\frac{4}{8}$ are the same

▲▲▲▲▲▲Figure 2 *In his paper, Salvador wrote about naming fractions, adding fractions, the usefulness of fractions, and equivalence.*

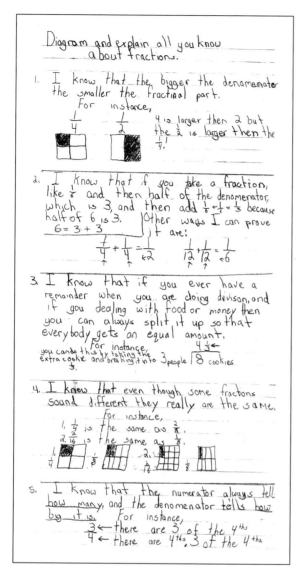

Diagram and explain all you know about fractions.

1. I know that the bigger the denomenator the smaller the fractinal part.
   For instance,

   $\frac{1}{4}$ $\frac{1}{2}$ 4 is larger then 2 but the $\frac{1}{2}$ is larger then the $\frac{1}{4}$.

2. I know that if you take a fraction, like $\frac{1}{6}$ and then half of the denomenator, which is 3, and then add $\frac{1}{6} + \frac{1}{6} = \frac{1}{3}$ because half of 6 is 3. Other ways I can prove it are:
   $6 = 3 + 3$
   $\frac{1}{4} + \frac{1}{4} = \frac{1}{2}$ $\frac{1}{12} + \frac{1}{12} = \frac{1}{6}$

3. I know that if you ever have a remainder when you are doing divison, and if you dealing with food or money then you can always split it up so that everybody gets an equal amount.
   For instance,
   you can do this by taking the extra cookie and breaking it into 3. $4\frac{1}{3}$
   3 people $\overline{\smash{)}8}$ cookies

4. I know that even though some fractions sound different they really are the same.
   For instance,
   1. $\frac{1}{4}$ is the same as $\frac{2}{8}$.
   2. $\frac{2}{16}$ is the same as $\frac{1}{8}$.

   1. $\frac{1}{4}$ $\frac{2}{8}$ 2. $\frac{2}{16}$ $\frac{1}{8}$

5. I know that the numerator always tell how many, and the denomenator tells how big it is. For instance,
   $\frac{3}{4}$ ← there are 3 of the 4ths
   ← there are 4ths, 3 of the 4ths.

▲▲▲▲▲▲**Figure 3** *In her second point, Laura explained her discovery about what happens to the denominator when adding two of the same unit fractions.*

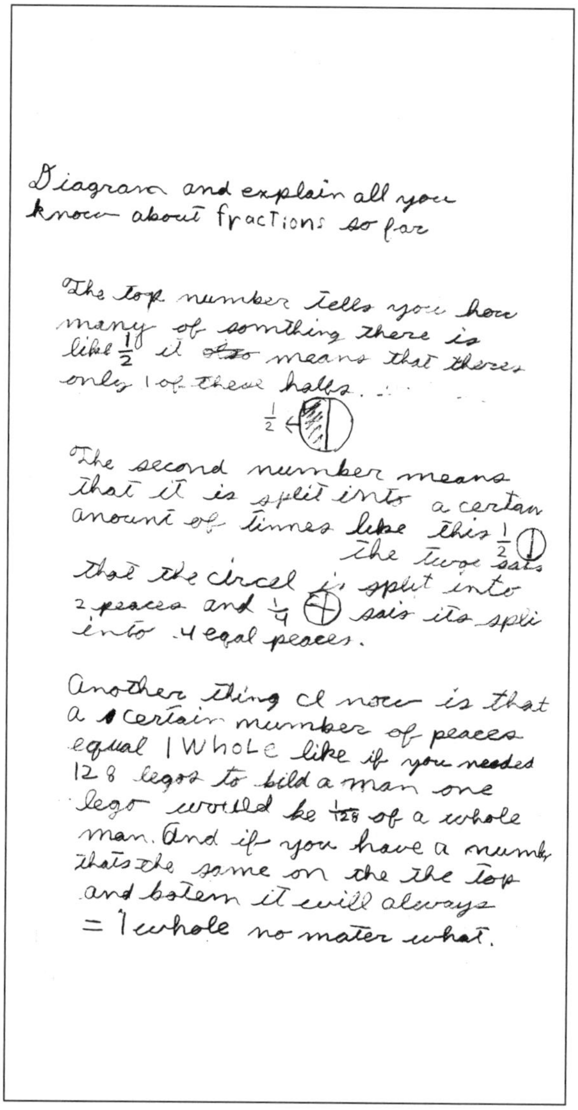

Diagram and explain all you know about fractions so far

The top number tells you how many of somthing there is like $\frac{1}{2}$ it means that theres only 1 of these halfs.
$\frac{1}{2}$

The second number means that it is split into a certan amount of times like this $\frac{1}{2}$ The two says that the circel is split into 2 peaces and $\frac{1}{4}$ says its spli into 4 equal peaces.

Another thing I noee is that a certain number of peaces equal 1 WHoLE like if you needed 128 legos to bild a man one lego would be $\frac{1}{128}$ of a whole man. And if you have a number thats the same on the the top and botem it will always = 1 whole no mater what.

▲▲▲▲▲▲**Figure 4** *Abe explained the meanings of the numerator and the denominator and then related fractions to building with Legos.*

166   Assessments

The Broth Problem

PROMPT

I was cutting a recipe in half. The recipe called for $\frac{3}{4}$ cup of broth. How much broth should I have used? Explain.

When first learning about fractions, it's typical for students to become comfortable with halves, fourths, and eighths. This assessment relies on just those fractions, presenting them in a measurement context. To solve the problem, three of the students changed $\frac{3}{4}$ to $\frac{6}{8}$. For example, Alan wrote: *Half of $\frac{3}{4}$ is $\frac{3}{8}$ because $\frac{3}{4}$ is the same as $\frac{6}{8}$, and half of $\frac{6}{8}$ is $\frac{3}{8}$.* Most students thought about $\frac{3}{4}$ as $\frac{1}{2} + \frac{1}{4}$ and found half of each part (see Elliott's solution in Figure 5). Some thought about $\frac{3}{4}$ as three $\frac{1}{4}$s (see Julio's solution in Figure 6). Five students gave the correct answer but were unable to give a clear explanation. Alec wrote: *It's $\frac{3}{8}$. I just knew. I can't explain.* Ally wrote: *$\frac{3}{8}$. I didn't need to figure it out. I just knew it. It was way to easy.* I initiated a follow-up discussion for students to share their explanations and then gave all of the students the chance to revise their explanations. This sort of practice helps students clarify and cement their understanding.

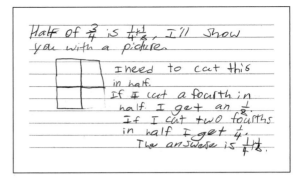

▲▲▲▲▲▲Figure 5   *Elliott drew a picture of $\frac{3}{4}$ of a square, then cut $\frac{1}{4}$ of it in half and the other $\frac{2}{4}$ of it in half.*

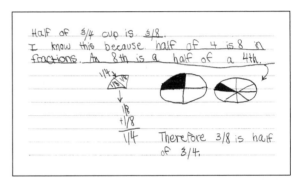

▲▲▲▲▲▲Figure 6   *Julio thought of $\frac{3}{4}$ as three $\frac{1}{4}$s and used this information to get an answer of three $\frac{1}{8}$s or $\frac{3}{8}$.*

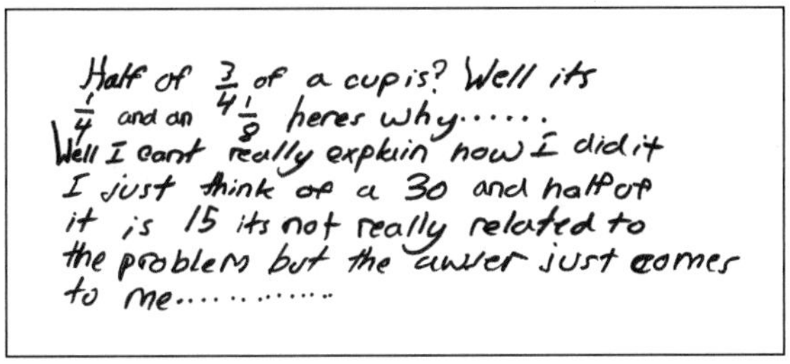

Half of $\frac{3}{4}$ of a cup is? Well its $\frac{1}{4}$ and an $4\frac{1}{8}$ heres why......
Well I cant really explain how I did it
I just think of a 30 and half of
it is 15 its not really related to
the problem but the answer just comes
to me............

▲▲▲▲▲▲Figure 7   *David was one of the students who knew the answer but couldn't explain his reasoning.*

A Class Party

PROMPT

Eight students volunteered to plan a class party. Three-fourths of them were boys. How many boys volunteered? Explain your reasoning. You can use words, numbers, and pictures.

This problem-solving assessment is appropriate after the students have experienced Chapter 3, "Balloons and Brownies." In that activity, the students find fractional parts of sets for unit fractions (one-half, one-third, one-fourth, and so on). This activity presents a similar problem for three-fourths, a fraction that isn't a unit fraction. Most of the students began solving the problem by organizing the eight students into four groups with two in each group. Three of the students began by changing three-fourths to six-eighths. Micah wrote: $\frac{3}{4} = \frac{6}{8}$, so 6 of the volunteered kids are boys and the other 2 are girls. Two students solved the problem by breaking the eight students into two groups of four each, figuring that three-fourths of each group was three students, and then combining two threes to get the answer of six (see Satya's paper in Figure 9). Griffith's solution was unique. He reasoned: $\frac{1}{2}$ of eight is 4 and $\frac{1}{2}$ of 4 is 2 and that's $\frac{1}{4}$ so $\frac{3}{4}$ would be $\frac{1}{2} + \frac{1}{4}$ and that's 4 + 2.

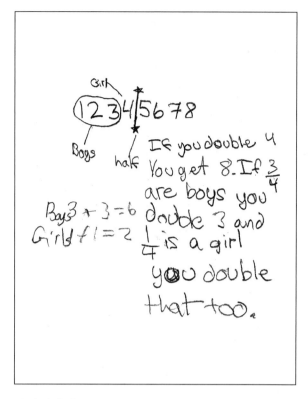

▲▲▲▲▲**Figure 9** *In her paper, Satya interpreted $\frac{3}{4}$ as 3 of the first 4 students and then 3 of the second 4 students.*

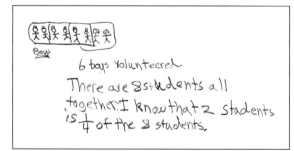

▲▲▲▲▲**Figure 8** *Niko explained that he knew that 2 students represented $\frac{1}{4}$ of the 8 students.*

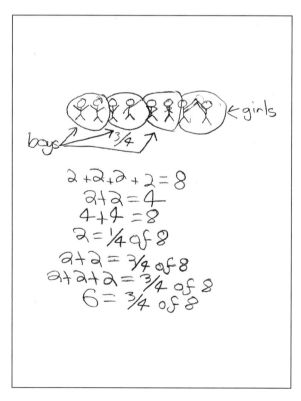

▲▲▲▲▲**Figure 10** *Tanya's explanation rested on her understanding that 2 is $\frac{1}{4}$ of 8.*

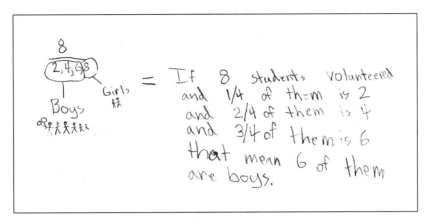

If 8 students volunteered and 1/4 of them is 2 and 2/4 of them is 4 and 3/4 of them is 6 that mean 6 of them are boys.

▲▲▲▲▲▲Figure 11   *Mac's paper showed his understanding of how to figure $\frac{1}{4}$, $\frac{2}{4}$, and $\frac{3}{4}$ of 8.*

7 Because 4 seems like the whole and the 3 is one less. So if 8 is the whole one less is 7.

BUT,

6 I also think 6 is the answer because,

6 Because, $\frac{1}{4}$ is 2 kids and $\frac{2}{4}$ is 4 kids and $\frac{3}{4}$ is 6 kids so 6 is the ANSWER

▲▲▲▲▲▲Figure 12   *Pia's confusion was evident in her first idea about why 7 could be the correct answer. She was also confused in her first explanation about why 6 could also be the answer, but she finally explained correctly why 6 was the answer. Her paper indicated that I needed to check her understanding in other ways.*

The Comparing Game Problem

PROMPT

Where would you put the numbers 2, 3, 4, and 5 to make the smallest possible fraction? (Two of the numbers go in the reject boxes.)

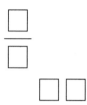

This assessment is appropriate after students have had time playing the *Comparing Game* (see Chapter 5). The students are already familiar with placing numbers in boxes to play the game, and this gives them all four numbers at one time, instead of rolling a die and writing each as it comes up.

▲▲▲▲▲▲Figure 14 *Elizabeth answered correctly, explaining her idea about "extreme" fractions.*

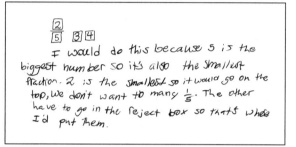

▲▲▲▲▲▲Figure 15 *Elliott's explanation was clear and correct.*

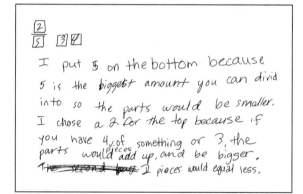

▲▲▲▲▲▲Figure 13 *Sonia's explanation about why she used the largest number for the denominator and the smallest for the numerator was typical.*

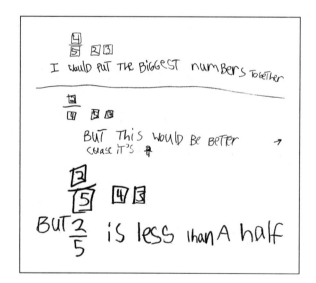

▲▲▲▲▲▲Figure 16 *Patrick gave three answers. He was the only student in the class who faltered, an indication that I needed to provide him with additional help.*

In-Between Fractions

PROMPT

Is $\frac{1}{4}$ in between $\frac{1}{2}$ and $\frac{1}{3}$? Explain.

Name a fraction that is EXACTLY halfway between $\frac{1}{2}$ and $\frac{1}{3}$. Explain.

This assessment is appropriate after the students have experienced Chapter 6, "In-Between Fractions." The students will be familiar with the assignment since they worked on a similar problem of deciding if one-fourth was in between one-sixth and one-half and then figuring out a fraction that was exactly halfway between one-sixth and one-half. In this problem, they work with the fractions one-fourth, one-third, and one-half. All but one student were clear that one-fourth is not between one-half and one-third. Many students' explanations were a variation on what

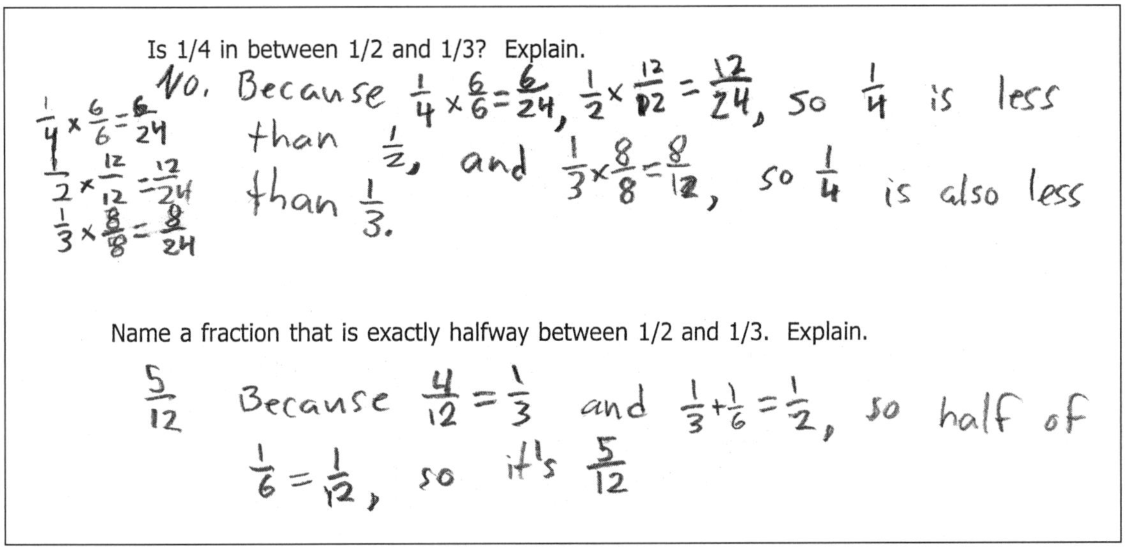

Is 1/4 in between 1/2 and 1/3? Explain.

$\frac{1}{4} \times \frac{6}{6} = \frac{6}{24}$
$\frac{1}{2} \times \frac{12}{12} = \frac{12}{24}$
$\frac{1}{3} \times \frac{8}{8} = \frac{8}{24}$

No. Because $\frac{1}{4} \times \frac{6}{6} = \frac{6}{24}$, $\frac{1}{2} \times \frac{12}{12} = \frac{12}{24}$, so $\frac{1}{4}$ is less than $\frac{1}{2}$, and $\frac{1}{3} \times \frac{8}{8} = \frac{8}{12}$, so $\frac{1}{4}$ is also less than $\frac{1}{3}$.

Name a fraction that is exactly halfway between 1/2 and 1/3. Explain.

$\frac{5}{12}$ Because $\frac{4}{12} = \frac{1}{3}$ and $\frac{1}{3} + \frac{1}{6} = \frac{1}{2}$, so half of $\frac{1}{6} = \frac{1}{12}$, so it's $\frac{5}{12}$

Figure 17 *Pedro converted the fractions to twenty-fourths to answer the first question; he used twelfths for the second question.*

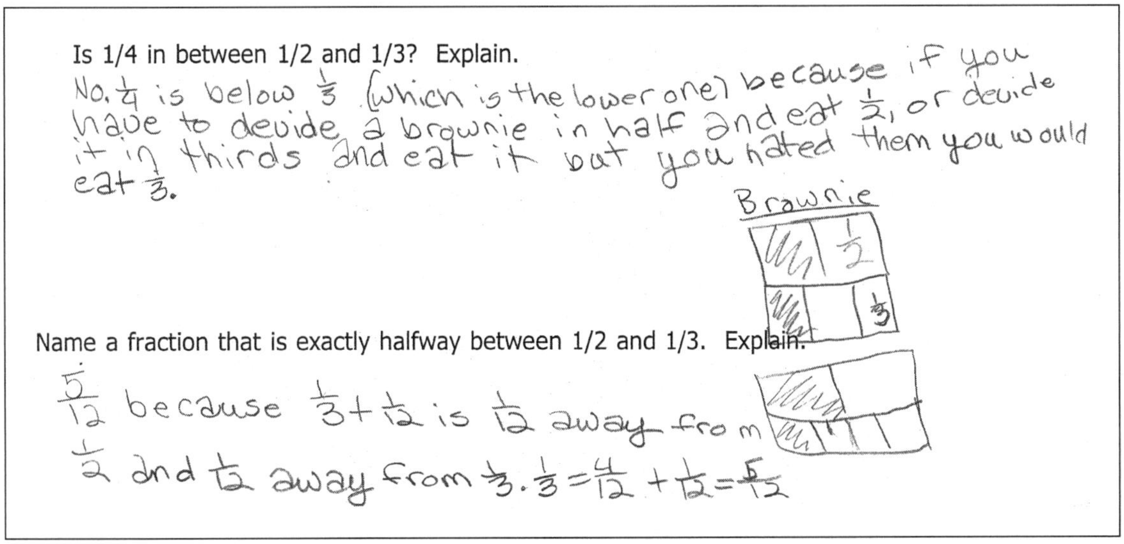

Is 1/4 in between 1/2 and 1/3? Explain.

No. $\frac{1}{4}$ is below $\frac{1}{3}$ (which is the lower one) because if you have to devide a brownie in half and eat $\frac{1}{2}$, or devide it in thirds and eat it but you hated them you would eat $\frac{1}{3}$.

Brownie

$\frac{1}{2}$

$\frac{1}{3}$

Name a fraction that is exactly halfway between 1/2 and 1/3. Explain.

$\frac{5}{12}$ because $\frac{1}{3} + \frac{1}{12}$ is $\frac{1}{12}$ away from $\frac{1}{2}$ and $\frac{1}{12}$ away from $\frac{1}{3}$. $\frac{1}{3} = \frac{4}{12} + \frac{1}{12} = \frac{5}{12}$

Figure 18 *Annie referred to brownies to answer the first question. While her answer was correct, her reasoning was not complete.*

Francis wrote: *No because $\frac{1}{3}$ is bigger than $\frac{1}{4}$ and so is $\frac{1}{2}$ bigger than $\frac{1}{4}$.* Another common explanation was expressed by David: *No. Because they all have a numerater of 1 and $\frac{1}{4}$ has a bigger denominator which means it's the smallest.*

Finding the fraction that was exactly halfway between one-half and one-third posed more of a challenge, but all but four students answered correctly. The student examples (Figures 17 through 20) show a variety of explanations.

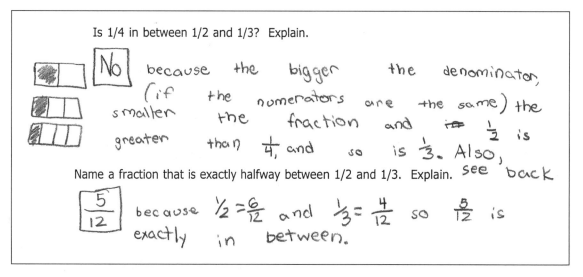

Is 1/4 in between 1/2 and 1/3? Explain.

No because the bigger the denominator, (if the numerators are the same) the smaller the fraction and $\frac{1}{2}$ is greater than $\frac{1}{4}$, and so is $\frac{1}{3}$. Also, see back

Name a fraction that is exactly halfway between 1/2 and 1/3. Explain.

$\frac{5}{12}$ because $\frac{1}{2} = \frac{6}{12}$ and $\frac{1}{3} = \frac{4}{12}$ so $\frac{5}{12}$ is exactly in between.

▲▲▲▲▲▲Figure 19 *Celia's answers were clear, concise, and correct.*

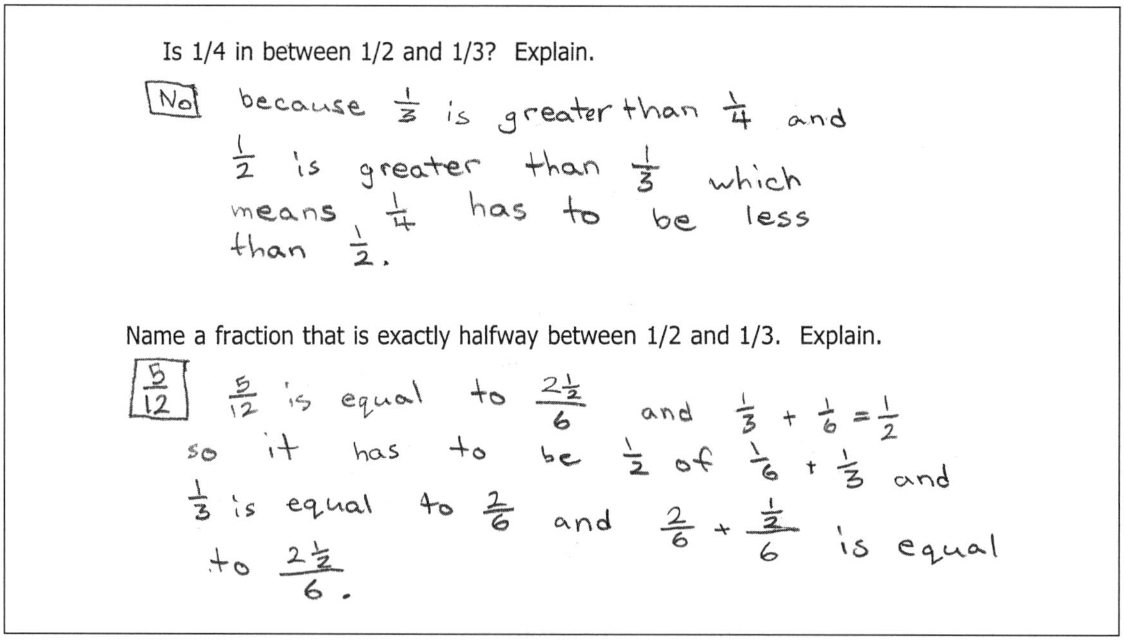

Is 1/4 in between 1/2 and 1/3? Explain.

No because $\frac{1}{3}$ is greater than $\frac{1}{4}$ and $\frac{1}{2}$ is greater than $\frac{1}{3}$ which means $\frac{1}{4}$ has to be less than $\frac{1}{2}$.

Name a fraction that is exactly halfway between 1/2 and 1/3. Explain.

$\frac{5}{12}$ $\frac{5}{12}$ is equal to $\frac{2\frac{1}{2}}{6}$ and $\frac{1}{3} + \frac{1}{6} = \frac{1}{2}$ so it has to be $\frac{1}{2}$ of $\frac{1}{6} + \frac{1}{3}$ and $\frac{1}{3}$ is equal to $\frac{2}{6}$ and $\frac{2}{6} + \frac{\frac{1}{2}}{6}$ is equal to $\frac{2\frac{1}{2}}{6}$.

▲▲▲▲▲▲Figure 20 *To answer the second question, Katia used complex fractions, representing $\frac{5}{12}$ as $\frac{2\frac{1}{2}}{6}$ and $\frac{1}{12}$ as $\frac{\frac{1}{2}}{6}$.*

True or False

PROMPT

Decide if each of the following statements is true or false. Explain your reasoning.

▲ $\frac{1}{8}$ *is* $\frac{1}{2}$ *of* $\frac{1}{4}$.
▲ $\frac{5}{8}$ *is greater than* $\frac{1}{2}$.
▲ $\frac{2}{2}$ *is* $\frac{8}{8}$.
▲ $\frac{1}{2} - \frac{1}{8} = \frac{3}{8}$.

Write the prompt on the board. Tell the students that for each statement, they should explain their reasoning using words, diagrams, and/or numbers and also indicate for each if it was too easy, just right, or too hard. For this assessment, I chose four statements that all were true. I repeated the assessment from time to time, sometimes including sentences that were false.

In this class, papers from five of the twenty-nine students showed either weaknesses or misunderstandings, which gave me information about further work they needed to do. Several students found the statements, as Andrew expressed, "Way too easy!" Most, but not all, of the students included sketches in their explanations, some using circles for all, some using rectangles for all, and some using a combination. I looked through the papers for ideas for follow-up class discussions.

Teachers have asked me why I sometimes ask students to indicate whether the difficulty of an assignment was easy, medium, or hard. I use assessments not only to learn as much as I can about what students are learning but also to assess my instructional choices. Asking students to evaluate the difficulty of an assignment gives me feedback about the appropriateness of the assignment and about students' attitudes toward it. It's a technique I use from time to time when I'm not quite sure that an assignment matches students' understanding or level of confidence.

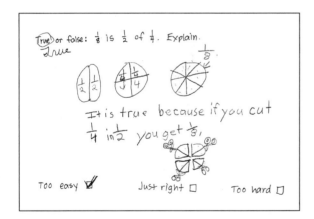

▲▲▲▲▲▲**Figure 21** *Dolores visualized cutting quarter pieces of a circle in half to get eighths.*

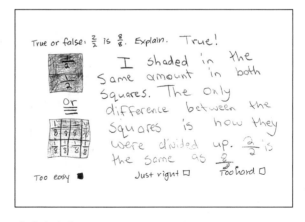

▲▲▲▲▲▲**Figure 22** *Andrea was confident that $\frac{2}{2}$ and $\frac{8}{8}$ both equal one whole.*

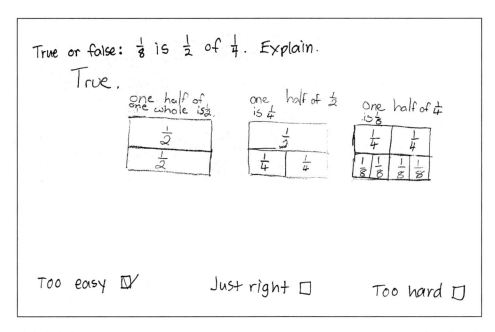

True or false: $\frac{1}{8}$ is $\frac{1}{2}$ of $\frac{1}{4}$. Explain.

True.

one half of one whole is $\frac{1}{2}$.

$\frac{1}{2}$
$\frac{1}{2}$

one half of $\frac{1}{2}$ is $\frac{1}{4}$

$\frac{1}{2}$	
$\frac{1}{4}$	$\frac{1}{4}$

One half of $\frac{1}{4}$ is $\frac{1}{8}$

$\frac{1}{4}$		$\frac{1}{4}$	
$\frac{1}{8}$	$\frac{1}{8}$	$\frac{1}{8}$	$\frac{1}{8}$

Too easy ☑   Just right ☐   Too hard ☐

▲▲▲▲▲▲Figure 23   *Diego included three drawings to explain that $\frac{1}{8}$ is $\frac{1}{2}$ of $\frac{1}{4}$.*

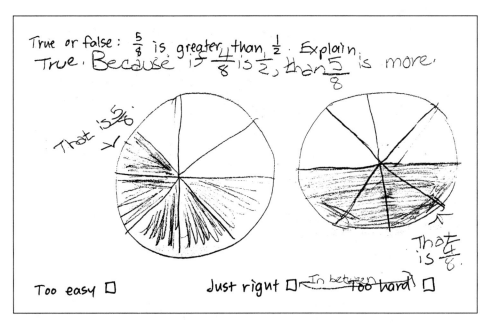

True or false: $\frac{5}{8}$ is greater than $\frac{1}{2}$. Explain.
True. Because if $\frac{4}{8}$ is $\frac{1}{2}$, than $\frac{5}{8}$ is more.

That is $\frac{5}{8}$

That is $\frac{4}{8}$.

Too easy ☐   Just right ☐ ← In between → Too hard ☐

▲▲▲▲▲▲Figure 24   *Cara divided a circle to explain why $\frac{5}{8}$ is greater than $\frac{1}{2}$. She felt the problem was in between "just right" and "too hard."*

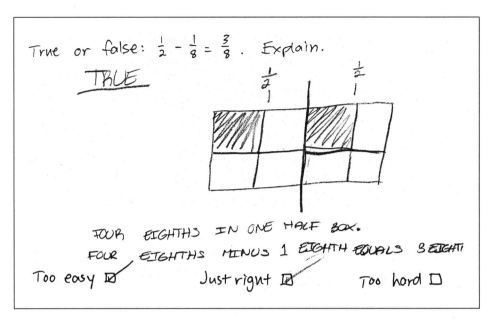

▲▲▲▲▲▲Figure 25 Darryl explained clearly why $\frac{1}{2} - \frac{1}{8} = \frac{3}{8}$. He first rated the problem "just right" but then changed his opinion to "too easy."

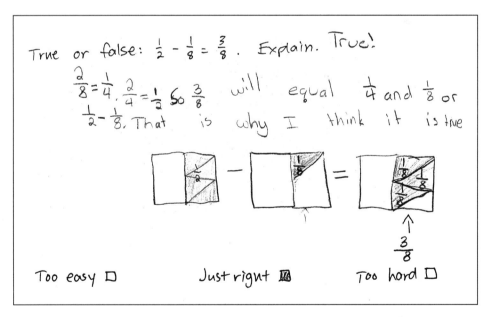

▲▲▲▲▲▲Figure 26 Sonya illustrated $\frac{1}{2} - \frac{1}{8}$ by dividing rectangles.

Sharing Apples

PROMPT

At one table, four people were given three apples to share equally. At another table, six people were given four apples to share equally. Where would you sit to get more apple? Explain.

This assessment asks students to apply their understanding of fractions to a problem-solving situation. To figure out the answer, practically all of the students drew pictures, figured out a person's share at each table, and used this information to answer the question. However, their explanations differed. One student, Alan, solved the problem without referring to fractional parts. He wrote:

> *At table 1 there are four people and 3 apples. But at table 2 they have 4 apples*

and six people. So instead of having 1 person more than there are apples at table 1, there are 2 more people than there are apples. (See Figure 29.)

Libby figured out each person's share by cutting the apples at the first table into four pieces (since there were four people) and cutting the apples at the second table into six pieces (since there were six people). She wrote:

> *At table 1 each person gets $\frac{1}{4}$ of an apple so $\frac{1}{4} + \frac{1}{4} + \frac{1}{4} = \frac{3}{4}$. Each person at table two gets $\frac{1}{6}$ of an apple so $\frac{1}{6} + \frac{1}{6} + \frac{1}{6} + \frac{1}{6} = \frac{4}{6}$. These people get more pieces but they are smaller. I think table #1 will get more because you only need one more apple for everyone to have a whole apple and at table #2 you need 2 more for everyone to have an apple.*

Three students answered that both tables would get the same amount; the others all answered the question correctly.

▲▲▲▲▲▲Figure 27 *Sadie drew each person's share and concluded that the people at the smaller table would get more apple.*

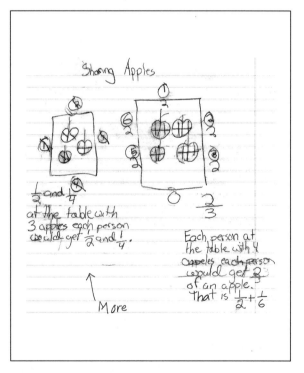

▲▲▲▲▲▲Figure 28 *Kendra's argument was that people at the small table would get $\frac{1}{2} + \frac{1}{4}$ of an apple while people at the large table would get $\frac{1}{2} + \frac{1}{6}$ of an apple.*

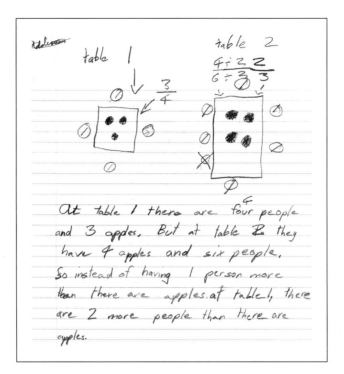

At table 1 there are four people and 3 apples. But at table 2 they have 4 apples and six people. So instead of having 1 person more than there are apples. at table 1, there are 2 more people than there are apples.

▲▲▲▲▲▲Figure 29 *Alan didn't use fractions in his explanation about why people at the small table got more apple.*

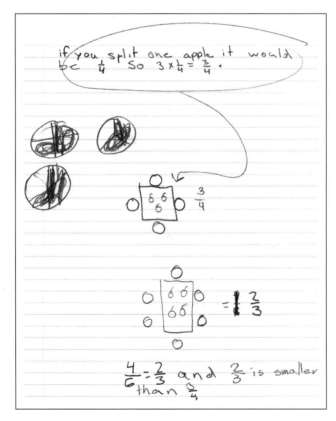

if you split one apple it would be $\frac{1}{4}$ So $3 \times \frac{1}{4} = \frac{3}{4}$.

$\frac{4}{6} = \frac{2}{3}$ and $\frac{2}{3}$ is smaller than $\frac{3}{4}$

▲▲▲▲▲▲Figure 30 *Tamika explained that people at the larger table got less apple because $\frac{2}{3}$ is smaller than $\frac{3}{4}$.*

The Pizza Problem
PROMPT

If a pizza is $\frac{1}{2}$ cheese, $\frac{1}{10}$ sausage, $\frac{1}{5}$ mushroom, and the rest anchovies, how much of the pizza is anchovies? Solve the problem. You must use words and numbers; you may also include a picture.

This is another assessment that I find useful both before beginning instruction and after the students have had some experiences. I gave this problem to a class of fifth graders who were comfortable representing fractional parts of circles and understood equivalence of fractions that were halves, fourths, eighths, and sixteenths. However, they hadn't had

a good deal of experience thinking about equivalent fractions with other denominators. The problem was accessible to about two-thirds of the class and gave me information about the additional work they needed with comparing fractions with other denominators.

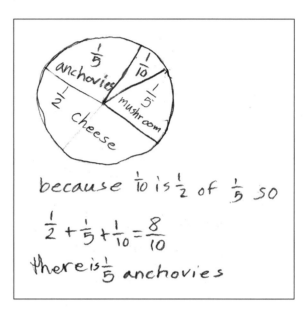

▲▲▲▲▲▲Figure 33 *Hannah was one of the few students who didn't divide her pizza into tenths or fifths. Her paper showed her ability to add $\frac{1}{2} + \frac{1}{5} + \frac{1}{10}$.*

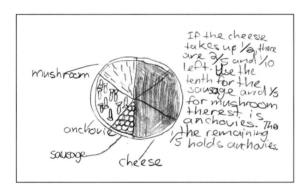

▲▲▲▲▲▲Figure 31 *Tara reasoned that if $\frac{1}{2}$ of the pizza was cheese, then she could think of the remaining $\frac{1}{2}$ as $\frac{2}{5}$ plus $\frac{1}{10}$. Her explanation and drawing were clear.*

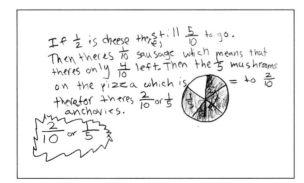

▲▲▲▲▲▲Figure 32 *While he didn't use the notation of subtraction, Nicholas did successive subtractions to solve the problem.*

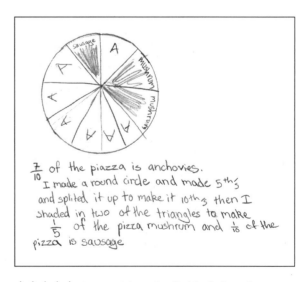

▲▲▲▲▲▲Figure 34 *Pia divided the pizza into tenths. While she correctly showed that two of the tenths represented the $\frac{1}{5}$ that was mushroom, she didn't account for the $\frac{1}{2}$ of the pizza that was cheese and, therefore, arrived at an incorrect answer.*

While including a picture was an option, every student chose to do so, seeing the drawing as an assist to solving the problem. About a third of the students divided the pizza they drew into tenths, most of the rest divided it into fifths, and two divided it the way Hannah did (see Figure 33). Pia forgot to account for the half of the pizza that had cheese and was the only student who arrived at the wrong answer (see Figure 34).

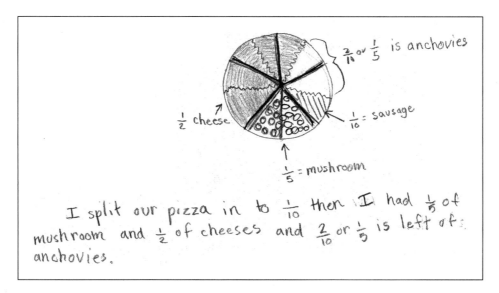

$\frac{2}{10}$ or $\frac{1}{5}$ is anchovies

$\frac{1}{2}$ cheese

$\frac{1}{10}$ = sausage

$\frac{1}{5}$ = mushroom

I split our pizza in to $\frac{1}{10}$ then I had $\frac{1}{5}$ of mushroom and $\frac{1}{2}$ of cheeses and $\frac{2}{10}$ or $\frac{1}{5}$ is left of anchovies.

▲▲▲▲▲▲Figure 35 *Jamila was another student who divided the pizza into tenths. She correctly assigned each portion and figured the answer that $\frac{2}{10}$ or $\frac{1}{5}$ of the pizza was anchovies.*

Fraction Capture

PROMPT

Write about what you think about the game of Fraction Capture. *Use the following questions for ideas:*

- ▲ *What did you like about playing the game* Fraction Capture?
- ▲ *What did you find confusing when you were playing?*
- ▲ *What strategies did you use?*
- ▲ *What do you think* Fraction Capture *can help a student learn?*

It's useful at times to get feedback from students about how they responded to an activity. This kind of information can help you assess students' attitudes toward and feelings about their learning experiences. Also, in the course of their writing, students often reveal information about the mathematics about which they are uncertain. This assessment is appropriate after students have learned how to play *Fraction Capture* (see Chapter 12).

I liked how you could fill in someone's circle if they didnt get more than half. But that was also hard if you didn't have the same denominator.
Nothing really confused me. I just liked playing the game.
I diant really have a strategy but if they didn't fill more than half a circle, I'd always try to fill it in somehow.
The game could help you if you were just starting to learn about fractions. I thought it was pretty easy.

▲▲▲▲▲Figure 36 ***Midori responded to each of the four questions I posed and indicated that the game was easy for her.***

I liked this game because it was a very good game for using fractions. It was very complecated when you could add one you have to change the circle. My stratagy was to talk to the dice and that seems to work. This game is good for fractions and how to draw them.

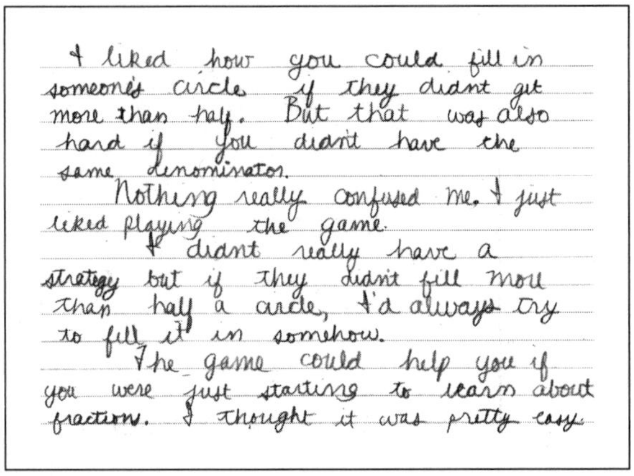

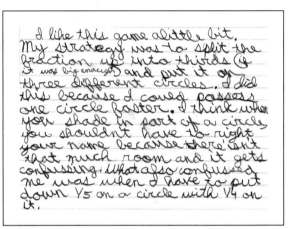

▲▲▲▲▲Figure 37 ***Letitia felt that the game was helpful for learning to draw fractions.***

I like this game alittle bit. My strategy was to split the fraction up into thirds (if it was big enough) and put it on three different circles. I did this because I coued passes one circle faster. I think when you shade in part of a circle you shouldn't have to right your name because there isn't that much room and it gets confussing. What also confused me was when I have to put down 1/5 on a circle with 1/4 on it.

▲▲▲▲▲Figure 38 ***Dario, who tended to write his letters and numbers large, was frustrated because he felt that there wasn't enough room on the worksheet. Also, he indicated his difficulty adding $\frac{1}{5}$ on to a circle with $\frac{1}{4}$ already shaded.***

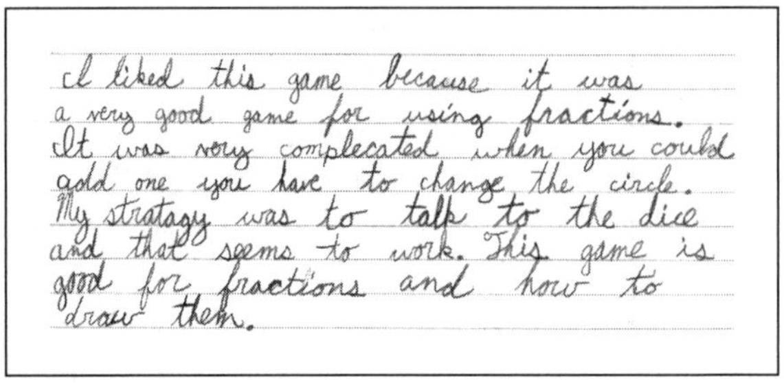

Which Fractions Will Capture?

PROMPT

If a circle has $\frac{1}{4}$ shaded, which of these fractions will result in a capture—$\frac{1}{3}$, $\frac{1}{6}$, $\frac{3}{8}$, $\frac{1}{4}$?

As with the previous assessment, this is appropriate after students have had experience playing *Fraction Capture* (see Chapter 12). Write the prompt on the board and ask the students to copy it on their papers and answer it. Tell the students to use words, numbers, and drawings to explain their reasoning for each fraction.

In this class, most of the students came to the conclusion that one-third and three-eighths would result in a capture while one-sixth and one-fourth would not. However, their reasons differed. For

why one-third would capture, for example, some students figured out that one-fourth plus one-third equals seven-twelfths. Kendra did this and wrote: $\frac{7}{12}$ *is more than a half* (see Figure 39). Tamika also did this but explained that seven-twelfths was more than one-half by writing: $\frac{7}{12} = \frac{3.5}{6}$. Manuel reasoned: $\frac{1}{3}$ *will work because $\frac{1}{4} + \frac{1}{4} = \frac{1}{2}$ and it would not capture but $\frac{1}{3}$ is more than $\frac{1}{4}$ so it does*. Some students relied on sketches. Libby, for example, wrote: $\frac{1}{3}$ *will capture because when you color it in it is more than half as you can visually see*.

For follow-up assessments, I used the following prompts:

If a circle has $\frac{1}{6}$ shaded, which of these fractions will result in a capture—$\frac{1}{3}$, $\frac{1}{4}$, $\frac{2}{4}$, $\frac{2}{5}$? Explain your reasoning for each.

If a circle has $\frac{1}{3}$ shaded, which of these fractions will result in a capture—$\frac{1}{5}$, $\frac{1}{4}$, $\frac{2}{6}$, $\frac{2}{5}$? Explain your reasoning for each.

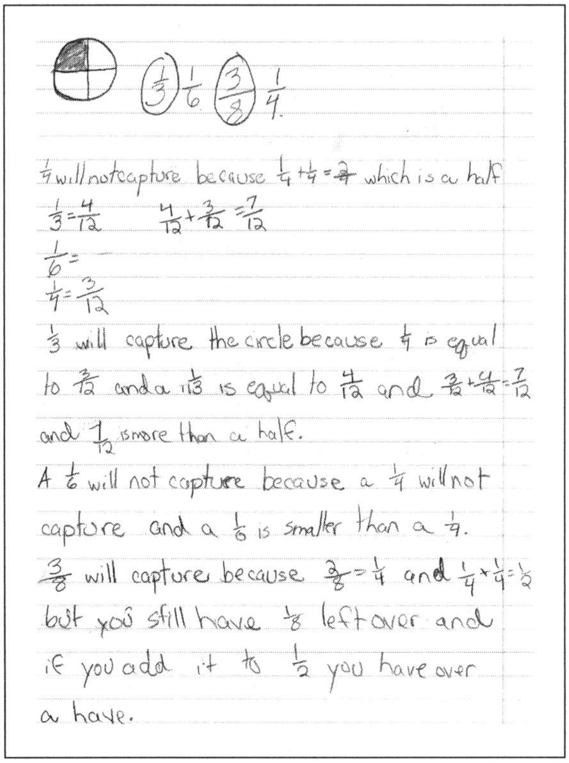

▲▲▲▲▲▲**Figure 39** *Kendra's explanations were clear and correct.*

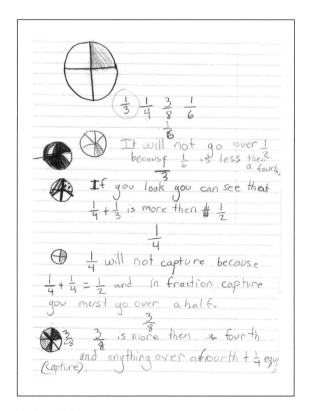

▲▲▲▲▲▲**Figure 40** *Carlotta relied on her sketches to explain her reasoning.*

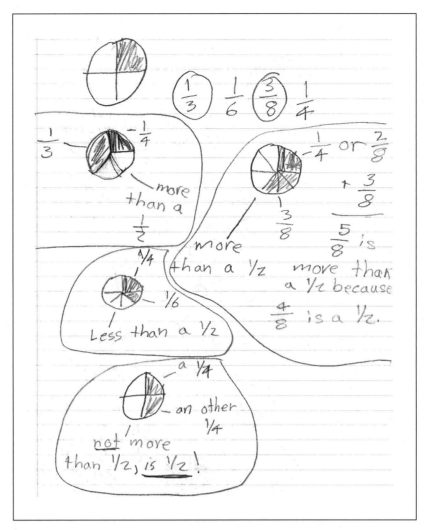

Figure 41 *Sadie used only sketches to explain why $\frac{1}{3}$ would work and $\frac{1}{6}$ would not. For $\frac{3}{8}$ and $\frac{1}{4}$ she also included written explanations.*

Comparing Five-Eighths and Two-Thirds

PROMPT

Is this true or false: $\frac{5}{8} = \frac{2}{3}$? Explain.

While students generally develop proficiency comparing unit fractions (one-half, one-third, one-fourth, and so on), learning to compare other fractions is more complicated. And comparing fractions where one denominator isn't a multiple of the other adds to the difficulty for some students. It's useful to vary the fractions and give an assessment like this one from time to time.

The students' explanations differed. A common strategy was to compare both fractions to one-half. Juan, for example, wrote:

I think that $\frac{2}{3}$ is bigger because $\frac{1}{3} + \frac{1}{6}$ is equal to $\frac{1}{2}$ so if you add $\frac{1}{6}$ more you get $\frac{2}{3}$ wich means $\frac{2}{3}$ is $\frac{1}{6}$ over a $\frac{1}{2}$. $\frac{5}{8}$ is $\frac{1}{8}$ over $\frac{1}{2}$ and $\frac{1}{8}$ is smaller than $\frac{1}{6}$ so $\frac{2}{3}$ is bigger than $\frac{5}{8}$.

Other students changed the fractions to twenty-fourths, comparing sixteen–twenty-fourths to fifteen–twenty-fourths to decide that two-thirds is larger. Nick gave this argument a unique twist. He wrote: $\frac{15}{24} = 7\frac{\frac{1}{2}}{12}$ which is almost a $\frac{2}{3}$ ($\frac{8}{12}$). A few students changed the fractions so that they had the same numerators—$\frac{10}{16}$ and $\frac{10}{15}$.

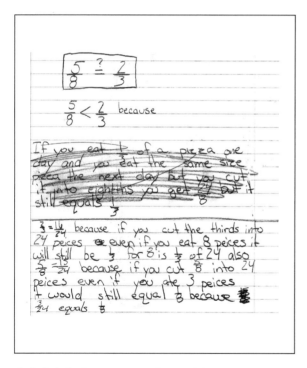

▲▲▲▲▲▲**Figure 42** *After a false start, Indira changed both fractions to twenty-fourths.*

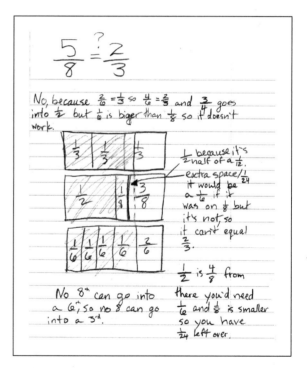

▲▲▲▲▲▲**Figure 43** *Althea used pictures and a written explanation to relate the fractions to $\frac{1}{2}$.*

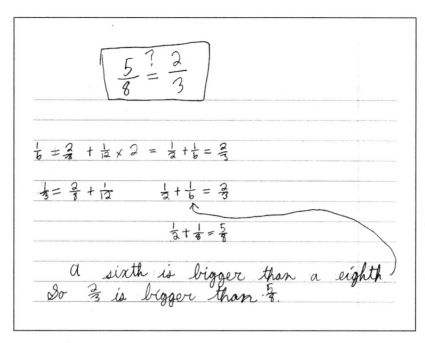

▲▲▲▲▲▲**Figure 44** *Angelo explained numerically how much more each fraction was than* $\frac{1}{2}$.

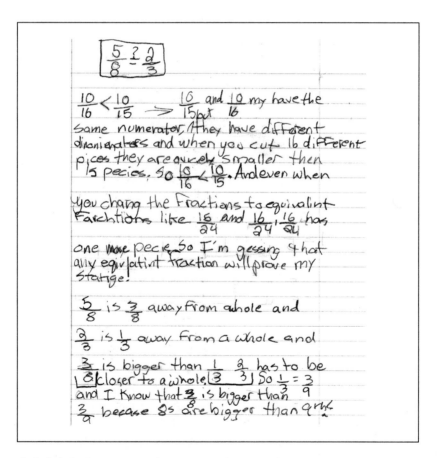

▲▲▲▲▲▲**Figure 45** *Eliana gave three explanations, first changing the fractions to equivalent fractions with the common numerator of 10, then changing them to equivalent fractions with the common denominator of 24, and finally explaining that* $\frac{2}{3}$ *is closer to 1 whole and, therefore, is larger.*

Does $\frac{2}{1} - \frac{10}{6} = \frac{1}{3}$?

PROMPT

A student reasoned that $\frac{2}{1} - \frac{10}{6} = \frac{1}{3}$. Do you think the student is right? Explain your reasoning.

A student, Claudia, produced this problem after experiencing the lessons *Exploring Fractions with Pattern Blocks* and *How*

Much Is Blue? A Pattern Block Activity (see the Teaching Arithmetic book *Lessons for Introducing Fractions, Grades 4–5*, Chapters 4 and 12). Her idea sparked a wonderful class discussion at the time, and since then I've used it as an assessment. It's not necessary for students to be familiar with pattern blocks in order for this to be a useful assessment. In this class, two students referred to pattern blocks pieces while others relied on other ways to reason.

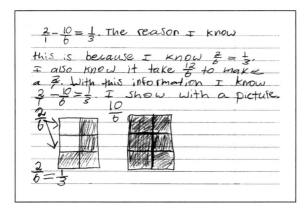

▲▲▲▲▲▲Figure 46   *Eduardo's explanation was clear and concise.*

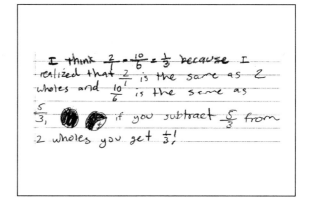

▲▲▲▲▲▲Figure 48   *Lily changed the problem to $2 - \frac{5}{3}$; she drew circles to show her reasoning.*

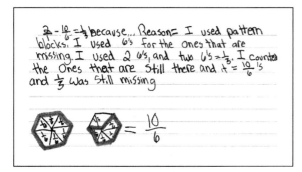

▲▲▲▲▲▲Figure 47   *Gabe referred to pattern blocks and found that two $\frac{1}{6}$ pieces were missing from covering two wholes. He knew that $\frac{2}{6} = \frac{1}{3}$.*

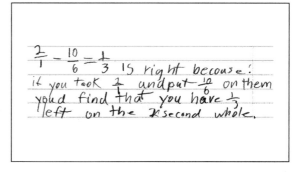

▲▲▲▲▲▲Figure 49   *William did not include any drawings with his explanation.*

BLACKLINE MASTERS

Fractions on Grids
(4-by-4 Squares)

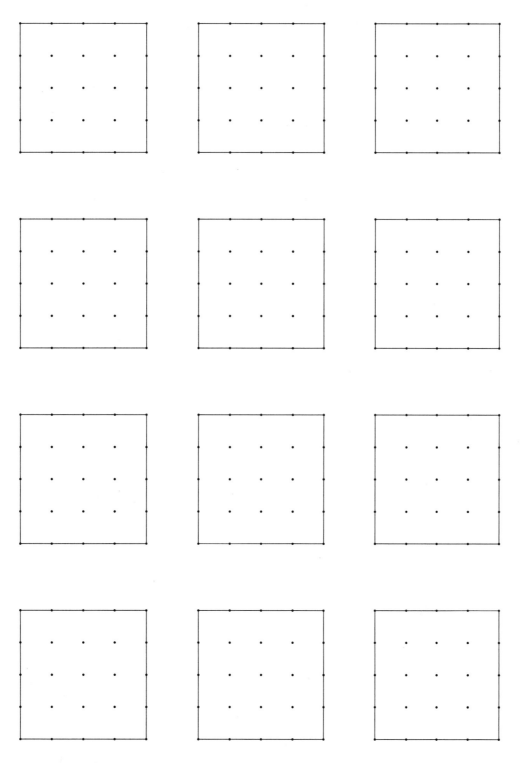

Fractions on Grids
(6-by-4 Squares)

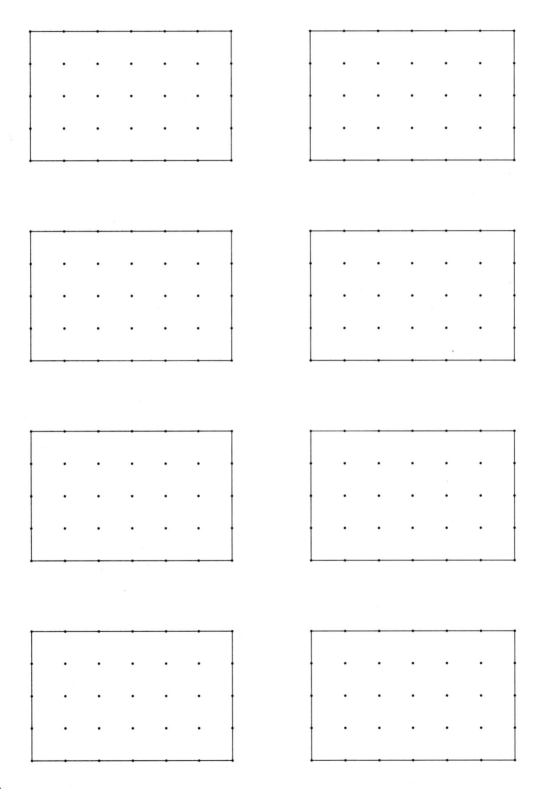

From *Lessons for Extending Fractions, Grade 5* by Marilyn Burns. © 2003 Math Solutions Publications

Large 4-by-4 Grids

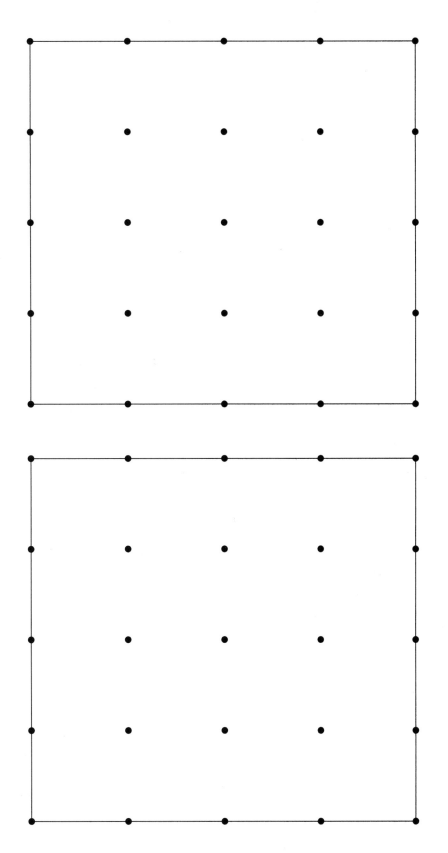

Large 6-by-4 Grids

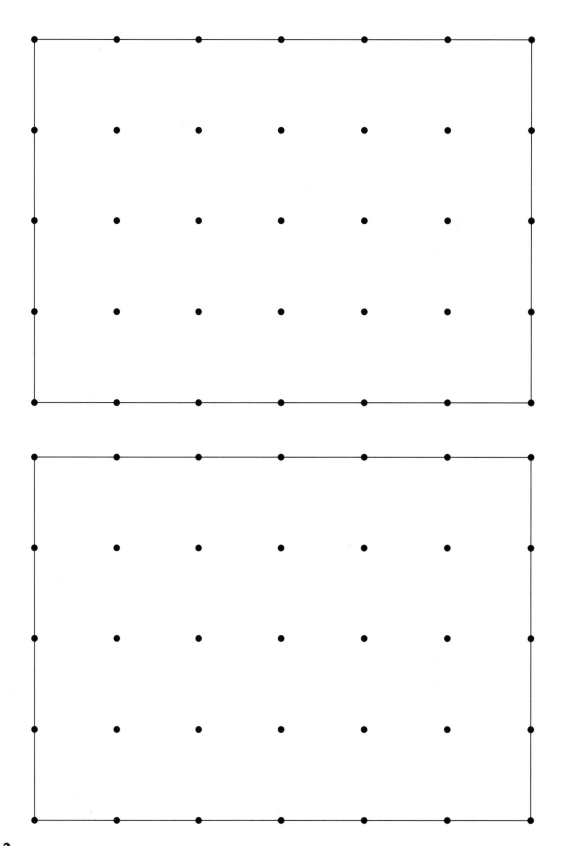

From *Lessons for Extending Fractions, Grade 5* by Marilyn Burns. © 2003 Math Solutions Publications

	Balloons	Brownies
$\frac{1}{2}$		
$\frac{1}{3}$		
$\frac{1}{4}$		
$\frac{1}{5}$		
$\frac{1}{6}$		
$\frac{1}{8}$		
$\frac{1}{10}$		
$\frac{1}{12}$		

Fractions and Venn Diagrams

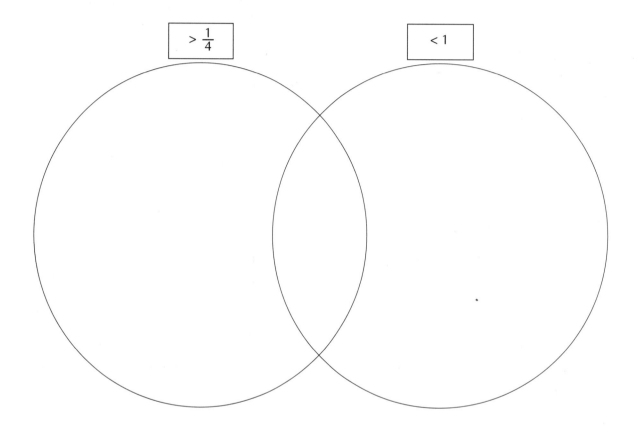

Write at least three fractions in each section of the Venn diagram. Choose one fraction from each section and explain below how you know it's in the correct place.

 From *Lessons for Extending Fractions, Grade 5* by Marilyn Burns. © 2003 Math Solutions Publications

The Comparing Game Rules

You need:
  a partner
  a die, a 1–10 spinner, or a bag with slips of paper numbered 1 to 10

Rules

1. Each player draws a game board as shown.

2. Players take turns rolling the die (or spinning the spinner, or drawing a number from the bag) and writing the number in one of the spaces on the game board. Once a number is written, it cannot be changed. The boxes to the side are reject boxes for numbers you don't want to use in your fraction.

3. When you have written a number, pass the die, spinner, or bag of numbers to the other player.

4. Play until both players have recorded a fraction. (One or both of your reject boxes may be empty if you used your rolls to complete your fraction.)

5. Compare fractions to see whose is larger. Make drawings to show the fractions, first agreeing on the shape to use for the whole.

6. Write a math sentence to show whose fraction is larger (for example, $\frac{3}{4} > \frac{2}{3}$).

7. Play at least three rounds.

Version 1: The larger fraction wins.
Version 2: The smaller fraction wins.
Version 3: The fraction closer to one-half wins.
Version 4: The fraction closer to one wins.

In-Between Fractions

Is $\frac{1}{4}$ in between $\frac{1}{6}$ and $\frac{1}{2}$? Explain.

Name a fraction that is EXACTLY halfway between $\frac{1}{6}$ and $\frac{1}{2}$. Explain.

    From *Lessons for Extending Fractions, Grade 5* by Marilyn Burns. © 2003 Math Solutions Publications

The Orange Problems

Three friends were eating oranges.

David ate $\frac{3}{8}$ of an orange.

Elissa ate $\frac{1}{4}$ of an orange.

Freda ate $\frac{1}{2}$ of an orange.

How many oranges did they have? _____

How much is left? Explain your thinking. _____

Three friends were eating oranges.

George ate $\frac{2}{3}$ of an orange.

Hiro ate $\frac{3}{4}$ of an orange.

Ian ate $\frac{1}{2}$ of an orange.

How many oranges did they have? _____

How much is left? Explain your thinking. _____

Three friends were eating oranges.

Jamaal ate $\frac{1}{8}$ of an orange.

Katie ate $\frac{1}{3}$ of an orange.

Laura ate $\frac{1}{2}$ of an orange.

How many oranges did they have? _____

How much is left? Explain your thinking. _____

Make a One

1. $\dfrac{\square}{\square} + \dfrac{\square}{\square} + \dfrac{\square}{\square} + \dfrac{\square}{\square} + \dfrac{\square}{\square} = 1$

— Round 1

2. $\dfrac{\square}{\square} + \dfrac{\square}{\square} + \dfrac{\square}{\square} + \dfrac{\square}{\square} + \dfrac{\square}{\square} = 1$

— Round 2

3. $\dfrac{\square}{\square} + \dfrac{\square}{\square} + \dfrac{\square}{\square} + \dfrac{\square}{\square} + \dfrac{\square}{\square} = 1$

— Round 3

4. $\dfrac{\square}{\square} + \dfrac{\square}{\square} + \dfrac{\square}{\square} + \dfrac{\square}{\square} + \dfrac{\square}{\square} = 1$

— Round 4

5. $\dfrac{\square}{\square} + \dfrac{\square}{\square} + \dfrac{\square}{\square} + \dfrac{\square}{\square} + \dfrac{\square}{\square} = 1$

— Round 5

Total Score _____

 From *Lessons for Extending Fractions, Grade 5* by Marilyn Burns. © 2003 Math Solutions Publications

Make a One Rules

You need:
   deck of forty cards, ten each of 1s, 2s, 4s, and 8s (for
   Version 1)
   deck of forty cards, ten each of 1s, 3s, 6s, and 12s (for
   Version 2)
   Make a One worksheet
   a partner and another pair to play with

Rules for Version 1
1. One person mixes the Version 1 deck of cards and
    leaves them facedown.
2. Each pair takes ten cards.
3. Try to use as many of your cards as you can to make
    fractions that add to one. Write the fractions on your
    worksheet and fill in your score. You score one point for
    each box you fill in when making your fractions.
4. When everyone has completed the round, return to Step
    1 and continue.
5. Play five rounds and figure your total score. The team
    with the highest score wins.

Rules for Version 2
Play the same way as you do for Version 1, but use the
Version 2 deck of cards.

Rules for Version 3
Play the same way as you do for Versions 1 and 2, but shuffle both decks of cards together.

From *Lessons for Extending Fractions, Grade 5* by Marilyn Burns. © 2003 Math Solutions Publications

Fraction Capture

 From *Lessons for Extending Fractions, Grade 5* by Marilyn Burns. © 2003 Math Solutions Publications

Fraction Capture Rules

You need:
  Fraction Capture worksheet
  two dice
  pencils or thin markers in two different colors
  a partner

Rules for Version 1
1. Each player uses a different color pencil or marker.

2. Take turns rolling the dice. On your turn, use the numbers that come up to make a fraction that is less than or equal to one. If a 5 comes up on one or both of the dice, replace it with an 8. For example, if you roll a 3 and a 5, the fraction you use is $\frac{3}{8}$.

3. Draw and shade in a pie-shaped piece equal to your fraction in one of the circles. You may do this in a blank circle or add to a circle that already has a shaded piece. Record your fraction outside the circle. For example:

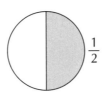

4. If you wish, you may shade parts of more than one circle on your turn. For example, if your number is $\frac{2}{3}$, you may either color $\frac{2}{3}$ of one circle or $\frac{1}{3}$ of one circle and $\frac{1}{3}$ of another circle. You can only split a fraction by keeping the same denominator; that is, you can't split $\frac{2}{3}$ into $\frac{1}{6}$ and $\frac{3}{6}$, even though $\frac{4}{6}$ is equivalent to $\frac{2}{3}$.

5. When you've shaded in more than half of any circle, write your initial beside it to show that you have captured it.

6. The winner is the player who captures more circles.

Rules for Version 2
Play the same way as you do for Version 1 except that when you roll a 5, do not substitute an 8 for it. For example, if you roll a 3 and a 5, the fraction you use is $\frac{3}{5}$.

From *Lessons for Extending Fractions, Grade 5* by Marilyn Burns. © 2003 Math Solutions Publications

Score the Difference

Round 1

Round 2

Round 3

Round 4

	Scores	
Names		
Round 1		
Round 2		
Round 3		
Round 4		
TOTALS		

Score the Difference Rules

You need:
  a partner
  a die

Rules
1. You need a game board for four rounds like this:

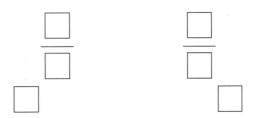

2. Players take turns rolling the die and writing the number in one of their spaces on the game board. Once a number is written, it cannot be changed. The boxes to the side are reject boxes that give you one chance to write a number that you don't want to use in your fraction.

3. After writing a number, pass the die to the other player.

4. Play until both players have recorded a fraction. (Your reject box may be empty if you used your first two numbers to make a fraction.)

5. Whoever has the smaller fraction wins the round and scores the difference between the two fractions.

6. After four rounds, total your scores. Whoever has the larger total is the winner.

The Smaller Answer Wins

Round 1 $\dfrac{\square}{\square} + \dfrac{\square}{\square} =$ $\qquad$ $\dfrac{\square}{\square} + \dfrac{\square}{\square} =$

$\square$ $\qquad\qquad\qquad\qquad\qquad\qquad\qquad\qquad$ $\square$

Round 2 $\dfrac{\square}{\square} + \dfrac{\square}{\square} =$ $\qquad$ $\dfrac{\square}{\square} + \dfrac{\square}{\square} =$

$\square$ $\qquad\qquad\qquad\qquad\qquad\qquad\qquad\qquad$ $\square$

Round 3 $\dfrac{\square}{\square} + \dfrac{\square}{\square} =$ $\qquad$ $\dfrac{\square}{\square} + \dfrac{\square}{\square} =$

$\square$ $\qquad\qquad\qquad\qquad\qquad\qquad\qquad\qquad$ $\square$

 From *Lessons for Extending Fractions, Grade 5* by Marilyn Burns. © 2003 Math Solutions Publications

The Smaller Answer Wins Rules

You need:
  a partner
  a die

Rules

1. You need a game board for three rounds like this:

$$\frac{\square}{\square} + \frac{\square}{\square} = \qquad \frac{\square}{\square} + \frac{\square}{\square} =$$

$$\square \qquad\qquad\qquad\qquad \square$$

2. Players take turns rolling the die and writing the number in one of their spaces on the game board. Once a number is written, it cannot be changed. The boxes to the side are reject boxes that give you one chance to write a number that you don't want to use in your problem.

3. After writing a number, pass the die to the other player.

4. Play until both players have recorded two fractions. (Your reject box may be empty if you used your first four numbers for the fractions.)

5. Add your two fractions. Check each other's sums. The winner of the round is the player with the smaller sum.

6. Play three rounds. Whoever wins more rounds wins the game.

INDEX